Undercover Investigations in the Workplace

Undercover Investigations in the Workplace

Eugene F. Ferraro CPP, CFE

BUTTERWORTH
HEINEMANN

Boston   Oxford   Auckland   Johannesburg   Melbourne   New Delhi

Library of Congress Cataloging-in-Publication Data
Ferraro, Eugene.
    Undercover investigations in the workplace / by Eugene F. Ferraro.
        p. cm.
    Includes bibliographical references and index.
    ISBN 0–7506–7048–7 (pbk. : alk. paper)
    1. Undercover operations.   2. Employee crimes.   I. Title.
HV8080.U5F37   1999
363.25′2—dc21   99–38455
                                                                    CIP

British Library Cataloguing-in-Publication Data
A catalogue record for this book is available from the British
Library.

The publisher offers special discounts on bulk orders of this
book.
For information, please contact:
Manager of Special Sales
Butterworth–Heinemann
225 Wildwood Avenue
Woburn, MA 01801-2041
Tel: 781-904-2500
Fax: 781-904-2620

For information on all Butterworth–Heinemann publications
available, contact our World Wide Web home page at:
http://www.bh.com

10 9 8 7 6 5 4 3 2 1

Printed in the United States of America

*In fond memory of my friend
and teacher,
Tracy A. Schnelker
(1918–1992)*

Table of Contents

Preface   xi

Introduction   xiii

1. The Justification and the Legitimacy of Undercover
Investigation in the Modern Workplace   1

The Birth of a New American Culture   1
The War on Drugs   2
Corporate America Joins the Fight   5
Rationalization and Doper Logic   8
The Role of Undercover and the Drug-Free Workplace   9
The Pursuit of a Crime-Free Workplace   10
Gangs in the Workplace   13
Workplace Violence   16
Obligations of Employers   22
Risks of Undercover   25

2. Preinvestigation Preparation and Operative Placement   27

Management Commitment   28
Meaningful Objectives   38
Preinvestigative Preparation and Strategy Proposals   56
Profile of the Professional Operative   61
Preinvestigation Actions and Final Preparation   72
Who Exactly Should be Involved?   74
Common Mistakes   78

3. Case Management and Communications   81

Case Management   81
Communication   87
Case Files   101

4. Drug Investigations   105

The Human Cost of Substance Abuse   106
The Role of the Employer   106
Understanding Employee Substance Abuse   107
Addiction and Chemical Dependence   110
Employee Drug Users and the Opportunities of
   the Workplace   112
The Progressive Nature of Substance Abuse in
   the Workplace   113
Destructive Behaviors   115
Intervention   119
Progressive Discipline and Corrective Action   121
Prevention   123
The Process of Investigation   124
Investigating Employee Substance Abuse   129
Employee Prosecution   137

5. Theft Investigations   139

Why Employees Steal   139
Theft as a Process   141
Undercover Theft Investigations   144
Corroborating Evidence   154
Recoveries   156
Theft Prevention   157

6. Organized Labor and Other Important Management
Considerations   159

Common Misconceptions   159
Labor Relations   163
Grievances and Arbitrations   165
Unemployment Hearings   172
Public Relations   172
Employee Relations   173

7. Case Closure and Shutdown   177

Selecting the Appropriate Outcome   177
Administrative and Operational Preparations   178
Restitution and Recovery   180
Employee Interviews   181
Role of Law Enforcement   187
Operative Removal   189
Employee Communication   190

8. Litigation Avoidance   191

Potential Liability for Failing to Investigate Reported
Workplace Drug Abuse, Threats, and/or Assaults   192

Legal Responsibilities of Employers Who Hire Private
Investigative Firms   195
Avoiding Discrimination Lawsuits   196
Sexual Harassment   198
Avoiding Unfair Labor Practice Claims   200
Workplace Privacy   202
Investigative Interviews   217
False Imprisonment; Assault and Battery   219
Use of Consumer Credit Reports and
   Investigative Consumer Reports   221
Honesty Testing   223
Workplace Searches   225
Investigating Threats of Violence   228
Wrongful Discharge   231

9. Measuring Results   233

Benchmarking   233
Information and Data Collection   235
Leveraging Your Successes   239

10. The Future   241

New Roles and New Challenges   241
Workplace Undercover Investigation for the Government   244
Workplace Evaluations   245
A Final Word   245

Appendixes   247
Bibliography   285
Index   287

Preface

Corporate undercover is like no other form of investigation. It can be exciting or terribly boring. It can yield extraordinary results or fail miserably. It can be incredibly cost-effective or precipitate costly lawsuits. This much is clear, however: undercover is not for everyone. The organizations that will be most successful conducting such investigations are those with courage and the willingness to invest time, money, and patience.

Amazingly, the literature is devoid of any noteworthy or authoritative work on the subject. Even those who have addressed the topic have failed to approach it from the perspective of the corporate user. No one has adequately addressed how this important form of investigation should be used, or puzzled over the complex legal issues and liabilities associated with it. Confronted with the challenging demands of loss prevention and asset protection as well as ever-expanding employee rights, security professionals, human resource directors, corporate executives, and the lawyers who represent them need better information about workplace investigations—and about undercover investigations in particular.

This book is designed to fill this conspicuous void in the literature. I have attempted to provide the insight and tools you and your organization need to make informed business decisions regarding the use of undercover investigation in today's workplace. Whether you have successfully used undercover techniques in the past or contemplate using them sometime in the future, this book is designed to be a practical, user-friendly tool. My goal—and expectation—is for the reader to achieve the best results legally possible.

One perhaps doesn't truly appreciate the help and encouragement of others until he or she attempts to convert many years of experience into an organized, cogent, and entertaining text. For my part, I would like to acknowledge the efforts of several important people. The first are my editors, Laurel A. DeWolf and Rita Lombard. Without their vision, professionalism, and tight deadlines, this book would have never made it to press. I also wish to thank my friend and trusted colleague Michael Gips, senior editor of *Security Management*. For years, Michael has been a trusted critic and counsel. He encouraged me to begin this project and *finish it*. I also wish to express a special thanks to Jean Chaney for her enormous contribution and legal insight. Jean gave freely of her time, energy, and editorial skills in preparing the chapter entitled *Litigation Avoidance*. Without her assistance this work would not be a reality. I also want to thank my loving wife, Shelley. Without her patience and encouragement, this book, as well as everything else meaningful in my life, would not be possible.

EFF
Golden, Colorado

Introduction

Workplace undercover investigations are not new. Used for decades by employers in the United States and elsewhere, these complex and sometimes lengthy operations often produce results impossible to achieve by other means. By definition, "undercover" is the surreptitious placement into the workforce of a properly trained and skilled investigator posing as an employee. Once placed, the investigator-employee pursues the desired information. In most cases, the investigator seeks information on various forms of employee misconduct or crimes against the business. At the completion of a successful investigation, the culprits are disciplined or terminated, and in some cases are prosecuted.

But undercover can be much more. It is one of the few forms of investigation that are interactive: undercover not only makes it possible to gather evidence through observation but also gives the investigator the unique opportunity to deal personally with the offenders as they commit their crimes. This allows for increased insight into how and why employees commit the wrongful conduct, that is to say, insight into their motive.

In criminal cases, motive is not always important. What matters most to the prosecution is convincing the jury or judge that the person accused is in fact the person who committed the crime. By contrast, in workplace settings, employers should focus on motive. For if the employer knows and understands motive, it can likely take the necessary steps to prevent the problem from recurring. In this sense, understanding motive is the purest form of corporate loss prevention and asset protection.

Consider the following example. Several years ago, the operator of a large distribution operation called my office desperately seeking help. His firm sold and distributed supermarket notions, he explained, and he believed employee sabotage to be rampant. He told me that his newly opened distribution center in central Los Angeles, which employed mostly women, had suffered huge losses caused by poor productivity and costly damage—obviously intentional—to the mechanical picking line used to fill orders. Almost with panic in his voice, he told me that he wanted the problem stopped and those responsible "put in jail." He asked for an under-cover operation.

Upon meeting him and more closely examining the situation, I agreed that an undercover investigation would be appropriate. Several days later, one of our female investigators was placed into the distributor's workforce. Within a week, she had been accepted by the other women on her shift, who began to confide in her. Just as our client had suspected, some of the women were intentionally disrupting the operation and sabotaging equipment. But, as our investigator soon learned, the women were motivated not by wanton malice but by maternal instincts. Specifically, the investigator learned that most of the female employees were single mothers. Many had young children in child care or at home alone after school. She also learned that mandatory overtime was common: with little or no notice, the women would be required to work up to four hours beyond their regular shift. But the most interesting discovery was that the new facility had only one pay telephone available to employees. Upon learning that the entire shift would have to work overtime, many of the 150 or so women on that shift would race to the single pay phone and scramble to make last-minute arrangements for their children. With only ten minutes between the end of the shift and the start of overtime, most women could not get in touch with their children or their care providers. In desperation, these parents did what they believed was necessary for the welfare of their children: they prevented any possible overtime by sabotaging their employer's equipment and disrupting production.

This is a good example of not only how simple consideration for others can resolve what seem to be intractable problems but also why it is often so important to know a perpetrator's motive. And as is often the case, once the motive is known, prevention is relatively easy. Upon learning of the predicament that he himself had created, my client did the logical thing. He installed more phones. In fact he installed *19* more phones. He also provided his management team with sensitivity training. Thus, with a relatively small investment and a little compassion, my client solved what had been a perplexing and costly problem.

Motive is crucial, but it is equally important to understand how the offense was committed. Here again, undercover can provide insight. Unlike many other forms of investigation, undercover lets investigators learn firsthand how the crime was committed. Although surveillance arguably can accomplish that task, surveillance is not perfect. What's more, surveillance raises significant privacy concerns. Undercover investigation, though more complicated than surveillance, bypasses many of the privacy issues associated with surveillance and provides the user far greater insight into the matter under investigation.

Consider another example. A lawyer representing a large telecommunications company recently asked me to install a hidden camera in the office of a supervisor suspected of selling drugs from his desk. According to the lawyer, even if the camera failed to capture the supervisor in the act of selling the drugs, merely recording his discussions about intended transactions would be enough to terminate him and his customers. As logical as that might sound, this approach raised concerns. First was the issue of privacy. The supervisor probably enjoyed some reasonable expectation of privacy in his office. For example, couldn't the supervisor have expected enough privacy to change clothes in his locked office? Most likely. Therefore, the use of a hidden camera could foreseeably give rise to an invasion of privacy claim. Second, secretly recording conversations may run afoul of the law. In most states, statutes prohibit secretly recording the conversations of others. In places where it is permitted, state law requires that at least one party to the conversation have knowledge of the recording, which certainly would not have been the case in this instance. Consequently, I told the attorney that the proposed approach was neither appropriate nor legally prudent. Strange as it might sound, the attorney admitted that he hadn't thought through the legal ramifications of video surveillance.

Instead of surveillance, I recommended undercover investigation. The attorney agreed and our investigation began immediately. To no one's surprise, the supervisor *was* selling illegal drugs from his desk. He soon sold to our investigator and was terminated for it. The real surprise, however, was that his best customer was his manager, a respected professional with years of tenure at the company—an unlikely customer to say the least. Out of fear of being caught, however, she only purchased from him at his home and rarely entered his office. Before the end of our investigation, she confessed to the possession of illegal drugs on company premises, and she too was terminated.

If a hidden camera had been used, much less would have been learned about the problem and the employees involved; the manager, for instance, may well have avoided suspicion. As is true in most cases, only by understanding the *how and why* of the offense could the client take appropriate action and prevent the problem from occurring again.

Undercover has the further value of allowing the investigator to interact with and ask questions of others, thereby getting a better feel for the workplace culture. This ability enables the investigation to move more quickly and with more specificity. Hours of fruitless surveillance, tedious research, and wasted corporate resources are often avoided. Instead, the investigation can be narrowed and precisely focused, saving the business and employer time and money.

It is precisely this ability to engineer an investigation to yield the highest possible return on investment that forms the heart of this book. In fact, if used properly, this book is designed to allow you to engineer *all* investigations to maximize your investment of time and money. The result will be a powerful value-added service to the customers and clients you serve.

CHAPTER 1

The Justification and the Legitimacy of Undercover Investigation in the Modern Workplace

Never had corporate undercover played a bigger role in the fight against workplace crime than it did in the 1980s. As that decade began, America was desperately clawing its way out of the second most severe economic recession in 50 years. Hobbled by successive oil embargoes and an energy crisis that lasted nearly five years, the economy was flat on its back. The nation was still reeling from the psychological devastation and human indignities of the Vietnam War, while the Cold War raged on under vast oceans, in deep space, and in the minds of the world's greatest scientists.

The military-industrial complexes of the world's two superpowers—the United States and the Soviet Union—were also at war. With unbridled restraint they were designing and building some of the most powerful weapons and war machines the world had ever seen. In an almost cruel paradox, the American corporations that quietly proxied for their customers, enjoyed some of the most profitable years of their existence. The U.S. military needed and wanted everything; it seemed as if its growth would never stop. Meanwhile, almost silently, something else was going on. Illegal drugs had found their way into the American workplace. And although alcohol had been there for years, illegal drugs soon became corporate enemy #1.

The Birth of a New American Culture

Alcohol and drugs have always played some role in American history. The logbook of the famous colonial warship *Constitution* reveals that during our war for independence she attacked the island of Jamaica and made a night raid on the Scottish coast at the Firth of Clyde for the procurement

1

of rum and whisky for her crew.[1] Later, during the Civil War, morphine was so indiscriminately used that the war ended with nearly half a million addicted survivors. And more recently, of course, there was the cocaine epidemic of the early 1990s. Clearly, America has always been a nation steeped in drugs and drug abuse. But we were not prepared for what was to unfold in the mixed up 1970s and 1980s.

The 1950s were a time of national excitement and enthusiasm. Although the threat of Communism was so exaggerated out of proportion as to become something of a national preoccupation, Americans by and large were optimistic. The postwar years were decidedly behind us and most every American shared in the nations greater collective prosperity. The Unites States was indeed an economic and military superpower, and we became the leader in space exploration and were first to put a man on the moon. Yet America was also a nation that had tragically lost a beloved president, and racial tensions had never been greater. Life seemed faster, harsher, and more demanding. In many ways we had lost our innocence. In retrospect, we can now look back and see that the world had already begun to become a global community and America was locked into a race to maintain global economic dominance.

America's youth had also changed. The new generation decided their parents and the government could no longer be trusted. They created a new language, new music, and a new way of living. They claimed to be free from conventional society and desperately sought out the meaning of life and the purpose of their existence. Unwittingly the younger generation of the 1960s created a new American culture. Regrettably, part of that new lifestyle was to evolve into what became known as the *drug culture*, with its own look, style, and message. It was a counterculture almost in every regard. It ran counter to traditional religion and family values and to the law. By the early 1970s what had seemed almost innocent in its beginning had become a national epidemic. With the reinventing of the Federal Bureau of Narcotics in 1968 and the creation of the Drug Enforcement Agency (DEA), a new war was declared. That war soon became known as the *war on drugs*.

The War on Drugs

As governments around the world began to funnel billions of dollars into the war against drugs, so did the enemy. That enemy, as employers were soon to find out wore two faces: that of the producer and the consumer. The producers immediately recognized the threat of government interven-

---

[1] Jonathon Wapperly, Quartermaster's clerk. From the logbook of the U.S. warship *Constitution*, Library of Congress, 1779–1780.

tion and interdiction and took decisive action. Without the constraints of public debate or congressional hearings, they were able to swing into immediate action. First they eliminated their weakest competition and then they went after the agencies and governments that opposed them. They increased production to overcome losses caused by government interdiction and interception. They corrupted government officials, criminal justice systems, and eventually entire governments. They defended themselves and protected their enterprises with violence, murder, and assassination. They then banned together to create massive criminal enterprises called *cartels*. Without national boundaries, access to vast sums of money and the organizational savvy of a large international corporation, the drug cartels instantly thrived. Their power and influence made the Italian-American Mafia appear almost impotent. With global receipts of nearly $1 billion a day, collectively the business of international illicit drug production and distribution became the largest industry on the planet. The impact on the industrialized world was, and still is, nothing short of devastating. Almost overnight, mind-altering drugs of all kinds poured onto our streets. Addictive and expensive, these substances made billions for the producers.

With drugs also came crime. In the mid-1970s, America quickly began to realize illegal drugs and crime were synonymous. Contrary to the often ridiculous claims of vocal members of the drug culture, Hollywood, and late-night talk show guests, drugs in America had another, more sinister side: the people who used them, sold them, and produced them frequently engaged in other criminal activity. In every large American city, the statistics for burglary, robbery, and murder began to rise. In nearly every urban center, local law enforcement responded by creating narcotics investigation units and criminal drug task forces. Eventually even the Federal Bureau of Investigation concluded that illegal drugs had become a problem and began to pursue offenders. Before the end of the decade, J. Edgar Hoover was reluctantly led to admit that America had a drug problem.[2]

By the late 1970s parents began to wake up. Parents and educators alike admitted that illegal drugs had found their way into their schools and onto their campuses. Substance abuse awareness programs like D.A.R.E. had sprung up everywhere. Evidently because it appeared the producers and their toxic products could not be controlled, progressive thinkers began to focus on the consumer. And just as Eric Clapton and other popular musicians of the day made fortunes singing about their drug of choice and, in doing so, glamorized drug abuse and America's drug culture, teachers, parents, and drug counselors told our kids to *just say no*. The outcome should have been obvious. Pathetically, although well-meaning adults of almost all walks of life tried their hand in discouraging drug abuse, the

---

[2] Curt Gentry, *J. Edgar Hoover: The Man and the Secrets* (New York: Norton, 1991).

impact was negligible. The media, with the help of people like Timothy Leary, continued to popularize the drug culture while doing all they could to minimize the adverse effects drugs had on our nation.

Then just when it seemed things could not get worse, someone discovered *rock cocaine*. Most likely accidentally invented while trying to purify street quality cocaine, this powerful and extremely addictive substance nearly devastated an entire generation of poor inner-city kids in just several short years. Users claimed they became addicted to it the first time they used it. Addicts consumed it at the astonishing rate of $100 per hour, sometimes more. Abusers spent hundreds a day on it and street dealers made tens of thousands. The devastation was incomprehensible. Young children sold their bodies for it, mothers sold their children for it, and husbands left their families for it. Even doctors, lawyers, and politicians used it. If America ever had a drug problem, this was it. The war on drugs by any measure appeared to be an utter failure.

By January 1, 1980, the cocaine epidemic had not even begun to peak. Cocaine poured into the country and onto our streets by the ton. Police departments in cities like Los Angeles did not even have the resources to destroy all that it had seized. Several cash seizures by the Drug Enforcement Agency (DEA) were so large that agents resorted to weighing the money instead of counting it. The crusaders in the war against drugs told the American public that illegal drug trafficking had become a $100 billion industry.[3] The U.S. army, navy, air force, and coast guard were called into action. The DEA and U.S. Customs Service blanketed airports, harbors, and waterways. The Research Triangle Institute 1984 study based on data collected in 1980 set the annual economic cost of the American drug problem at $46.9 billion, or the equivalent of $472 for every working adult in the country.[4] Ten years later, that cost had swelled to $114 billion.[5] The magnitude of the problem could not have been more poignantly made than by the remarkable testimony of defendant Donald Steinberg before a federal grand jury.[6] Steinberg—a notoriously successful marijuana smuggler known for his aversion to violence—while describing his fleet of smuggling vessels, off-handedly told a roomful of astonished listeners and a federal judge that his best *one day* take was $600 million! Steinberg and others like him had successfully fed America's craving for drugs. In doing so, they made fortunes, and destroyed millions of lives. Several bold federal law enforcement

---

[3] This number has been continuously debated. Because the organized crime syndicates and drug cartels do not publish annual reports and by their very nature are secret organizations, the true cost and economic impact is impossible to determine.

[4] Harwood, Napolitano, Kristiansen, and Collins, "Economic Costs to Society of Alcohol and Drug Abuse and Mental Illness: 1980," Research Triangle Institute, June 1984.

[5] William C. Cunningham, "The Hallcrest Report II," Hallcrest Systems, Inc., 1990.

[6] James Mills, *The Underground Empire: Where Crime and Governments Embrace*, Doubleday & Co., Inc. 1986. NY.

officials even asserted it would only be a matter of time before one or more of the worlds drug cartels took over an entire South American government. Local and state law enforcement, the criminal justice systems, and the military in some parts of the world had already been compromised. Seizure of political control seemed like the next logical step. Even in our country, the criminal justice system was beginning to show the strain. According to the Office of National Drug Control Policy (ONDCP), the federal drug control budget increased from $1.5 billion in fiscal 1981 to $13.2 billion in fiscal 1995.[7]

By the mid-1980s, nearly 300,000 Americans were behind bars for drug offenses; one in five of them were first time offenders.[8] More than half of all federal prison inmates were incarcerated for violations of federal drug laws. Yet law enforcement officials continued to consistently recite the claim that they were seizing "only 10 percent" of all drug shipments into the United States. By 1988, an estimated 27,971,000 people in the United States aged 12 and up had used an illicit drug at least once in the past year, and 14,479,000 were estimated to have used illicit drugs in the past month.[9] That same year, the city of New York reported that 83 percent of all male arrestees tested positive for a controlled substance, while the city of Detroit claimed that 81 percent of its female arrestees tested likewise.[10] Then it happened. In the midst of one of our greatest social tragedies, corporate America awoke to the reality that substance abuse had come to the workplace.

Corporate America Joins the Fight

As alarms resounded across the land, the sleeping giant awoke. And as it so often seems in so many cases, the government and the public looked to big business for answers. After a string of spectacular workplace mishaps, fatal industrial accidents, and railroad tragedies, everybody demanded corporate America to do something. Suddenly, the entire nation became aware that alcohol had become the most widely used and destructive drug in America. A 1983 survey reported that nearly half of all convicted inmates had been under the influence of alcohol at the time of the crime for which they were convicted.[11] The same report claimed that alcohol was involved

---

[7] "Drugs and Crime Facts, 1994," U.S. Department of Justice, Bureau of Justice Statistics, June 1995.

[8] Ethan Nedelmann and Jann S. Wenner, "Toward a Sane National Drug Policy," *Rolling Stone*, 4 May 1994, p. 24–25.

[9] "National Household Survey on Drug Abuse," National Institute on Drug Abuse, 1988.

[10] "1988 Drug Use Forecasting Annual Report: Drugs and Crime in America," National Institute of Justice Research in Action, March 1990, p. 3.

[11] National Council on Alcoholism, "1983 Facts on Alcoholism and Alcohol-Related Problems," NIAA Sixth Annual Report.

in 54 percent of all violent crimes, 40 percent of crimes of property, and 64 percent of offenses to public order. In 1984, the equivalent of 2.65 gallons of absolute alcohol was consumed per person over age 14 in the United States.[12] In 1984, the National Council on Alcoholism, an independent health organization dedicated to combating the disease of alcoholism reported the following statistics:

- Of the estimated 100 million adult Americans 18 years and older who consumed alcohol, approximately 10 million suffered from alcoholism and alcohol-related problems. Only 15 percent of the 10 million received formal treatment
- For each American alcoholic, another four people were directly affected
- Alcohol was the direct or indirect cause of approximately 95,000 deaths a year. Cirrhosis of the liver alone was the cause of nearly 30,000 deaths that year. Alcoholism and alcoholic psychosis accounted for approximately 5,000 deaths. Accidents, homicides, and suicides related to alcohol accounted for approximately 60,000 more fatalities
- Drunk driving was involved in 50 percent of all highway traffic fatalities
- Between 5 and 10 percent of all employees suffered from alcoholism
- Approximately 3.3 million American teenagers were heavy drinkers and showed signs of potential problems with alcohol[13]

By 1985 nearly 18 million adults had a problem with alcohol dependence or abuse. In 1986 the economic cost of alcohol in the United States was estimated at $123.3 billion, while lost employment and reduced productivity accounted for more than half of it.[14] The infamy of alcohol in the workplace was not fully realized, however, until four minutes after midnight on March 24, 1989 off the coast of Alaska in a place called Prince William Sound. Carelessly, the supertanker *Exxon Valdez* piloted by an unqualified third mate ran aground on Bligh Reef and spilled 11.2 million gallons of crude oil into the sea. The resulting oil slick blackened over 500 square miles of sea and destroyed thousands of birds, fish, and sea mammals. It was later alleged that the ship's captain, Joseph Hazelwood had been drinking just hours before the mishap and that his employer, Exxon, was aware that he had a severe alcohol problem.[15] Although Exxon claims that it monitored Hazelwood after he voluntarily entered an employee assistance

---

[12] Ibid., p. xix.

[13] National Council on Alcoholism, "1984 Facts on Alcoholism and Alcohol-Related Problems," July 1984.

[14] "The Alcohol Problem and Loss of Productivity in the U.S.A.: Interview with Otis Bowen," World Congress for the Prevention of Alcoholism and Drug Dependency, 1988, p. 57.

[15] Behar, "Joe's Bad Trip," *Time*, 24 July 1989.

program, there is evidence that Exxon repeatedly missed signs that Hazelwood had continued to drink heavily.[16]

But alcohol hasn't been the only drug in the American workplace. Marijuana, cocaine, and even heroin began to appear in factories, warehouses, and corporate boardrooms. No place was safe and no organization immune. As the demands for action grew louder, American corporations began to respond. Instinctively their first resort was to local law enforcement. But these agencies already were themselves overwhelmed; there simply weren't enough resources or manpower to effectively fight drug abuse in the streets and the schools and in the workplace as well. Federal and state legislatures in an effort to help often made matters worse. Mandatory jail sentences, obligatory rehabilitation programs, and an ever-larger tangle of rules, regulations, and policies often frustrated the efforts of law enforcement and stretched the resources of the criminal justice system to the breaking point. Compensating while earnestly looking for solutions, corporations promulgated new work rules and policies. Some began to experiment with drug testing and others toyed with employee counseling programs. Scientific terms and phrases like *false positive, window of detection, enzyme multiplied immunoassay technique (EMIT)*, and *gas chromatography/mass spectrometry (GCMS)* found their way into the workplace lexicon. Employee drug education programs and supervisor and management training became the order of the day.

But corporate America wanted more. Business owners, executives, and security directors wanted to attack the problem at its root. They wanted the dealers. Unable to consistently obtain assistance from law enforcement, corporations looked to the private sector. Although industry leaders in physical security like Pinkertons, Wachenhut, and Burns had been offering their clients undercover services for decades, it remained only a sideline. In 1981, innovators from both the public and private sector began to offer workplace undercover drug investigations. Yet by 1983, only half a dozen private investigation firms in the country claimed to specialize in undercover. The battle for businesses like General Motors, Proctor & Gamble, and Hewlett-Packard gave birth to unique organizations like Professional Law Enforcement (PLE) in the east and Krout & Schneider, Inc. in the west. By 1986, these two firms alone provided undercover drug investigations for more than half of the Fortune 500 companies of their day.[17] What had become a nightmare for law enforcement and industry became a blessing for a small, specialized segment of the security industry. In essence, private entrepreneurs were able to effectively provide a service that the government could not.

---

[16] Ibid.

[17] Based on author's personal experience (employed by Krout and Schneider, Inc. between 1983 and 1994) and the interview of former PLE employees for this book.

The recruitment of the private sector in the war against drugs was not without its problems. Competency, credibility, and liability all became issues. Every law enforcement agency, every prosecutor, and every court had its own perspective on how cases of drug abuse in the workplace should be handled. Encumbered by state licensing requirements, jurisdictional policies, and unwritten departmental rules, private investigators and their clients worked awkwardly at first with law enforcement, but in time they began to achieve what law enforcement was unable to do alone. Together, they fought the war against drugs in the trenches and pursued not the producers but the consumers: the American workplace substance abuser. The impact was impressive. Headline after headline exalted the success of extraordinary workplace undercover investigations performed by private industry. At one point, the National Institute on Drug Abuse (NIDA) reported that a full 23.8 percent of all full-time working American males (females were polled separately) had used an illegal drug at least once in the 60 days prior to its study. About the same time, the DEA asserted that at least 60 percent of all illicit drugs produced in the world were consumed in the United States.

Many employers at first, however, targeted only the dealers. Like their governmental predecessors, they insisted on interdiction. The reasoning went like this: if one could eliminate the source, one would naturally control consumption—and combined with enough publicity, the prosecution of employee dealers would not only eliminate the source but impart a significant and memorable deterrent effect as well. This approach, though largely effective, failed to consider one essential point: substance abuse is not a form of recreation, it is a way of life. Consequently, simply eliminating the dealers and scaring the abuser was often not enough. I personally saw the disappointing effects of this approach a number of times in conducting my own investigations. I, too, had not yet understood the dynamic between supplier and user.

Rationalization and Doper Logic

Particularly in large organizations (those with over 1,000 employees), employee drug dealers are not usually liked. Though they enjoy the benefits of the highest perch in the workplace drug cultural hierarchy, they have often used force, deceit, and intimidation to get there. Many employees also owe them money. Furthermore, their customers are irrationally envious. Not only do the workplace dealers have all the drugs, they also make small fortunes on the backs of their coworker abusers. Therefore, not only does the removal of employee drug dealers not always deter substance abuse as one might assume, it may in fact even exacerbate the problem by creating new business opportunities for employee abusers. Several times my own investigations have exposed abusers rushing to fill the vacancies created when employee dealers are brought to justice. Contrary to expectations, the fear of prosecution is easily overcome by rationalization and greed. Typically, the development of new clientele is not even necessary. The abuser, like the predatory dealer, knows the identity of all of his coworker abusers. With the elimination of the dealer, enterprising abusers can assume that role and in some cases even collect on debts. Look at it another way: the abuser reasons he is already breaking the rules. Is the risk of termination or prosecution that great? If it were, wouldn't the abuser have already been caught? This is called *doper logic*. As remarkable as it may seem, prosecuting drug dealers is simply not enough to solve the problem of drugs in the corporate setting. Employers today have learned that properly dealing with the abuser plays an important and critical role in creating and maintaining a drug-free workplace.

The Role of Undercover and the Drug-Free Workplace

The question remains as to how private industry can go about filling the shoes of public law enforcement. The federal legislature actually began to answer that question in the late-1980s. When Congress passed Title V of the Omnibus Drug Initiative Act of 1988, it included a provision with the short title of the Drug-Free Workplace Act of 1988.[18] The Act requires that all businesses contracting with the federal government and all grantees receiving federal financial assistance certify that they have in place policies and practices addressing workplace substance abuse and have taken certain steps to create and maintain a drug-free workplace. The Act applies to any contract over $25,000 and to any grant from any federal agency regardless of the amount. It became law on March 18, 1989.

Though the intent was commendable, the Act fell pathetically short on substance. In essence it required the promulgation of employer policy statements regarding substance abuse and some nonsensical reporting of workplace drug offenses and employee convictions. What it did accomplish, however, was to heighten employer awareness. Combined with the loosely constructed provisions of the "general duty" clause in the Occupational Safety & Health Act of 1970 (OSHA) regarding an employer's obligation to provide a workplace free from recognized hazards likely to cause death or serious harm, employers not only felt statutorily obligated but empowered. Corporate decisionmakers everywhere were suddenly encouraged by their lawyers, security directors, and human resource managers to go after the workplace drug problem. Not surprisingly, undercover became their weapon of choice.

---

[18] Public Law No. 100–690, Title V, Subtitle D, User Accountability, November 18, 1988.

Undercover investigation is efficient and effective. It is also exciting. Businesses of all sizes that used it quickly learned that roughly 20 percent or more of their workforce was involved in drugs at work. My own research at the time, based on the results of hundreds of undercover cases my organization had conducted, revealed the problem was more serious than that. By 1987 on average, our investigations showed that 23 percent of our clients' employees had committed at least one workplace drug policy violation and as many as one-half of them had also sold illegal drugs at work. Quickly employers of all sizes learned that employees both used and sold drugs at work. The drugs included marijuana, hashish, cocaine, heroin, LSD, PCP, and prescription drugs of all sorts—and of course alcohol. In one of my own undercover investigations in a southern California aerospace firm in the mid-1980s, we discovered that fully nine out of ten employees (including those in management) were involved with illegal drugs at work. It seemed like everybody was involved. In more than one case, the very person who engaged my firm to investigate an employee substance abuse problem was in fact involved himself. On one remarkable occasion in the late 1980s, during a meeting while offering my services to examine an alleged workplace substance abuse problem, the prospective client offered me cocaine! The stuff was simply everywhere.

The Pursuit of a Crime-Free Workplace

The corporate undercover investigations of the 1980s, however, did not just uncover drugs. The investigators of the day and the employers who hired them found the American workplace had become a mirror image of society. Human resource and labor relations professionals had always known the workplace reflected the people and cultures that constituted it, but the image was never fully clear until the proper implementation of undercover. In some instances, in as little as several days, skilled undercover investigators uncovered prostitution, theft, embezzlement, loan sharking, and gun smuggling. Employers' worst fears were becoming realities. Not only did many of them have workplace substance abuse problems, *most* of them had workplace crime problems.

In one notable case for a midwestern distribution company, the breadth of employee criminality was almost enough to overwhelm even law enforcement. Only weeks after placing a team of undercover investigators into the client's workforce we knew they had big problems. Immediately, each of our investigators was approached and encouraged to remove company property without permission. The employees hounded our investigators to steal and break company rules. We knew prior to our engagement that our client had suffered the loss of $600,000 worth of cigarettes. Who was responsible was the big question, and the amateurs who had initially approached us did not appear to be perpetrators. After attempting to compromise the new employees (our investigators), our new "friends" then introduced the undercover investigators to alcohol. They were not just drinking while at work, but drinking while driving company vehicles. In several days, these same employees were asking our investigators to bring marijuana to work. Under circumstances like these, most new employees would either have quit or acquiesced. Our investigators did neither.

After they had completed their new-employee probationary period, they were carefully dispersed in different departments on all three shifts. Within a short period of time, each investigator discovered employee drug use and trafficking. Interestingly, the dealers used different colored felt-tipped markers carried in exposed belt pouches to advertise the availability of specific drugs for sale. The dealers felt they could now trust the new employees not to squeal (they had "stolen" company property in the presence of the dealers and others just weeks before) and openly pursued them as new customers. After making the necessary arrangements with local law enforcement, our investigators purchased all the drugs they could. Hand over fist our operatives purchased marijuana, cocaine, and methamphetamine from the employee dealers.

After meeting the minimum of three purchases from each dealer of a controlled drug as mandated by the district attorney overseeing our case, we reversed the very tactics used against us by the dealers. Very carefully and selectively our investigators approached the dealers one at a time and told them we thought *they too could be trusted*. The dealers were told that the investigators were also part of an organized ring, not for moving dope but for diverting large quantities of inventory. The dealers were also warned that if they ever told anyone about the plan, their drug dealing activities would be reported to management. They were told that some of the drugs they had sold our people had been retained and would be used as evidence against them if necessary. However, the dealers were not asked to steal; they were asked only to identify *who was*. In fact, the dealers were warned that any stealing on their part from that moment forward would also result in management learning about their drug activities. Our investigators explained that stealing was risky business, and that if others were carelessly stealing at the same time they were, everyone could get caught; that the only way to avoid a problem was to know who else was stealing and when. Apparently it made perfect sense to the dealers. In several days they not only identified the bad guys, they introduced them to us. And as is typical in these sort of complex cases, the investigators then introduced a nonemployee "acquaintance" (another investigator) to the ringleaders ostensibly as their "fence." The undercover investigators then became "cutouts" and were no longer permitted to associate with the thieves unless specifically told to do so. In an apparent act of greedy back-stabbing, the thieves were told that the guys who had made the introduction (our undercover investigators) were inexperienced and were known to be careless, that their role would only be that of lookouts and low level assistants if necessary. Appealing to their sense of greed they were also told that the fewer involved, the less the risk and bigger the opportunity. The bad guys were delighted with what they heard and to have another eager customer.

Our fence then went about the process of "qualifying" them. He insisted they prove their qualifications as capable thieves by producing several references and providing a demonstration. Eagerly, the thieves told our investigator that they had been stealing from their employer for years. They also identified several employees who would vouch for them. Subsequent follow up confirmed their claims. In so doing and to the delight of the district attorney, they negated any future ability to claim entrapment (more on this subject in later chapters). With a little preparation and some coordination with law enforcement, several large purchases of stolen cigarettes were purchased from the group. All purchases took place under the watchful eye of the police and were carefully videotaped. But the real surprise came sometime later. Not only were these employees into trafficking stolen property (cigarettes apparently their specialty), they also had an elaborate distribution network specializing in pornography, auto parts, stolen motorcycles, and guns. Agents from the FBI and the Bureau of Alcohol, Tobacco and Firearms (ATF) who soon joined our efforts quickly identified our subjects as members of an international motorcycle club with ties to organized crime. With our cooperation, they cut out our fence and substituted their own. And, although we had already met our client's objectives, the government's investigation went on for several more months. In the end, a dozen fun-loving motorcycle enthusiasts went to jail and an equal number of very unhappy employees lost their jobs.

By 1989 the U.S. Chamber of Commerce was reporting that one out of three business failures was due to employee theft and that three out of four companies in the United States were likely to be victims of some form of fraud. Half of the business owners polled at that time considered employee theft and fraud to be a major concern for the 1990s. In 1993, a report by the U.S. Justice Department's Bureau of Justice Statistics entitled "Survey of Criminal History Information Systems" suggested their concerns were valid. The FBI reported that arrests for all crimes had risen almost 40 percent between 1982 to 1992.[19] In fact, by 1993, state and local law enforcement agencies were making a mind-boggling 15 million arrests a year, with over 1 million of them for drugs.[20] Just the recordkeeping is hard to imagine, not to mention the reports, investigations, and court hours related to these arrests. In 1995 the Association of Certified Fraud Examiners reported that fraud and abuse were costing employers an average of

---

[19] "Drugs & Crime Data Fact Sheet," U.S. Department of Justice, Bureau of Justice Statistics, November 1994.
[20] Ibid.

$9.00 a day per employee, or roughly $400 billion a year.[21] The report also revealed that small businesses with less than 100 employees were most at risk. Among the victims, the median loss per occurrence was roughly $120,000. Companies of 10,000 employees or more had a median loss of $126,000.[22] A year later, the Association of Certified Fraud Examiners was reporting that fraud and abuse was costing American corporations 6 percent of their annual revenues.[23] The U.S. General Accounting Office estimated that, in that same year, fraud and abuse had consumed about 10 percent ($100 billion) of the $1 trillion spend on health care. Clearly, employee theft and dishonesty was costing this country billions of dollars.

Gangs in the Workplace

Gangs have existed for centuries. Nothing more than people bound by a philosophical (or practical) allegiance to a common purpose who consistently engage in inappropriate, violent, or criminal behavior, gangs have plagued the American landscape for more than 150 years. Their formal presence into our urban centers, however, did not occur until the turn of the century. In the ports of entry like New York and Boston, frightened immigrants first banded together for protection. These small, seemingly mysterious groups naturally spoke their native tongue and had many unusual customs. Their strangeness alone gave them power. Quickly some of these subcultures gave birth to bands of vigilante hoodlums. Using intimidation, extortion, and violence, they terrorized not only their own people but entire cities. Ever evolving, some of the organizations become sophisticated criminal syndicates like those of Al Capone and John Dillinger. Others enjoyed relative obscurity, like those of Los Angeles's White Fence and New York's West Side ethnic neighborhood gangs.

However, it was not until the 1970s and early 1980s that the significance of America's *street gangs* operating in our urban centers became fully recognized. In Los Angeles the problem was particularly apparent. There, in the almost exclusively black neighborhoods of the area known as South Central, several powerful black street gangs emerged. They were the Pirus, Hoover Street, Crips, and Bloods. On the east side of the city, characteristically territorial Hispanic gangs like White Fence, Tortilla Flats, and 13th Street ruled most of the lower income neighborhoods. Elsewhere in the country, other gangs became visible: the Latin Kings and Latin Disciples (both of Chicago), the Black Gangster Disciples, the Triads (Chinese), the

---

[21] "Report to the Nation, Occupational Fraud and Abuse," The Association of Certified Fraud Examiners, 1995.

[22] Ibid.

[23] "Report to the Nation, Occupational Fraud and Abuse," The Association of Certified Fraud Examiners, 1996.

Ghost Shadows (Chinese), Skinheads, and of course the Hell's Angels. In 1988 the Los Angeles Police Department (LAPD) estimated that there were 250 active gangs operating in Los Angeles County with approximately 80,000 members. By 1992 gang membership countywide had risen to over 100,000 (consider that the entire U.S. Marine Corps has barely 190,000 members).[24] All told, gangs in Los Angeles had taken 10,000 lives.[25]

Regardless of their age, color, name, or place of origin, gangs exist because they provide their members with power, prestige, protection, and money. And in the mid-1980s, we saw gangs everywhere expand their horizons and enter the workplace.

Supervising the large number of undercover cases I had at the time, I knew full well that some of those we were watching had gang affiliations. Many were also active gang members ("gang bangers") living otherwise normal lives. But by 1987 we began to see organized street gangs intentionally infiltrating the workplace. It didn't take a degree in rocket science to realize that most substance abusers had jobs. And for the gangs, whose principle source of revenue was from trafficking illegal drugs, what better market to dominate than the workplace. I am sure that they realized very quickly not only the magnitude of the customer base but also the very obvious absence of law enforcement. Most if not all of law enforcement's efforts were directed at street enforcement. Not yet had law enforcement realized the significance of the workplace as it relates to substance abuse and other criminal activity. Business owners, managers, and security professionals too had not yet fully appreciated how fertile the workplace is for criminal activity.

In time it became clear in many parts of the country that street gangs and other criminal organizations were using the workplace and the security it provided to further their criminal activity. And as on the streets, they effectively used intimidation, coercion, and violence to get what they wanted. By taking advantage of poor business controls, ineffective policies, and simple managerial ignorance, some of the infiltrators got away with *murder*. In at least two of my cases between 1987 and 1990, gang violence that erupted in the workplace ended in homicide. Theft, diversion, extortion, and drug trafficking were far more common.

In an interesting case several years ago, a small group of employee gang bangers were discovered to be active gun traders. The facility in which they worked was beside a Social Security Administration office that provided a steady stream of customers all day long. Apparently management did not find it peculiar that visitors were regularly entering the facility through the shipping and receiving area and mingling with employees who should have been working. I personally interviewed the ringleader at the conclusion of

---

[24] Burt Larson and Wendell Amstutz, "Youth Violence and Gangs," National Counseling Resource Center, 1995, p. 6.
[25] Ibid., p. 6.

our investigation and actually found him rather personable (his predisposi-
tion to breaking the law aside). He was on medical leave and receiving
benefits for a persistent injury he had received on the job at the time but
agreed to submit to some questions. He readily admitted that in the two
months in which he had been out on leave he had continued to move guns
and had sold marijuana to 32 employees at the site. Before we concluded
our interview I asked him if he had any remorse or some sense of guilt for
what he had done. He answered casually with a question, "Why should I?
If they wanted computers I would have sold computers."

It was not until the end of 1989 that employers began to fully realize
the effect and danger of gangs in the workplace. Although I had publicly
spoken on the subject for several years, the issue had not received
much attention. Following a presentation on the topic before a large trade
group in Los Angeles, a number of the attendees contacted me and asked
for help. Just as our investigations were beginning to uncover increased gang
activity in the workplace, apparently many employers were starting
to suspect the same thing. Instantly the demand for undercover mush-
roomed. In the next 24 months, we placed dozens of investigators into every
imaginable environment to address workplace gang problems. Our investigators uncovered gang activity in factories, hospitals, and even office
environments.

One large metropolitan law firm alone had been infiltrated by more
than two dozen *gangstas*. They had recognized that the firm's mailroom
and message center were perfect places from which to distribute illegal
drugs throughout the city. Employing nearly 30 full-time messengers, the
operation was tailor-made for the distribution of drugs and other contraband. We placed two investigators into the mailroom and quickly discovered that the firm was in fact the host to two gangs, not one. The rival gangs
were the Crips and the Bloods. Both vying for control of the distribution
opportunities the mailroom afforded, they quietly but aggressively com-
peted. Theft of personal property, vandalism, and verbal insults gave way
to threats, shouting, and pushing. Then in a restroom door jamb, visible
only with the door fully open, one of our investigators discovered a cryptic
and significant message. Written with what appeared to be a black felt-tip
marker in one-inch block letters was *BKC*. The message does not mean
"bankrupt-no cash" as one lawyer nervously later quipped; its chilling
translation is *Bloods Kill Crips*. I suggested to the client to not remove the
message and see what happened. And just as I suspected, about a week later
the letters were crossed out and beside them was scrawled *CKB*. The translation was obvious, the Bloods had challenged the Crips and the Crips had
accepted the challenge. Fearing a nasty confrontation between the two, the
authorities were summoned and our investigation was brought to a quick
conclusion. Fortunately, our investigators had already identified enough
policy violations to justify the termination or arrest of the dangerous
individuals.

Many gangs mark their territory. Like dogs, they mark the perimeter of their domain as a warning to intruders. The gang graffiti that defaces our urban (and now suburban) landscape demonstrates the point. In the workplace, gang members also mark their territory. Common on restroom walls, lockers, toolboxes, and sometimes even products, the symbols and marks are often innocuous. Clearly indicating the presence or affiliation with a gang are messages like the following:

Symbol or Mark	Translation
AB	Aryan Brotherhood (a white supremacist prison gang)
AFFA	Angels Forever, Forever Angels (greeting of brotherly affection used by the Hell's Angels)
FFF	666 (Satanic)
K3	Ku Klux Klan
M	Mexican Mafia or marijuana
13	Marijuana user or dealer (m is the thirteenth letter of the alphabet, used largely by Hispanic gangs)

Today gangs continue to play a role in many workplaces. Employers everywhere need to be concerned. Unfortunately, in some workplaces applicants are still selected based on gang affiliation, not qualifications. Gangs can be disruptive, intimidating, and dangerous. Employers can protect themselves by improving their employment screening practices, training managers and supervisors, and aggressively investigating allegations or evidence of gang activity in their workplace. Undercover has been and remains the single best investigative weapon available.

Workplace Violence

No discussion about today's workplace would be complete without mention of workplace violence. According to an October 1994 Bureau of Labor Statistics report, homicide accounts for 17 percent of all occupational fatalities. More alarming, the report indicates that homicide is the leading cause of occupational fatality for women, accounting for 41 percent of all female deaths in the workplace.[26] And of course, murder is only the tip of the iceberg. Incidents of workplace assault, rape, and psychological abuse occur by the thousands every year. Clearly, workplace violence touches everyone,

---

[26] "Crime Data Brief: Violence and Theft in the Workplace," U.S. Department of Justice, 1994.

not just the victims. It affects the way we think, feel, and behave. The threat of workplace violence affects the emotional stability and productivity of employees and ultimately corporate profitability.

Although the incidence of actual physical violence at work is relatively low, workplace violence nevertheless affects the lives of thousands of innocent Americans each year. Even when the act of aggression is only psychological, it can be painful and costly.

More locks and guards are not the answer, however. Employers need strong policies, effective security protocols, and a well-conceived strategy to confront the potentially violent employee and prevent workplace violence. Employers have a moral duty to provide a safe workplace for their employees. They also have statutory obligations under federal and state law to provide and promote a safe and violence-free work environment. Illustrative of these responsibilities is the requirements under the Occupational Safety and Health Act (OSHA) and state workers' compensation laws. Employers also have responsibilities to the public. Either vicariously or directly, employers may be liable for the harm brought to others by workplace violence. Moreover, employers have additional legal obligations to job applicants.

This intricate web of statutes, standards, rules, and regulations creates a legal minefield for employers. Picking one's way through that minefield is precarious at best; employers must protect their employees and other parties without infringing on the rights of others. Rarely has the challenge for employers been greater. Fortunately, there are solutions.

Profile of an Aggressor

Research shows that workplace aggressors follow a typical sequence of behavior, called a *progression*, that may ultimately lead to violence. They usually suffer a traumatic, insoluble (or so they believe) experience and they project the blame for that experience on others. Egocentric by nature, they believe that everyone is against them and the world is out to get them. Unable to resolve personal, interpersonal, and work-related problems, these individuals typically resort to violence.

Progressions can be detected, though predicting an aggressor's behavior is a considerable challenge. Most experts agree that without careful evaluation and analysis it is reckless, if not dangerous, to predict an individual's future behavior. Without the help of an experienced clinician or other qualified professional, it is impossible for the typical employer to psychologically assess an emotionally troubled employee and determine his or her fitness for duty. However, many workplace aggressors share certain characteristics. They often relate poorly to people, have difficulty getting along with others, strongly believe they have been wronged, have recently been adversely influenced by something or someone outside of their control, and *have a history of violence* (domestic, public, or workplace).

Though it is important to stress that no two aggressors are alike, there are other characteristics they are likely to share:

- Withdrawn and considered a loner
- Owns or is familiar with weapons
- Has few interests outside work
- Depends heavily on the job for self-esteem
- Unjustly projects blame on others
- Has a history of substance or alcohol abuse
- Functions in a *"toxic work environment"*

Motivation toward Violence

We are a culture steeped in violence and a society burdened with enormous economic pressures. The threat of a corporate downsizing, restructuring, or layoff looms over many of us. As a result, many people have rid themselves of traditional values and chosen to accept less personal responsibility while expecting more from their employers and government. Many people are afraid and angry. Truly, the sanctity of the workplace is being challenged.[27]

Research suggests that perpetrators of workplace violence generally fall into six motivational categories:

1. *Economic.* The aggressor believes the target is responsible for undesirable economic conditions affecting him, his family, or a particular group.
2. *Ideological.* The aggressor believes that the target is imperiling principles the attacker considers extremely important.
3. *Personal.* The aggressor possesses distorted feelings of rage, hate, revenge, jealousy, or love.
4. *Psychological.* The aggressor is mentally deranged or clinically psychotic, a condition often exacerbated by drugs or alcohol.
5. *Revolutionary.* The aggressor obsessively desires to further political beliefs at any costs.
6. *Mercenary.* The aggressor is motivated by opportunity for financial gain.

Those who commit workplace violence don't simply snap without warning, however. Research has shown that aggressors tend to exhibit inappropriate and disruptive behavior prior to committing an act of violence.[28] To the

---

[27] R. J. Simmons, *Employer's Guide to Workplace Security and Violence Prevention* (Los Angeles: Castle Publications, Ltd., 1994).

[28] James S. Cawood, "A Plan for Threat Management," Protection of Assets Manual, Merrit Company, 1994.

observant supervisor or manager, this behavior serves as a warning sign and allows time for preventive action to be planned and implemented. Typically, over time the behavior becomes increasingly inappropriate. This incremental escalation, or *ramping up*, should serve as a warning to the employer. However, once set in motion, rarely does a progression reverse without intervention.

Threat Management

Intervention is the process of returning the employee to a structured work environment and helping him regain control of his life. To successfully intervene, management must have the will to redefine boundaries and overcome the aggressor's base of power. The intervention process must be well planned and executed. That strategy is developed and implemented by what is often called the *threat* (or *incident*) *management team*. Depending on the circumstances, the threat management team should consist of professionals from the following areas or disciplines:

- Executive management
- Human resources
- Security/executive protection
- Employment/labor law
- Public law enforcement
- Clinical psychology/psychiatry
- Private investigation
- Incident/crisis management

Though each member of the team has an important role, that of the clinician is probably the most critical. The clinician should be a licensed psychological or psychiatric professional, preferably at a Ph.D. or M.D. level. He or she should have experience in dealing with the criminally insane, conducting hostage negotiations, and trauma management. He or she should also be familiar with local and state employment and labor law. The other team members should also be carefully selected. Each should have the necessary skill and experience to make difficult decisions quickly.

Once the members are identified, the team should meet and decide on preliminary objectives based on available information. The safety of the intended target (if known) should always come first, of course. Protection of property, inventory, and equipment is secondary.

Lacking critical information, the team is often unable to make decisions. When this situation occurs, one or more team members must be assigned the task of collecting the information that is needed. That process may involve discreetly interviewing the target, witnesses, coworkers, supervisors, and former employers and may also require background investigation, surveillance, and in some cases the use of undercover.

In most cases of aggressive and threatening employee behavior in the workplace, time does not permit the placement of an undercover investigator for the specific purpose of gathering information. However, in many instances the investigator is already there. Under these circumstances the undercover investigator can be used like a surgical tool to discretely and unobtrusively gather information that may otherwise be impossible to obtain. Unlike the sort of cases considered previously, where the transgressor is involved in drugs or guns for profit and violence is a potential outcome, in these cases violence *is the outcome*. Plainly, the objective of those engineering the intervention is to avoid that outcome. The use of sophisticated tools like undercover can be a terrific advantage in meeting that objective.

Effective undercover investigators establish elaborate networks in the workforces in which they are placed. In a matter of months, an investigator can get to know dozens of people and be widely accepted as an "insider." Once networked the investigator easily collects information regarding employee misconduct, behavior, and attitudes. As an insider the investigator can also identify dysfunctional personalities, emotional irregularities, and inappropriate behavior. I am not suggesting that the typical undercover investigator is able to psychoanalyze his coworkers or even come close to predicting the level of danger posed by them. However, I am suggesting that the undercover investigator who is properly trained and supervised can flag early warning signs and potential trouble. He can be an employer's eyes and ears and warn not only of potentially aggressive behavior but also of the real threat of violence itself.

Several years ago, during a routine undercover drug and theft investigation for a large midwestern meat processor, one of our investigators stumbled onto a real psychopath.[29] We'll call him Oscar. Oscar was a 42-year-old white male. He lived alone and had few friends. He often wore camouflaged military fatigues to work and always carried a black backpack. He was so protective of the backpack that he once told our investigator, who had unwittingly walked between Oscar and his backpack, that if the investigator ever did it again, he'd kill him. It was much later in the investigation, however, that we began to see the real Oscar. He frequently hinted he had seen action in Viet Nam—later proven to be untrue—and that he enjoyed torturing animals in his spare time. He claimed to have killed a neighbor's horse as well as several neighborhood dogs because its owner had offended him. During breaks and lunch Oscar frequently discussed the killing power of military weapons and his familiarity with handguns. For years the entire workforce had been frightened of Oscar. But over time he became comfort-

---

[29] For the purposes of this book, the word *psychopath* shall mean a person with an antisocial personality disorder, especially one manifested in aggressive, perverted, criminal, or amoral behavior. Though not clinically diagnosed, Oscar's behavior at work and elsewhere fit this definition.

able with our investigator, with whom he began to share some of his inner secrets.

Oscar told us he had had a tormented childhood. He said he had been physically and mentally abused by his mother and abandoned by his father. He hated women and openly discussed his desire to physically dominate them. He also confided that he wanted to hurt people and the desire to do so was escalating. Considering the threat he had made to our investigator, several incidents of sabotage (all tied to Oscar), and his deteriorating mental state, our client and we decided it was time to intervene. After considerable preparation we withdrew our undercover and confronted Oscar.

We chose to interview him in a small conference room, but took all of the necessary precautions in view of our suspicion that his backpack contained a weapon. To our surprise (and that of everyone else), Oscar was cooperative and quite lucid. Apparently recognizing the stir he had created, he readily emptied his pockets and allowed us to search his backpack. It contained some toiletries, a newsmagazine, a sweatshirt, his wallet, car keys, and several best-selling paperbacks, but no weapon. In fact, the search of his locker, work area, and automobile produced similar results. Our background investigation failed to substantiate any of his claims and he had no criminal record. Other than his threat and unusual choice of conversation, he was in most regards just like anyone else. Having my own doubts, however, I suggested he submit to a psychological assessment. Not surprisingly, he refused and while his employer was deciding what to do next, he resigned and has not been heard of since. Who was Oscar? What was his plan and what really went on in his head? No one will ever know.

The background investigation and overall coordination of the intervention process are usually the responsibility of the team consultant/coordinator or corporate security manager. In any event, the expeditious collection of reliable information will assist in the determination of dangerousness and potential solutions. Predicting the future behavior of the aggressor is another matter. As discussed earlier, this complicated task is best left to experts.

Management should rely only on the assessments made by qualified professionals. If termination, hospitalization, or prosecution is appropriate, the team must strategize to achieve that result without provoking a violent response. Even if management intends to work with the troubled employee, the threat management team must still create a workable strategy. That strategy should redefine performance and behavior boundaries for the aggressor and tolerance thresholds for management, and, if appropriate, contemplate the use of undercover.

Prevention

In summary, employers must take the following steps to ensure a violence-free workplace:

- Make a commitment to workplace safety
- Create practical and sound policies that address workplace violence and aggression
- Better screen applicants and identify problem individuals before they are hired
- Allow all grievances to be heard and solve problems early
- Quickly address poor performance and inappropriate behavior
- Hold supervisors and managers accountable
- Teach kindness

Obligations of Employers

It is difficult if not impossible to argue that employers do not have an affirmative obligation to maintain a safe and orderly workplace. It is the duty of employers to protect employees from real and potential dangers. Employers also have the legal duty to investigate any claim of unlawful discriminatory harassment. As business managers, employers have the further duty to protect the public and all those with whom the business and its employees interact. And for publicly traded companies the burden is even greater. Corporate executives have a duty to protect the financial interests of their investors. Employee theft, substance abuse, and criminal misconduct threaten a business's ability to meet these obligations and as such increase its liabilities. Employee malfeasance impairs a business's ability to effectively function and compete. It effects its ability to raise capital, attract and retain quality talent, and generate a reasonable return on investment. Let's look at these obligations a bit more closely.

Moral Obligation

I think most readers would agree that every employer has several significant moral obligations. As a corporate parent, the employer has the moral obligation to maintain peace and order among those it employs, at least while at work. It is expected that the employer provide a safe and healthy work environment, free from known hazards and risks. It is expected that the employer do all that it can to ensure that the employee, who walks through the front door in the morning, exits by the same means at the end of the day. Many contend that the employer has the obligation to create an environment that stimulates creativity and personal growth, and, if at all possible, one that is mentally challenging. I personally think, and am sure many readers would agree, the employer has the obligation to ensure that employees are not subjected to the immoral or unlawful conduct of others—that they not be exposed to those who steal, use drugs, hurt people, and detract from the general enjoyment of a peaceful work life.

As a corporate citizen the employer's moral obligations are equally great. The communities in which businesses reside expect those businesses to behave properly and professionally. They expect businesses to pay their taxes, create meaningful and well-paying jobs, and protect the environment. No community knowingly permits business abuses, immoral conduct, and criminal practices. And businesses that don't meet the expectations of the communities in which they reside often pay dearly. Consider the public outcry and the tarnished images of specific corporations (or entire industries in some cases) in the aftermath of public spectacles like the congressional hearings investigating the tobacco industry, the grounding of the *Exxon Valdez*, and the huge class action sexual harassment case against Mitsubishi.

American corporations have the moral responsibility to keep a clean house. They also have the moral responsibility to maintain a workplace free of dishonesty, substance abuse, and inappropriate behavior. Consistent with that responsibility, employers of all sizes have the obligation to investigate all matters involving employee malfeasance and criminal activity in their workplace. To do otherwise is negligent and immoral.

Legal Obligation

Though I will discuss the topic in greater detail in a later chapter, businesses have a vast array of legal obligations to both the public and their employees. They are bound by statute to provide a safe and healthy work environment, free from known hazards and risks, under federal and state laws like that of OSHA. They are also legally obligated under Title VII of the U.S. Code to ensure that their workplaces are free of discrimination and harassment. And in many states businesses are legally restricted as to how far they may pry into the private affairs and activities of their employees. Businesses also have myriad banking, securities, and accounting rules that impose guidelines with which they must comply with or face stiff penalties and even prosecution.[30]

If that were not enough, businesses can also be civilly punished for their own misconduct or for that of their employees. Inappropriate behavior or misconduct, whether intentional or not, can give rise to claims of emotional distress, false imprisonment, illegal search and seizure, defamation of character, invasion of privacy, discrimination, wrongful discharge, and negligence. In many instances the defendant may face compensatory as well as punitive damages. And because punitive damages are

---

[30] See "Sentencing Guidelines for Organizational Defendants," part of the Federal Sentencing Guidelines that were promulgated by the U.S. Federal Sentencing Commission and became federal law on November 1, 1991. Violations of the Guidelines result in severe penalties, in some cases up to $290 million in fines.

meant to punish the defendant, awards can sometimes be astronomic. They can even bankrupt a financially healthy organization.

Sound policies and proactive prevention programs can significantly reduce these exposures. But when problems surface there is no substitute for a properly conducted investigation. In fact a failure to conduct an investigation could, by itself, constitute ratification by the employer of the unlawful conduct. Additionally, the regulations under Title VII require an employer both to investigate and to take immediate corrective action, if appropriate, depending on the outcome of its investigation when dealing with allegations of discrimination or discriminatory harassment (29 C.F.R. §1604.11(d)). Furthermore, the courts have said that the employer must not just conduct an investigation, it must conduct *a thorough and meaningful* investigation.[31] In addition to whatever legal protection it may afford, a thorough investigation will also likely produce better information and more facts that will allow corporate decisionmakers the opportunity to make legally defensible decisions regarding discipline and/or corrective action. By using a "good faith and reasonable" standard of proof, employers can minimize their exposure even in cases where their conclusions may be incorrect.[32] There can be few more compelling reasons to conduct a thorough investigation than that of reducing personal and corporate liability.

Financial Obligation

Those who manage businesses also have an obligation to their owners or investors to ensure that their investment is reasonably protected from fraud, waste, and abuse. Managers and supervisors have a fiduciary duty to protect those who employ them from the effects of employee theft, substance abuse, and workplace criminal activity. Protecting the organization's assets through a comprehensive loss prevention and asset protection effort is not only the law but also makes financial sense. And as most managers know, an effective loss prevention and asset protection program requires policies, sound practices, and the ability to investigate. Because undercover investigation is interactive and discrete by design, it is among the most effective forms of investigation available. Engineered and executed properly, undercover is more successful than any other form of investigation in obtaining information and uncovering workplace misconduct and criminal activity.

It seems to me that businesses are financially irresponsible when, confronted with proof (or at least a credible allegation) of gross employee misconduct or malfeasance, they choose to ignore it. I know of organizations that passively endure inventory shrink exceeding 5 percent. I know of others that have suffered very unsophisticated employee diversion schemes for

---

[31] *Fuller v. City of Oakland*, 47 F.3d 1522 (9th Cir. 1995).
[32] See the recent California Supreme Court decision, *Cotran v. Rollins Hudig Hall*, (1998).

years and have done nothing. I know of still others that have been defrauded of millions of dollars by a trusted employee, and yet simply allowed that person to resign. The fraud, waste, and abuse that goes on in the typical organization is deplorable. Yet we simply allow it. What's more, we often encourage it.

Consider for a moment your own organization. How effective are its employee access control procedures? Does it have a functioning prop-erty pass system for employees? Are all applicants drug tested? Are inter-nal audit and finance separate functions? Are blank company checks kept under lock and key? Is there a functioning security awareness program? And most critically, *are all losses, thefts, and allegations of substance abuse properly investigated?* Your answers tell a lot about your organiza-tion and how it operates. Is it not financially irresponsible not to control ones assets and the corporate environment? It is—and it is therefore also true that while employee transgressors actively seek out our vulnerabili-ties, we must aggressively try to identify them first. For it is also true that the transgressor will exploit the system to the extent the system will allow. For that reason alone, businesses must demonstrate their resolve to main-tain order and protect their interests by aggressively investigating all offenses against them. No other form of investigation better suits that need than undercover.

Risks of Undercover

There can be no gain without risk. The argument for undercover is no excep-tion. Undercover investigations are fraught with risk and opportunities to stub one's legal toe. In many situations, however, there are no other options. This is particularly true in the workplace where most misconduct and crim-inal activity is perpetrated: on private property behind the secure walls of an impressive building protected by fences, a trained security force, and exotic electronic gadgetry. Regardless of the type of workplace, those who undertake an undercover investigation must possess the skills, experience, and resources to do the job properly. All too frequently the small yet eager private investigative agency accepts an undercover assignment without the ability to properly carry it out. These small vendors often lack the sophis-tication to run the case effectively and avoid the legal minefields created by the myriad laws and regulations at the federal, state, and local level. Many of these small vendors do not provide their employees proper train-ing or supervision. Many are either uninsured or underinsured. Most simply lack the experience to do the job right. The result is very often predicable. The client's objectives are barely met (if at all); any potential criminal cases are usually so defective they cannot be filed; financial recoveries are rarely made; and so many rules, laws, and personal rights are violated that every-one becomes a defendant except the subjects of the original investigation.

And as is usually the case, bad facts make bad law. In the end everyone is a loser.

Undercover investigation still plays a very special role in today's workplace. Few investigative tools rival its effectiveness and return on investment. While it can be incomprehensibly complicated and fraught with liability, undercover permits a "behind the scene" view of the internal workings of an organization while allowing a rare peek into the criminal mind in action. But, for this marvelous tool to work, strategy and process are necessary. Without these essential elements no undercover investigation can succeed.

CHAPTER 2

Preinvestigation Preparation and Operative Placement

The process of investigation is dynamic and fluid. The approach must be reasonable and the investigator flexible. However, in order to be successful, every investigation must have a meaningful purpose and be executed ethically and lawfully.

By definition, corporate undercover investigation is nothing more than the surreptitious placement of a properly trained and skilled investigator, posing as an employee, into an unsuspecting workforce for the purpose of gathering information. Simple you say? Hardly. Although on its face, undercover appears deceivingly simple, it is in fact the most complicated and demanding form of investigation available. It is fraught with legal challenges and if improperly executed it can create untold liabilities for both the client-employer and the investigator. Undercover also requires the investment of time, patience, and resources. It requires a highly structured process and flawlessly detailed plan.

For these reasons and others, undercover investigation is neither for everyone nor for every organization. Undercover does, however, serve a very specific purpose and, as previously mentioned, it enables the collection of information and ultimately the solving of problems not possible by other means. The successful undercover investigation requires the following elements:

- Management commitment
- Meaningful objectives
- Well-conceived strategy
- Properly pooled resources and expertise
- Lawful execution

Let's take a closer look at each of these components and how they affect the investigation.

Management Commitment

Because undercover investigations require the investment of time, patience, and resources, management determined commitment to the undercover operation is paramount. From the very beginning, management must be prepared to see the process through. For example, suppose the typical undercover investigation requires a budget of about $100,000 and takes something on the order of five to six months to complete. Should that be the case, management needs to be emotionally prepared at the outset for that kind of investment. Management must also be prepared to withstand the temptation to react to the information as it is developed by the investigator(s).

This is often a significant challenge. Consider for a moment discovering early in an undercover drug investigation that your company suffers a huge employee theft problem (which is often the case). Imagine daily losses of thousands of dollars because of employee theft and yet learning that the investigator has only scratched the surface of the problem. The bleeding may seem unbearable. However, reacting too soon may expose only a portion of the problem and permit only temporary corrective action. The net yield is therefore significantly diminished and the return on investment reduced.

The Investment of Time

Obviously not all undercover investigations are alike. They vary in purpose, approach, and design. They also vary in length. The investigation's objectives and the size and scope of the problem under investigation will determine its length, along with the skill and the ability of the investigator and his or her handler. The better trained, skilled, and experienced the investigative team, the shorter will be the investigation.

Typically, once the investigator is placed and has begun his cover position, some period of time is required for him to build relationships of trust and acceptance with supervisors. During this relationship-building phase, the investigator also familiarizes himself with the facility, his job, and the general environment in which he is working. He establishes himself as a hardworking, dedicated employee who listens to instructions and completes his assignments. This element is critical, for after the relationship-building phase the investigator wants the opportunity to freely wander and associate without attracting unnecessary attention from supervisors.

During this phase the investigator also must do what is necessary to become accepted by his coworkers. Depending on the environment this can be a particularly difficult challenge. In cases where there have been recent layoffs, downsizings, or some form of workforce reduction, tension between management and labor may be particularly high. New employees introduced into such an environment are likely to not be well received and will be thought of and treated as outsiders. Tenured employees may be outwardly hostile to them and make their work life miserable. There are methods to overcome this situation (discussed in the next chapter) and the investigator must be prepared to use them if necessary.

Cliques, gangs, and family relationships can also prolong the relationship-building phase. Lifestyle, education, and ethnicity also affect the rate at which new hires are accepted. Tightly knit and often closed subcultures do not easily allow newcomers. Sometimes, these subcultures practice hazing or employ unique acceptance rituals involving dangerous or even aberrant behavior. I have encountered situations in which new hires were expected to steal or use drugs in front of their coworkers. I have encountered another where the new hire was expected to publicly have sex with a mentally disabled employee in order to be accepted. I have even come across a situation where our investigator was required to urinate in a supervisor's coffee cup or defecate in her office in order to just sit at the same lunch table as our subjects. Of course the investigator did neither of those things, and consequently our investigation moved forward more slowly than if he had.

In any event, the investigative team must be aware of such obstacles to developing trust in advance and prepare for them to whatever extent possible. Without such obstacles, the typical relationship-building phase takes somewhere between four to six weeks. Under normal circumstances in real life, it takes something on the order of three to six months for an individual to fully integrate into a new organization. The existence of subcultures and the inability to freely associate with one's coworkers will significantly lengthen that time. The skilled undercover investigator, however, is usually able to compress that length of time into something much shorter. Her inability to do so results in a longer, more expensive investigation for the client.

In organized labor environments where the union is particularly strong or where antimanagement feelings are unusually strong, two months or more may be necessary just for the investigator to be allowed to eat lunch with his coworkers, which is ironic given organized labor's alleged commitment to brotherhood. My experience is that union workshops are often the most difficult to penetrate. Not only is new employee hazing common, unionized environments tend to be very hierarchical. By their very nature they value seniority over skill. Consequently, new hires are relegated to menial and labor-intensive tasks while their more senior "brothers" are given the more desirable or easier work. In circumstances such as these, the investigator is cast into an employee underclass that is overworked, undertrained, and sometimes viciously harassed. This counterproductive form of new hire orientation often goes unnoticed by the employer. Management does not see the hazing, teasing, and sabotaging of productivity. Instead, it simply looks like some people are cut out for the work while some are not.

For the undercover investigator, however, survival in the workplace is necessary for success. The investigator must overcome the challenge and prevail—often against significant opposition.

Although it is difficult to pinpoint the day when the investigator is finally accepted and no longer considered a new hire, the defining moment is usually different for different people in the organization. For example, supervision and management will generally recognize a focused, hard-working employee and accept them sooner than the individual's coworkers. Even in the most healthy work environments, some employees see enthusiastic and productive new hires as threats. The skilled investigator understands this double standard and uses it to her advantage. She carefully exhibits different behaviors and work ethics for different audiences. This technique is particularly effective in union environments, where union members and labor leaders can discourage productivity and efficiency while, conversely, management pursues it.

The successful undercover investigator will also recruit a *sponsor*. A sponsor is a carefully selected coworker that the investigator can use to create the appearance of having coworker friends that seem to trust her and without hesitation will vouch for her. Without attracting undue attention, then, the skilled investigator transitions from relationship building to proactive investigation.

As mentioned above, the length of the investigation will be determined by a number factors. The proactive portion of the undercover investigation may take weeks or months depending on the objectives and the nature and size of the problem. I have conducted drug investigations that lasted only several weeks and have conducted theft investigations that went on for 18 months. Today, most of my undercover investigations last somewhere between four and six months.

Drug investigations tend to move faster than other types of investigations. This is largely because substance abuse is a shared social behavior. In the case of illegal drugs, dealers must seek out users and, conversely, users must seek out dealers. This dynamic is exaggerated in the workplace where by design people are often caused to associate in small groups (called *work groups* or *teams* by management consultants) for long periods of time. Over time the members of these groups tend to undergo a sort of social and behavioral alignment. Interestingly, if sufficiently isolated, these groups evolve to create their own work ethic (called a *self-directed work group* when that work ethic meets management's expectations and an *experiment in employee empowerment* when it doesn't), values, and rituals. When employee substance abuse is introduced into one of these groups, a simple management experiment can become a management nightmare. Without effective supervision and no managerial oversight, these small teams can do pretty much as they please. Sufficiently isolated, they can use and sell drugs at their leisure with little risk of getting caught. However, these tightly knit groups are sometimes difficult for the undercover investigator to penetrate, thus increasing the length of an otherwise routine investigation.

Drug investigations are not always of shorter duration, however. If the employee substance abuse problem is particularly acute or an unusually large number of employees are involved, the investigation can be very lengthy. One recent case in Maryland produced almost 150 drug purchases from nearly 50 employees. It took four undercover investigators working for more than six months to penetrate the problem. And given more time, I'm sure the body count would have been even higher.

On the other hand, theft investigations generally tend to take more time and skill. With the exception of large theft rings and elaborate conspiracies, most workplace theft cases involve employees working alone or in relatively small groups. The participants tend to be very cliquish and secretive. They tend to be less social than substance abusers and appear to prefer isolation and solitude, probably with very good reason. Unlike the employee drug dealer, most workplace thieves don't need their coworkers knowing their dirty little business. In fact the more who know of their behavior, the greater the risk of discovery. Although this is also true for the drug dealer, his customers too are breaking the law. In the case of the lone thief, no one needs to know of his scheme, not even his fence. For the undercover investigator these situations pose obvious challenges.

Theft investigations also tend to run longer because they frequently spill out of the workplace. Clearly, it will take more time and resources to investigate a pair of shipping and receiving clerks who are diverting their employer's finished goods to an international network of autopart resellers than it would a small group of forklift drivers who routinely smoke marijuana in the company break room at night. Theft investigations can be exceedingly tedious and consume huge amounts of physical and financial resources because the perpetrators are so secretive.

Barring cases involving a high degree of employee complacency, most undercover theft investigations take months to solve. Later I will discuss ways to accelerate theft investigations using multiple investigators, cutouts, and a simple technique I call the "wedge."

Patience

Undercover investigations also require patience, sometimes a lot of patience. Because undercover is both labor and time intensive, it is easy to loose focus. Many employers have difficulty with undercover because it takes so long. Unlike other forms of investigation (like interviews) that typically provide instant gratification, undercover is usually slow and tedious. It is also fraught with complications.

First to contend with is the selection of the investigator. Then the investigator must be placed. Often this is not an easy task. The investigator-applicant must undergo multiple interviews, often with hostile interviewers hoping to hire a preferred candidate, a rigorous background investigation, and of course a drug test. Each phase of the hiring process possesses its own set of challenges and obstacles. Unfortunately, sometimes the investigator does not pass the grade and is not hired as planned. Though this outcome is often avoidable, when it does occur it is a setback which consumes time and delays the entire investigation.

I often have had cases in which the client could not influence the hiring process and our investigator had to be hired cold. In these cases, a lot of *front-end* had to be put into preparing and briefing the investigator-applicant. Even with the best of efforts, we have sometimes failed and the investigator was not selected. On more than one occasion it has taken as many as five investigators applying for a job before one was finally hired. These sorts of frustrating situations consume time and resources and delay the achievement of the investigation's intended objectives.

Once hired the investigator must next infiltrate the workforce. And as mentioned above, this too can require a great deal of time and patience. Optimally, the investigator should work a position that provides him the greatest amount of movement within the target facility and the least amount of responsibility. When this does not occur, the investigator's information-gathering ability is hampered and the investigation moves more slowly. Rotating shifts, staggered shifts, and production schedules will also affect the investigator's effectiveness. Interestingly, I have observed that an investigator working four 10-hour days produces less information than an investigator working five 8-hour days. Even though both investigators work the same number of hours a week, the one working fewer days produces less information. Thus, it seems that shorter shifts and longer workweeks tend to produce better and faster results.

Another frustration often encountered is law enforcement. All investigations involving drugs and most of those involving theft require some assistance from law enforcement. However, because the mission of law enforcement (the enforcement of public law) differs from that of most private employers (producing profits and creating wealth), conflicts sometimes arise as to mission and purpose. While law enforcement is chartered with the enforcement of public law, it recognizes it is also a public servant. Thus, it is typically eager to help employers address workplace problems involving violations of the law. On the other hand, the employer is not always particularly pleased with the nature and amount of help law enforcement has to offer.

The conflict occurs when law enforcement's resources don't meet the public's demands. By their very nature, workplace undercover investigations are very time consuming. Employee drug dealers are often unpredictable and employee thieves are typically very inexperienced and nervous. Law enforcement rarely has the resources to work these types of cases and dedicate the personnel necessary to properly develop them. Employers are easily frustrated when local police tell them they cannot provide the personnel to investigate their problems.

Even with the assistance of their hired private investigators, employers often find it difficult to obtain help from the local authorities. I've had cases in which our investigators were ready to buy drugs from an employee dealer and we could not get an appointment to see the local sheriff for four weeks. Meanwhile, the dealer began to question the motives of our investigators and my client had no choice but to continue to pay our fees. Matters are further complicated where local policy requires the district attorney's office to be involved. In these instances, after arrangements have been made with the local authorities, our investigators introduced and cleared, and our process approved, the case still cannot proceed without the approval of the local district attorney. Only after several meetings and receiving high-level government approval can these cases move forward.

Please let there be no misunderstanding. In no way am I criticizing law enforcement, district attorneys, or the criminal justice system. I am simply pointing out that the needs of the government and those of the private employer are not the same. Consequently, the investigative process may be affected and the undercover user needs patience.

Resources

In the business world of today, the term *resources* is synonymous with *cost*. For the purpose of our discussion here, it means much more than that. When I use the term, I am referring to time, money, and expertise. It is the proper pooling of resources that makes the undercover investigation possible. Let's first examine time.

Although I have previously discussed *the investment of time*, I restricted that discussion to the investment of time made by the investigator. The investigator's handler (typically called the *case manager* or *case supervisor*) and the client-employer's investment of time must also be considered. And although they will undoubtedly not invest the same amount of time the investigator does, their investment is considerable. For the present, I'll discuss only the investment of time by the client-employer.

The client-employer is usually not a single individual. More often it is a team that consists of several executive or managerial decisionmakers, a security manager, a human resources manager, corporate labor counsel, and any other essential participant. Through the course of the investigation, team members will need to review reports, periodically meet with the investigator and his supervisor, and make decisions. All of this consumes time. In more complicated cases, team members will also have to meet with law enforcement and other government officials.

What's more, at the completion of the investigation, the team must decide upon corrective and disciplinary action. The planning and preparation for such actions can be very time consuming and demanding. Once decided, these actions must be put into motion. If discharges are to take place, that process must be choreographed and replacements obtained. If prosecutions are intended, arrests must be coordinated and made; lockers and desks may need to be searched; and automobiles might need to be removed from company premises. Then during the aftermath, arbitrations, unemployment hearings, and employee prosecutions may require team members to appear as witnesses and testify. In the case of a complex criminal action, complete adjudication may take months. Such cases may require several appearances in court, the production of documents, and hours of preparation.

A successful undercover investigation also requires another resource— money. The size, scope, and nature of the problem will determine the amount of money the client-employer must invest. Today most experienced undercover investigation firms charge by the week (or some larger increment). The weekly rate is usually based on a 40-hour workweek and some minimum cover wage paid to the investigator by the client-employer. Although weekly rates vary, they generally range between $1,500 and $2,000 per week for a quality investigator. The minimum cover wage is usually fixed at something around $15 to $20 per hour. The weekly rate includes charges for both the investigator's time and that of his or her supervisor, as well as report writing, transcription, postage, and communications with the client-employer's designated point of contact. This all-inclusive fee includes just about everything except out-of-pocket expenses and the cost of other special investigations used to augment the undercover effort.

Here's how it works: let's say the cover position—a forklift operator— pays $14 per hour; the difference between it and the minimum cover of wage of, say $16 (an amount decided by the vendor) is $2; it is multiplied by 40 hours, producing a *differential* of $80 per week. The differential is then added to the weekly billing rate of, say, $1,500 for a total weekly charge of $1,580 to the client-employer. Expenses such as rent for the investigator's apartment (if not local), furniture rental, utilities, and union dues are additional.

When billed in this fashion, the investigator keeps his cover pay of $14 and is paid the difference between it and his wage with the agency. Wages for experienced investigators today run anywhere from $15 to $25 per hour, depending upon experience and special skills. In cases where the investigator holds a professional license (like a registered nurse), the wage may be as high as $40 per hour. In these sorts of cases the weekly billing rate and differential will both be above the norm.

Some agencies try to be cute. They claim to have several levels of skill or classifications for their undercover investigators. One small west-coast firm makes the ridiculous claim of having *ten different investigator levels*. I find that claim laughable and think most clients would think it an insult to their intelligence. Most agencies don't even have ten undercover investigators (for the majority of agencies undercover is a sideline), not to mention the means to differentiate investigator skill to the point of creating multiple levels. My firm, for example, has only one level. In order for an investigator to be placed undercover he or she must meet our demanding qualifications, be thoroughly screened, properly trained, and possess the experience necessary to do the job. After years of experience, I've decided we will field only the highest quality investigators available. We have no second or tenth best. My clients desire the best and quite frankly they deserve it.

Some inexperienced agencies charge by the hour. I used to do this too. I've found, however, that most clients don't want to be nickeled and dimed to death. Billing by the hour and charging for report preparation, photocopies, and every telephone call gets to be a bit much. Clients tend to resent complicated invoices that suggest everything is passed on to them and every minute is billed. Moreover, experienced clients know this type of billing scheme can be a foundation for hidden charges. Those who bill undercover by the hour will bill for their investigator's report writing time, his travel time, and any of his overtime. When all said and done, a relatively competitive looking $33 per hour can translate to as much as $2,500 per week after overtime and all the incidental fees are added in. Small and inexperienced agencies usually aren't aware that the experienced client can see through the policy of billing by the hour. Their lack of sophistication is often obvious and the investigation's outcome is consistent with such a lack of skill and experience.

Another common scam is charging a differential based on the investigator's experience. As mentioned above, some agencies go to great lengths to create the appearance of having huge flocks of investigators stratified by experience. Nonsense! If you are shopping for an undercover agency and come across such a claim, ask to see the written descriptions and qualifications for each level, then ask for the agency to tell you how many investigators they have in each level currently working undercover. Also suggest to the agency you want to interview one investigator *and supervisor* from each level. After reading my comments above about this kind of scam, the response you receive should not surprise you.

Also beware of agencies that claim that they have investigators available for immediate placement. Reputable agencies that are actively in the undercover business don't have qualified and experienced investigators just sitting around. Good undercover investigators are worth their weight in gold. It is true that sometimes even my organization has several investigators between assignments (*on the beach*, as we call it in the trade). But top investigators have a very short shelf life. Most often they are assigned their next assignment before the current one ends.

While overcharging is common, undercharging is far more typical. Although one would think that is a blessing for the consuming client-employer, in reality it is not. Undercharging upsets the market. It causes good but struggling agencies to cut corners. It unfairly erodes the profits of the healthy agencies. It causes weak agencies to take unnecessary risks. It diminishes every agency's ability to pay their investigators properly and provide them proper benefits. Any way you cut it, undercharging is a net loss for the client-employer. Businesses, even good businesses, do not continue to provide products and services for which they cannot make a profit. Undercharging creates a market filled with inexperienced cutthroats chasing eroding margins all the while providing the consumer products and services of ever-declining quality. Unfortunately, the undercover business is no different.

Not long ago the director of security for a large brewery proudly told me his firm does a lot of undercover. He said he pays only $400 per week for his investigators and laughingly said he would never pay my rates (at the time, about four times what he was paying). He said he could get investigators a dime a dozen and that his agency (the use of the word *his* later proved to be significant) paid them about $7 per hour. I told him I could not come anywhere near the rate of $400 a week, for most of my investigators were paid nearly twice that alone. What's more, the cost of employee benefits, overtime (we do pay our investigators overtime, even though we don't pass it on to our clients), contributory taxes, and insurance made the rate of $400 per week categorically impossible. The security director smugly suggested I obviously did not know what I was doing, for others had found $400 per week a rate they could charge and still make a profit. I knew his assertion was asinine, but nevertheless walked away scratching my head.

Some time later I learned his undercover investigation had been blown and his case had come apart. Somehow his investigators were compromised and subsequently admitted to have used drugs during the assignment. One of them also admitted to have retained some of the drugs he had purchased for himself while undercover. The security director himself was accused of taking kickbacks from the vendor and was ultimately terminated. To this day, the brewery refuses to use outside investigators despite my repeated attempts to offer my services.

I should note that I am not suggesting that if he had paid his vendors more he would have gotten a different result. Given the qualifications of the vendors, their shortage of experience, and complete lack professional ethics, a higher fee (no matter how large) would not have altered the outcome. What I do want to emphasize is that you get what you pay for. Even today, I occasionally hear of an agency charging less than $1,000 per week; and there is an agency in Atlanta that currently still charges half that. The truth of the matter is that it's just not possible to charge that kind of money, provide competent undercover, and still make a profit.

Consider this: if the investigator's wage, contributory taxes, and benefits total a mere $15 per hour and the investigator works an average of

50 hours (ten of which are overtime at time-and-a-half) per week, he's costing his employer about $800 per week. If the client is paying only a $1,000 per week, the gross profit is less than $200. From that, the agency must pay rent, communication expenses, taxes, recruit, train, market, purchase office supplies, buy equipment and insurance, and pay its staff. If the agency's operating expenses were a mere $20,000 per month, the agency would have to consistently run 25 undercover operations just to break even!

However, calculating differently, for an agency *to run* 25 undercover operations would require a staff of not less then ten people (excluding the investigators) and would have operating expenses on the order of *at least* $100,000 per month. (I should know. My agency is one of the largest of its kind in the United States and I've run as many as 29 undercover at one time.) It is easy to see that in order to charge less than $1,500 per week and remain in business for any length of time, an agency must cut corners. Agencies that undercharge usually don't have insurance, they don't pay their employees overtime as required by law, and they don't properly train their investigators. Most of them also don't pay competitive wages, and as a result don't attract or retain quality talent.

Another common scheme some less-sophisticated agencies pull in order to reduce their overhead is to use independent contractors. Employing their undercover investigators as contractors, they avoid the need to insure them and pay overtime. Though on its face this does seem to make good business sense, it is actually illegal. According to Internal Revenue Service (IRS) regulations, an undercover investigator managed by a private agency does not meet the legal requirements to be an independent contractor. The courts have generally articulated a five-factor test to determine employer as opposed to contractor status.[1] The test assesses (1) the nature and degree of control over the worker; (2) the degree of supervision, direct or indirect, of the worker; (3) the power to determine the pay rate or method of payment of the worker; (4) the right, directly or indirectly, to hire, fire, or modify the employment conditions of the worker; and (5) the preparation of payroll and the payment of wages.[2] Although no one factor may be determinative, the courts generally examine "the totality of the circumstances" in deciding status. Furthermore, the arrangement fails the test for independent contractor status under most state wage and hour regulations as well.

Independent contractors also create liability for the client-employer. Because the investigator is not covered by the agency's workers' compensation insurance, an on-the-job injury could result in an expensive claim against the client. The "contract" investigator probably does not have errors

---

[1] "Managing to Prevent Employment Liability," Sonnenschein Nath & Rosenthal, 1998. Section D, p. 2.
[2] See *Brock v. Superior Care*, 840 F.2d 1054, 1058 (2d Cir. 1988).

and omissions insurance either. Should the investigation precipitate any litigation, aggressive plaintiffs will pursue the deepest pockets available. In the end, should the plaintiff prevail or the case need to be settled, the client-employer will undoubtedly pay more than their fair share since their codefendant(s) are uninsured.

There's yet another risk. Should the independent contractor-investigator decide she no longer wants to be an independent contractor and wants the overtime pay she lawfully deserves, she could sue the client-employer to get it. Because the client, not the agency, provided most if not all of her wages, it is likely that the client would be on the hook for all of the back wages and unpaid overtime. Under the Fair Labor Standards Act of 1938, if all of the investigator's hours, including her overtime, were for a single client company (as is typically the case in an undercover investigation), that client is jointly responsible for ensuring that overtime and minimum wages are paid. What's more, at the completion of the assignment—or more likely when the investigator flat-out quits upon learning the agency cheated her—the investigator will likely file against the client-employer for unemployment benefits. Unless it wants to reveal that the applicant was co-employed and actually an undercover investigator, the claim will have to go uncontested and benefits undoubtedly awarded. What a mess!

I have therefore come to the conclusion that one simply has to pay in order to play. And as a general rule, agencies that undercharge produce poorer results, create unnecessary liability, and in the long run cost their clients more. As I said earlier, you get what you pay for.

In addition to the weekly fee, other costs should be anticipated. Most reputable agencies will charge for any ancillary services provided in support of the undercover. For example, if surveillance were appropriate at some point during the investigation, it would be charged on an hourly basis as an add-on. The booking and handling of evidence, client or attorney-requested meetings, and the creation of any special reports would also be chargeable. Like the fees for undercover, hourly rates do vary. Typically, hourly rates for support services range from $75 to $175 per hour depending on what service is provided. Though these rates may seem lofty and create the impression that the cost of the total project could quickly spin out of control, support services usually make up only a small portion of the total investment. However, in complex theft investigations that spill outside the workplace, fees for support services can add up and quickly become a significant part of the total cost of the project.

Meaningful Objectives

No investigation can be successful unless it has meaningful objectives. I am astounded by many investigative agencies and their investigators that begin an investigation without thoroughly formulating their objectives. How could one possibly measure success if he did not know what it was he was trying to achieve? As a matter of practice I begin every investigation, not just my undercover investigations, by articulating the project's objectives in writing.

In the written investigative proposals I prepare for the client, after discussing the genesis of the problem at hand and the scope of the project, I detail my objectives. By doing so I accomplish two things. First, it is a way to formally demonstrate my understanding of the client's needs or wants. And second, it establishes benchmarks that I can later use to measure results. Detailing an investigation's objectives at the beginning is smart practice and, quite frankly, it's the only way to do business.

Is There Evidence of a Policy Violation or Serious Misconduct?

Before I put pen to paper, however, I usually ask my prospective client a number of questions. The first question is really the most important one: Is there evidence or a credible allegation of a policy violation? Because an undercover investigation is so complicated and time consuming, there must be a very good reason in order to undertake one. Although occasionally businesses desire just a "look see" and want to know how their operations are functioning, clear evidence of gross misconduct or at least very credible allegations of misconduct precipitate most undercover investigations. Simple suspicion and unfounded allegations or rumors are usually not enough to justify such a massive undertaking. These typically suggest that a *preinvestigation* is more appropriate.

A preinvestigation is nothing more than an organized factfinding effort designed to determine if a "real" or professional investigation is actually necessary. Suspicion and rumors are often unfounded. People determined to carry out their own agendas will say things or suggest things that create the appearance of a bigger problem. Combined with circumstantial evidence or evidence suggesting an entirely different problem, decisionmakers can easily be influenced and led to authorize an investigation where none is necessary.

The converse is also true. Often decisionmakers don't authorize an investigation even when they should. Lacking any form of preinvestigation and not having the benefit of all the information that is reasonably available, decisionmakers sometimes make bad calls. By not asking the right questions or not looking in the right places, they can easily miss the obvious. When this happens, problems are not investigated when they should be and the situation remains unchecked.

This is most common in cases involving workplace substance abuse. Because of denial, a lack of will, or simple ignorance, employers sometimes don't recognize the problem until it's too late. Employee substance abuse is particularly insidious because most employers believe they have to catch the abuser using in order to take action. But this is a complete misconception. What's more, the sooner the employer responds to a substance abuse problem, the less expensive it is to fix. *And the fewer lives it will destroy.*

A little preinvestigation might expose an assortment of symptoms that, if examined individually, do not suggest the presence of any wrongdoing. But examined collectively, they may point to a bigger problem. Like the physician who must treat the underlying disease instead of just the symptoms, the business must resist the temptation to treat symptoms alone and have the courage to pursue the disease.

Is There a Duty to Investigate?

The next question I ask is whether the business has a *duty to investigate* and whether the person with whom I'm talking has the authority to authorize an investigation? A business may have very convincing evidence that employees routinely use marijuana on weekends, away from work and off company property. However, does such misconduct justify an investigation and, more importantly, does the employer have the duty to investigate it? The answer is probably no to both questions.

How about an employee theft ring operating outside the workplace? Here again, even in the face of very convincing evidence, an employer probably does not have the duty to investigate. However, the employer's antennae should go up. What is the likelihood this small band of thieves is stealing from others but never from their employer? I think it would be safe to assume that likelihood is quite small. It is probably the case that the employer simply has not yet been made aware of his own losses. In other words, no evidence of their misconduct has found its way to the employer . . . *yet.*

I also like to know that the person who is contemplating my services has the authority to engage me. This is not just because I'd prefer my time not be wasted, but also because someone else may already be working the investigation. In large organizations this is more common than one would think. I have conducted undercover investigations only to later find that another division in the same organization was simultaneously conducting its own undercover. I've actually had one case where my investigator reported the misconduct and drug use of a particular employee only to later learn the employee was actually another undercover investigator (not a very good one, but I guess good enough to fool me) working for another agency. How redundant and what a waste of money!

Would One's Failure to Investigate Have a Detrimental Effect on the Organization?

The last question I ask is whether our failure to investigate has a detrimental effect on the organization or its employees? In other words, what would happen if we did not conduct an investigation? Does the business's inaction create any liability, put people or assets at risk, or affect its reputation or profitability? Surprisingly, the answer is sometimes no. If that is the case, then why conduct an investigation?

It is more often the case, however, that the organization's failure to investigate clearly will have some detrimental effect on the organization or its employees. A good is example is a credible allegation of sexual harassment or race discrimination. Not only is the employer lawfully obligated to investigate, but also its failure to investigate significantly increases its liability and could have a devastating effect on morale and productivity. The answer to the question about detrimental effect, therefore, is often the motivator or precipitator leading the decisionmakers to take some action. If that action is to be taken and an investigation undertaken, clear and meaningful objectives are needed.

Defining Misconduct

In determining investigative objectives, one must first define *misconduct* and categorize the violations that are to be investigated. This rather commonsensical step seems simple enough. It is often overlooked, however, in which case everyone simply assumes they know the investigation's purpose and target. This makes it easy for the investigation to lose focus and direction. Imagine the chilling effect when, four months into the undercover investigation, the CEO angrily asks his lieutenants, "Is this a theft investigation and am I ever going to recover my stolen inventory or is this about a bunch of grab-assing and some stupid football pool?"

The misconduct and malfeasance to be investigated must be defined. Everyone involved in the investigation must understand what information is being sought and what sort of problems need the most attention. The undercover investigator must clearly understand what constitutes a policy violation and what does not. She and her supervisor can have no doubts as to what the client-employer considers misconduct and that which is actionable. It is a terrible waste of time and resources gathering information about issues that are of no concern or value to the customer.

Possible Outcomes and Measuring Results

Once misconduct is defined and the subject of the investigation identified, the client-employer must make clear to its investigators what it wants to do with the information that is uncovered. There are a number of choices at this point, but in the end they amount to only several basic outcomes. Each outcome will determine to some degree how the investigation is engineered and, to a much larger degree, will drive the investigative process. For example, an investigation designed to prosecute offenders will take more time and resources and by its very nature be far more complicated than one designed simply to result in the termination of the offender's employment. Let's examine some of the more typical outcomes and what they involve.

Prosecution

When businesses get hurt they often want revenge. Though it is more commonly called the *pursuit of justice*, the drive for revenge can easily consume an organization and its focus. And as primitive and unbusiness-like this instinct may be, many businesses pursue it with a vengeance. Many employers think employee prosecution creates an effective deterrent. Some believe employee prosecution is a civic duty, and still others pursue it just because they don't know what else to do.

However, employee prosecution can be expensive and risky. Our criminal justice system, though arguably the best in the world, is not perfect. It is cumbersome and slow. Moreover, it is designed to ensure that the accused retains certain rights and opportunities to challenge the accuser; it assumes innocence until guilt is proven. This concept of *due process* is constitutionally protected and buttressed by volumes of criminal procedure and decisions like *Miranda*.[3]

For the employer, the process is even more complex. By blending criminal prosecution and an employment action (e.g., termination), the employer may unwittingly bestow more rights to the subject of its investigation than intended. Not only will a criminal prosecution make it necessary to produce documents and witnesses not otherwise needed if a simple termination is the goal, the cunning defense lawyer may argue that the employer and its investigators pursuing criminal prosecution were agents of the government. If such a defense tactic is successful, agent status would significantly complicate the investigation for the employer. For if the employer (actually one or more of its employees, usually the point of contact or some other decisionmaker) or its investigators are deemed agents of the government, employees subject to interviews or questioning by those agents must be *Mirandized* and the claim of entrapment may be raised as a defense. The problem here, of course, is that neither the employer nor its investigators would know of its agent status until after the fact. Thus, the results of any defendant interviews (and confessions) absent a *Miranda* warning could potentially be thrown out or excluded from evidence. This may not be necessarily fatal to the prosecution assuming the case is based upon more than an employee's admission to his employer or investigator. However, it could very well be fatal to the employer's disciplinary action. What's more, it could give rise to a civil rights violation claim or some other cause of action against the employer. Interestingly, many unsophisticated investigative agencies and investigators actually seek agent status. Unwittingly they play into the hands of sharp

---

[3] *Miranda v. Arizona*. This important Supreme Court decision will be discussed in detail later.

defense attorneys and expose their clients and themselves to unnecessary risk and liability.

I will save the discussion regarding entrapment for later chapters. However, the reader should know that entrapment—contrary to popular belief—is not a crime, it is a criminal defense. Furthermore, a citizen cannot entrap another citizen. Only the government can entrap. Thus only if the employer or its investigators are deemed to be agents of the government can the claim of entrapment be raised. Therefore agent status not only expands the civil rights of the offending employee, it also allows him the opportunity to defend himself by using the otherwise unavailable defense of entrapment.

Employee prosecution can also be expensive and terribly disappointing. Though there are always exceptions, most employee offenders are first-time offenders. Certainly if an employer is effectively screening its applicants, most of those who have a serious record will be disqualified and not offered positions. Pre-employment drug testing, interviewing, and record checking contribute significantly to reducing the number of convicted criminals an employer unwittingly hires.

Thus, when the prosecution of an offending employee represents the first time they have been charged with unlawful conduct, the courts are often more sympathetic to the defendant, or should I say more lenient, than they might be otherwise. The result is often disappointing for the employer. Having possibly spent hundreds of hours and thousands of dollars in order to make its case, the defendant receives little more than a slap on the wrist. Rarely are small first-time offenders ever sent to jail. More rarely are they fined to any significant degree or forced to pay restitution. First-time drug offenders are usually given only probation. It is usually only repeat offenders and drug dealers who see any real punishment. Employers end up spending a lot of time and money perfecting a criminal prosecution and all the offender gets is a harsh admonishment and very inexpensive peek at the substance of the employer's investigation. For these reasons, prosecution often doesn't make a lot of sense to me. I prefer some combination of the next two options: termination and restitution.

Termination

As argued above, employee prosecution is not all what it's made out to be. But employers often justify it for what they consider to be its deterrent value. I, for one, question this alleged deterrent value. Sure, there is an immediate chilling effect as the offenders are marched out in handcuffs for all to see. But how long does that effect last? Not long at all, in my experience. I have conducted many undercover investigations for employers that produced huge "body counts," some of which involved the termination and or prosecution of over 70 employees. In some instances, we conducted as many as eight undercover investigations back to back. That is, upon completion of one investigation and dealing with the offending employees, we placed another undercover investigator and started all over again. On the eighth go-around, an employee approached our just-placed investigator and said, "Be careful, the company uses undercover investigators. . . . If you want anything (meaning drugs, of course) see me; I know who's cool and who's not." Incredible!

I prefer the outcome of termination. It is easier than prosecution largely because the standard of proof is lower. It simply takes less evidence to sustain a discharge than it does to successfully prosecute. What's more, even in cases in which the evidence is thin or even circumstantial, an employer may convince a suspected offender to resign. The time and resources necessary to effect an employment action like termination are far less than that which is required to prosecute.

Some argue, however, that a successful prosecution may justify a termination. It is even argued that a conviction may seal the fate of the offending employee and for all intents and purposes bar an action against the employer. Not true. A conviction affords no guarantees against an employee-filed action. Furthermore, the argument does not sufficiently contemplate what happens if the employee is by chance found *not guilty*. Logic would suggest that if the employee is found by a criminal court to be innocent of the very offense for which he was terminated, the termination might then be unjustified. In fact, that is often precisely the claim. It is not uncommon that a failed prosecution gives rise to a civil action against the employer. Claims could include malicious prosecution, wrongful discharge, intentional and negligent infliction of emotional distress, defamation, and, of course, discrimination. Unfortunately some of these causes of action not only allow compensatory damages but also punitive damages. And because punitive damages are designed to punish the defendant, in many states insurance is not permitted to cover or pay them when they are awarded.[4]

Fortunately employers have several remedies. The first remedy is actually preventive. From the very beginning of the investigation, the employer should carefully separate the criminal action from the employment action. That is, in no way should any employment decision be based on the outcome of a criminal prosecution. The employer should clearly demonstrate that its investigative objectives where quite different than law enforcement's and that it was not driven by employee prosecution. Furthermore, the employer and its investigators should do all that they can to avoid any semblance of agent status, effectively separating the criminal investigation and its outcome from that of the employer's efforts and actions. To successfully make this distinction, the employer must demon-

---

[4] However, state workers' compensation may preempt some claims involving physical or psychological injuries incurred while employed, thus barring further civil action and punitive damages.

strate that any cooperation with law enforcement was limited only to that which was required and necessary to fulfill its (the employer's) objectives. An example is cooperating with the police only in order to allow the undercover investigator to purchase illegal drugs and thus unequivocally prove a policy violation at work.

These measures allow the employer to point out that the standard of proof for criminal prosecution and employment actions are not the same. Thus, while on the basis of certain evidence one can quite easily be found not guilty of a criminal offense, one can, on the basis of that same evidence, be justifiably terminated. In fact employers do this all the time. For a moment, consider your own organization. Of those terminations that took place in the last year, how many of them were for criminal offenses and were summarily prosecuted? More than likely the answer is very few. Most terminations are not for criminal misconduct but for policy violations. Therefore, it makes good sense to engineer the undercover investigation so as to prove only policy violations, not criminal misconduct. There are exceptions to this strategy, however. I will discuss those in detail in Chapter 6 when we examine organizations subject to a collective bargaining agreement.

Restitution

Of all the investigative outcomes possible, restitution is the one least considered by employers. Remarkably, restitution is relatively simple and yet powerfully effective. What's more, restitution significantly increases the economic return on an expensive and protracted investigation. In many instances, the employer can recover not only its losses but also the cost of the investigation.

Restitution has many forms. In its simplest form the offenders either repay or return that which was taken. In its more complex form, restitution can involve contractual agreements, garnishments, and court-appointed facilitators. In these more complex situations, the offenders may not only have to pay compensatory damages but sometimes also punitive damages. A good example are actions under the Racketeer Influenced Criminal Organization Act (RICO), which statutorily permits treble damages. Under any circumstances, if an employer has suffered damages that can be quantified, restitution is usually possible. All that is necessary is an agreeable offender and a vehicle by which they can be bound to the agreement.

In simple matters, the offending employee is simply asked to return that which they have taken. Usually upon the return of the property the employee is terminated or allowed to resign. However, if the thief has made off with a consumable, such as perishable food, or has since disposed of the property, return of the goods is not always possible. Under these circumstances the employer may have to work out a deal with the employee and arrange for them to pay some form of restitution equal to the value of the property stolen. Employers, however, must be cautious in negotiating with the employee. It is unlawful to demand restitution in lieu of criminal prosecution. To do so is typically considered extortion and is in many jurisdictions both criminally and civilly actionable.[5] The employer must therefore be very careful to not even imply how restitution may influence the decision to prosecute or even to report the matter to the authorities.

Employers must also be careful how they construct their agreement with the offending employee. In some states, if an employer accepts an employee's verbal promise to pay restitution or return the stolen goods, a legal contract may be created, even though the terms have not been discussed or agreed upon.[6] The consequence for the impatient employer in these unfortunate circumstances is that the promise to repay may not be enforceable and prosecution legally barred. For this reason alone, it is advisable that no discussion regarding restitution take place until the employer has consulted an attorney familiar with state contract law. A qualified attorney can assist in the construction of a restitution agreement and even act as its facilitator. The attorney can also provide the guidance necessary to avoid an extortion claim or other legal complexities that may arise during the negotiations with the offending employee.

The employer should not overlook the opportunity to recover the cost of the investigation. Often the employer can ask for and receive repayment for the cost of its investigation in addition to the restitution for its actual losses. In one notable case for a world-famous manufacturer of women's undergarments, I recovered nearly $1 million in restitution and the entire cost of my investigation from the offending employee and her retired husband accomplice. The fraudsters and their attorney eagerly agreed to our terms hoping my client would not pursue criminal charges. Though criminal prosecution was never mentioned during our negotiations, the attorney obviously knew his clients were in big trouble and had undoubtedly contemplated the harsh reality of long prison sentences for them both. Because they had the money (well invested in California real estate), writing a million-dollar check was far easier than spending their golden years in prison.

Also recoverable may be management's time and the cost to the business for the inconvenience. Though it may be difficult to calculate hard dollars, rough numbers may work. There is nothing lost by asking the employee to pay restitution for the actual loss as well as a little more to

---

[5] California Penal Code §§153 and 519 make it a crime to threaten criminal action in order to obtain the settlement of a civil matter.

[6] Because verbal contracts are enforceable in many states, the reader is encouraged to seek the advice of counsel or research the appropriate state laws regarding contracts and their enforceability.

cover "costs." This option is particularly useful in cases involving third parties or others that are not employees. Several years ago one of our undercover investigators exposed a group of contract security officers planning to burglarize my client's facility. We subsequently intervened and foiled their plan. However, my client approached their employer and negotiated the forgiveness of several invoices he had not yet paid the contractor. The ultimate settlement included my fees for the undercover and several thousand dollars just for the "inconvenience of it all."

Selecting the Proper Standard of Proof

The *standard of proof* is nothing more than the measure required in a certain case to establish a particular proposition. The law recognizes many standards of proof and applies different standards based on the nature of the claim. It surprises my clients when I share with them that *they* can select the "standard of proof" they wish to apply when deciding corrective and disciplinary action. Most employers mistakenly apply the highest standard of proof possible: *beyond a reasonable doubt*. This lofty standard is the one the government must achieve in order to prevail in a criminal action against a defendant. Though this standard of proof is strict, it is not necessary that the defendant's guilt be proved *beyond all possible doubt*. It is only required that the government's proof exclude any "reasonable doubt" concerning guilt. A "reasonable doubt" is any doubt based upon reason and common sense that remains after careful and impartial consideration of all the evidence in the case.

On the other hand, to establish guilt by the standard known as the *preponderance of the evidence* means to prove that something is more likely so than not so. In other words, a preponderance of the evidence in a case means evidence that, when considered and compared with that opposed to it, has more convincing force and produces in one's mind the belief that what is sought to be proved is more likely true than not true. This is the standard of proof in most civil cases. It is a considerably less-strict standard than beyond a reasonable doubt, thus it is much easier to achieve.

The lowest standard of proof is that of *good faith investigation/reasonable conclusion*. This relatively easy-to-achieve threshold is generally the standard an employer must achieve in deciding an employment action. Significantly lower than either standards of beyond a reasonable doubt or preponderance of the evidence, this standard can be achieved by nothing more than conducting a good faith investigation and drawing some reasonable conclusion from it. In fact, the conclusion may even be wrong, yet the employer would have an affirmative defense against a claim if it had done all it practicably could to thoroughly investigate the matter and from it drew a reasonable conclusion. Not only is this threshold much easier to achieve, it is significantly less expensive to achieve.

In practice, a jury in a civil trial will expect an employer to have fully and promptly investigated an issue. Jurors tend to see employment decisions that result in discharge as extremely serious. Although instructed by the judge that they do not sit in place of the company, jurors are apt to be very impressed that an employer reached not only a decision that was supported by the evidence, but a decision that in the jury's opinion was the right thing to do. Whether the employer's investigation produced more evidence in favor of a proposition than not, or whether it produced clear and convincing evidence, or even if it produced evidence beyond a reasonable doubt, jurors will often consider only whether they think the employer was, in the end, right. This simple yet practical reality serves only to reinforce the need for a thorough, prompt, and professional investigation.[7]

Policy and Labor Contract Review

The next thing that must be done is to review company policies and any labor agreements that may exist. The employer and its investigators must determine what constitutes a policy violation and which violations are actionable. It no longer surprises me to find companies of all sizes with poorly conceived and ineffectual policies that do more to restrict management than dictate the standards for behavior and performance of employees. Common policies like this are progressive disciplinary procedures that are so detailed and complex that it is impossible for the well-meaning supervisor not to miss something and unwittingly violate the very policy he is attempting to enforce. Most of the newer workplace policies aimed at preventing violence that I've reviewed for clients tend to make the same mistake: they describe in exhaustive detail what managers "shall do" or "not tolerate" and barely mention inappropriate employee behavior and discipline.

Assurances should be made that the issues or problems subject to investigation are in fact actionable and properly addressed by written policy. Two common offenses overlooked (interestingly both of which are criminal) in many policy manuals are the possession of drug paraphernalia and the offer to sell drugs to another party. Though many substance abuse policies contemplate the sale or transfer of illegal drugs while on the job, few address the crime of offering drugs to others. Amounting to little more than what could arguably be idle talk, a cunning employee drug dealer could market his wares on company time and property yet never bring the drugs to work. Notwithstanding a decidedly aggressive interpretation, a dealer might be able to go so far as to even accept money on company time and property and yet not violate a policy prohibiting the sales of drugs at work. More safe and thus more typical is the employee-dealer who parks his car

---

[7] Substantial portions of the this section were provided by Bill C. Berger, Esq., Stettner Miller & Cohn, P.C., Denver, Colorado.

off company premises (say on a public street beside the business), where his customers are then brought for the actual money and drug exchange. You be the judge: would such conduct constitute a violation of your company's substance abuse policy?

Then consider the issue of drug paraphernalia. Does your company substance abuse policy prohibit the possession of drug paraphernalia on company time and property? My guess is that it does not.

The point I want to make is that the employer and its investigators must critically examine policies before assuming that common criminal misconduct constitutes a policy violation. As a rule, administrative law judges and arbitrators generally will not affirm terminations in cases lacking clear policy prohibitions and very good proof that those policies were violated willfully. With the exception of gross and willful misconduct that is in the direct conflict of the best interests of the employer (e.g., stealing or diverting company property), relying on criminal law in the absence of company policy will not fly. What's more, the punished employee may argue that if his employer is to use criminal law in place of policy, it should also apply the complimentary criminal standard of proof as well. And as discussed in the previous section, if the disciplined employee's claim prevailed, the employer might be saddled with a higher standard of proof than is otherwise necessary.

There are, however, a couple of simple and useful measures that can be taken. The first is also the most obvious. If a particular policy does not exist, create one! The employer with the assistance of competent legal advice could quickly write and disseminate a new policy. If, for example, the employer already had a substance abuse policy but felt it to be inadequate, the policy could be amended and republished. If the policy in any way changed the terms and conditions of employment—*prohibiting the offer to sell drugs at work does not change the terms and conditions of any work environment*—good sense dictates that the employer provide a short moratorium between the announcement of the change and its implementation. Depending upon the degree of change, that moratorium might be anything from one week to six months. Discuss the matter with your labor attorney if you have questions.

A second measure that employees can take is to enforce *public policy*. Although public policy violation claims are usually made by employees against their employers, employers can assert public policy violation claims as well by asserting that not only is the employee's activity not in the best interest of the public, and thus offensive, it is also not in the best interest of the employer. Therefore, not only is it in the best interest of the business to respond to the employee's behavior, but it is the company's public duty to so respond. Under this theory, the activity is thus actionable and the employer may punish employees who engage in it. As powerful as this argument may be, precedent, past practices, and labor contracts may restrict its effectiveness.

I will discuss the matter of precedent and past practices in the next section, so for the moment let me briefly address labor contracts. Labor contracts should be reviewed for an assortment of reasons while formulating the project's objectives and engineering the investigation. First, see if the contract prohibits the use of undercover (I've never seen one that does) or in any way restricts the conduct of a workplace investigation (I've seen plenty that do). A restriction I've seen several times dealt with the employer's use of covert surveillance. As I recall, they required the employer to notify employees when and where "covert surveillance" was to be used. Obviously, that practice would produce little or no results. The question begs to be asked: if privacy laws already provide adequate protection against an employer's invasion of employee privacy, why would the union contractually need to know if the company decided to use cameras to investigate suspected employee theft? My guess is that it is not because unions want to know about any internal investigations and help the company find members who were stealing.

Labor contracts may also stipulate how long the employer can sit on information regarding a policy or work rule violation before notifying the alleged violator of it. I've come to call these stipulations the "ten-day" or "thirty-day rule," with the number of days representing the corresponding *statute of limitations*. Either rule is problematic for undercover. Effectively, any policy violation beyond the stipulated statute of limitation is not actionable. In other words, regardless of the length of the investigation, the employer can only take corrective action for the most recent offenses. Fortunately for the employer handicapped by this type of contract language, there are several highly effective countermeasures that I will discuss in Chapter 6 when addressing some of the other complexities of undercover in a union environment.

The last labor contract provision to be aware of is the "three-day rule." This fairly common stipulation requires the employer to discipline the transgressor within three days of noticing an employee's policy or work rule violation. It is the union equivalent of a defendant's right to a speedy trial. The provision requires the employer to closely watch the calendar during the undercover shutdown. If the investigation yields a body count of any significant size, it may take the employer more than three days to process the offenders and disburse disciplinary action. An innocent three-day rule violation on the part of the employer could negate its prerogative to discipline or take corrective action.

Precedent and Past Practice

Another consideration when developing investigative objectives is precedent. Both the client-employer and the investigator should examine past practices and precedent relative to the intended course of action and the potential outcomes. If, for example, a retailer has never discharged an

employee for theft, even though many thieves have been caught and repri-
manded, an employee who decides to steal could expect only to be counseled if caught. If the retailer were to suddenly change its practice and
instead discharge, the offender could argue that the punishment was
not consistent with past practice and too harsh. Though under most
circumstances, an employer can change the terms and conditions of
employment, those potentially affected by the change should be given
notice and asked to acknowledge their awareness and understanding of the
new policy. In this example, the employer might simply publish and distribute a memorandum establishing that, from that moment forward,
anyone caught stealing would be discharged. To ensure that the new policy
was properly communicated, the employer might ask each employee to sign
off on it.

In a union environment, changing the terms and conditions of employment is not so easy. Typically, such changes must be bargained for by the
employer through negotiation with the union representing the affected
employees. This can be done either during scheduled contract negotiations
or via a letter of agreement prior to contract expiration. For example, the
employer of unionized workers that decides to institute random drug testing
for the purpose of establishing fitness for duty changes the terms and conditions of employment for all those affected. This change must clearly be
bargained before its institution.

But suppose random drug testing has already been properly instituted
and that those testing positive are routinely given a second chance, offered
rehabilitation if appropriate, and subjected to periodic drug testing for, say,
12 months. Over a period of time this practice establishes precedent and to
a significant degree restricts management prerogative. The impact of such
a precedent can be significant *even when the employer does not know one
exists.*

Several years ago one of my clients suffered a severe blow in arbitration as the result of its past practices and a precedent it had unknowingly
established. The client-employer had discharged over 30 employees for
workplace substance abuse offenses based on my undercover investigation.
Our case was airtight. We had written and tape-recorded confessions from
most of the offenders, and our evidence against the others was overwhelming. On behalf of the employees, the union filed a grievance and the
cases eventually went before the notorious San Francisco arbitrator Sam
Kagel. Upon hearing both sides, Kagel overturned every discharge, citing
the employer's disparate treatment of the offenders and an inconsistency
with past practices. Because several former supervisors had once consumed
beer in the company parking lot prior to a Saturday fishing trip and were
not so much as counseled for it, Kagel reasoned that the employer's discharge of the union employees who had been caught using and selling drugs
at work should be similarly treated. What's even more remarkable is that
the employer (the manufacturer of corrugated boxes) was not aware of the

supervisor's beer drinking until it was disclosed by the union during the arbitration. Not only had the alleged event taken place nearly three years before our undercover investigation, but the only witnesses to the alleged beer drinking were the grievants. The supervisors had long since been terminated for poor performance.

I think Kagel's opinion is a travesty. Not only did he abrogate management's prerogative to discipline for gross misconduct, he denied those needing drug treatment and counseling the impetus to obtain the help they so desperately needed. Though Kagel may not know it, such passive encouragement of drug use is called *enabling* and it is often what allows substance abuse to exist in the workplace. Although he handed the union what must have seemed to it a victory, Kagel's decision did no favors for those employees who were caught and not given the treatment they deserved.

Time Allocation and Requirements

The client-employer must also contemplate the amount of time it can invest in the investigation. An undercover investigation can take months to complete. In preparing to move forward, the employer must consider the potential impact on workplace safety by delaying corrective action until a thorough investigation is completed. The employer must decide if solving the bigger problem is worth the risk of possible mishaps, accidents, or even injuries. For while the undercover investigation is unfolding, the very incidents that the employer is trying to prevent may in fact occur. The employer must therefore ask whether this risk and associated liability are offset by the ultimate outcome. The answer to this question is a function of the seriousness of the problem and some guesswork as to the probability of an incident occurring while the matter is still under investigation. Logically, the more serious the problem, the greater the risk. However, even in the case of substance abuse that impairs a worker's performance so that significant danger and liability are risked, an employer can almost always justify the length of an undercover and the time it will take to solve the problem properly. For if the employer takes corrective action prematurely, and is able to only partially address a serious drug problem, many abusers and dealers may go undiscovered. Consequently, the potential of a mishap, accident, or injury occurring is only fractionally reduced while long-term liability remains relatively unchanged. By completing the investigation properly and getting to the root of the entire problem and identifying all of those involved, the employer can take more effective corrective action and reduce its substance-abuse related liability to zero.

Theft cases are no different. Upon discovering that access control procedure violations are contributing to an ongoing inventory shrink problem, an employer may be penny wise and pound foolish to correct that problem if the root of the trouble is in shipping and receiving. Reacting prematurely or taking interim corrective action while trying to solve a bigger shrink problem may not be wise. Frequently all that is accomplished is alerting the perpetrators and driving the problem deeper underground. I've had cases in which an angry client-employer, against my advice, distributed memorandums warning employees not to steal, just as my undercover investigator was making headway with the thieving employees. All that the client accomplished was to spook the crooks and extend the investigation by three months.

In addition to safety and liability, the employer must consider the operational implications as well. By delaying corrective action, there may be operational consequences that are not acceptable. The best example that comes to mind is one where the employer's business is seasonal. If, for example, the employer is a produce packer, it makes no sense to wait for the completion of an undercover and delay corrective action, only to disrupt the business operation at what may be the height of packing season. A better strategy would be to somehow accelerate the investigation or delay its conclusion until after the season.

Union organizing efforts pose a similar timing problem. Clearly it would not be wise to conclude an undercover investigation and discipline a large number of offending employees just prior to a unionization vote. Management's actions, though justifiable, may play into organizers' hands and become the subject of propaganda. Union organizers could fabricate a lot of benefit from such an action and perhaps turn a close election campaign into a victory.

I have, however, intentionally shut investigations down shortly before a vote. In these cases, we knew that those behind the campaign were professional union organizers planted into the workforce posing as employees (a lot like my undercover, but for a distinctly different purpose). By accelerating our investigation and taking decisive employment action against policy violators, my clients were able to significantly weaken union sympathy. Interestingly, the majority of employee offenders in these types of cases were also union sympathizers. Suffice it to say that the employer who is able to eliminate a serious employee drug or theft problem and coincidentally reduce the number of employees in favor of organizing is very fortunate indeed.

I should note, however, that intentionally penetrating a union or collecting information on union organizing by means of undercover is an unlawful violation of the National Labor Relations Act. It is also unethical, and is a form of misconduct employers are frequently accused of by unions attempting to organize their workforce. I don't advocate it under any circumstances.

Compatibility with the Organization's Culture

Organizational culture plays a critically important role in contemplating and engineering any workplace undercover. Because undercover investigation is commonly perceived as sneaky and deceptive, many employers are afraid of it. They mistakenly assume that the workforce and management would respond with intense anger and criticism should the investigation ever be exposed. Executive decisionmakers themselves may dislike the idea of *spying* on their trusted and loyal employees. Such cultural resistance is real and significantly impairs an organization's ability to solve workplace problems. I've had client-employers tell me they would never conduct an undercover investigation because it would violate the trust their employees had in them. Whenever I hear this claim of employee trust in management, my response is to ask why then won't those same employees trust management to properly solve complex workplace problems like that of employee theft, dishonesty, and substance abuse? To the employers that assert employee loyalty concerns, I ask why haven't those loyal employees come forward to reveal who the violators are and to provide the information necessary to deal with them so an investigation can be avoided. If employee loyalty is in fact so great, then why is there a theft, drug, or discrimination problem?

The truth of the matter is, even truly loyal employees won't come forward unless they feel safe. Employers need to do all that they can to create an environment of open communication where employees feel secure enough to come forward and voice concerns and discuss serious issues when necessary. Closed doors and poor workplace communication keep problems underground and away from problem solvers.

Another cultural obstacle is the liberal attitude toward employee theft and substance abuse. In some organizations, employee theft is culturally accepted. As long as employees don't steal too much, it is tolerated. In other organizations, employees are permitted to "take" (substitute "steal" if you prefer) only certain items, others are strictly off limits. Yet other organizations tolerate employee marijuana use during breaks and lunch, but then draw the line when it comes to drug dealing. Go figure.

Organizational culture and attitudes will affect the determination of investigative objectives and should be thoroughly contemplated before any investigation begins. The employer's failure do so will compromise the investigation's results and the utility of the information it generates.

Alternatives

Fundamental to the establishment of meaningful investigative objectives, and before choosing undercover, the employer should examine alternative responses to the problem. Clearly the employer could deny a problem exists and do nothing. In spite of convincing evidence or the credible allegations of witnesses or informants, the employer could choose to deny the existence of a problem that requires aggressive investigation. This type of denial is common in even the largest and most sophisticated organizations. Serious problems, however, rarely go away by themselves. As I have mentioned previously and will repeat again, employee substance abuse problems not only don't go away without some form of intervention, they usually get worse. It can be categorically stated that denying a serious workplace problem exists and putting off investigation of it enables the problem to grow and fester, damages employee morale, increases the organization's liability, and invariably decreases its profitability.

Another alternative is to allow or cause someone else to undertake the investigation. This alternative is very popular, particularly among young or closely held and managed organizations. Entrepreneurs and inexperienced owners often defer problems that in any way appear criminal to law enforcement. Though in some cases this is precisely what should be done, proxy punching of timecards, ghost employees, petty theft, and beer drinking in the company parking lot are not the sorts of things most law enforcement agencies routinely investigate. In many large metropolitan areas, city policy generally will not investigate business crimes where losses are less than $10,000. Public law enforcement does not have the manpower or resources to undertake such efforts. What's more, it is a commonly held belief on the part of much of the law enforcement community that businesses have the obligation to manage their own affairs and prevent many of the small problems that routinely plague them. This is not to say that anyone in law enforcement has chosen to turn a blind eye to workplace crime or is not sympathetic to the problems of the modern workplace. But let's face it; a corporation whose proprietary security force is larger than the entire police department of the town in which it resides is going to find it difficult to get the authorities to investigate the loss of $100 from a petty cash fund. Conversely, the small business in which every employee knows where the cash is kept and has access to it will not likely receive much help from a large metropolitan police department for a similar loss.

Employers need to be realistic. They need to assume some responsibility for themselves and for the protection of their organization. Asking someone else to solve their problems is naive and costly.

Lastly, the employer must objectively ask if there is a better investigative approach than undercover. Because undercover investigation can be very time consuming and expensive, impulsively selecting undercover as the best way to solve workplace problems is not always wise. Before I undertake any undercover investigation I work with my client to see if there is not a better way. My commitment to every client is to engineer the investigative solution I prescribe so as to obtain our objectives as quickly as possible and provide the highest return on investment. And that, of course, does not always mean undercover is the only answer. Like me, the client-employer must be committed to bringing about solutions that are better, faster, and less expensive than conventional approaches. Because undercover is but one form of information gathering, both the employer and its investigators have the ethical and financial obligation to objectively assess alternative forms of investigation. In some instances, for example, video surveillance may be most appropriate and still very cost effective. In other instances, some form of audit and forensic analysis may be the way to go. In still others, highly structured employee interviews may work.

Articulating the Investigation's Objectives

Other than my preliminary notes, the first document to go into my case file is one that details my investigative objectives. Together with my client, I will have reviewed policies, work rules, labor agreements, past practices, and corresponding precedents. We will have discussed the resources that will be allocated and who shall participate. We will have considered organizational culture and employee attitudes. Last but not least, we will have examined all possible investigative alternatives. Therefore, the objectives of the proposed investigation will reflect the uniqueness of the workplace in question and the human dynamic that embodies its culture. The objectives will almost always articulate the desire to:

- Seek out and identify the true nature and scope of the problem
- Identify who is involved and why
- Gather any and all information in such a fashion as to allow the proper distribution of appropriate disciplinary and/or corrective action
- Effect the process in the way that is least disruptive to the organization and its operations
- Engineer the process to provide the best return on investment

This is no small order to say the least. However, implementing a well-planned and properly structured investigation, these objectives are remarkably quite obtainable. While they are not only achievable, collectively they are the benchmark of a successful workplace investigation. Like any group of objectives, they can be altered or modified in order to fit a particular circumstance or situation; but those listed above serve well as a foundation from which to begin. What's more, these investigative objectives acknowledge fundamental management concerns. They communicate an appreciation for fairness, thoroughness, and caution. The objectives communicate that the planners and investigators who will conduct the investigation understand the client-employers needs and know how to fulfill them.

Preinvestigative Preparation and Strategy Proposals

Upon mutual agreement of the investigation's objectives I will formally present a written investigative proposal. The proposal will contain the following elements:

- A detailed analysis of the project's scope and purpose
- Investigative objectives
- My recommendations how to achieve the objectives
- Logistical aspects associated with the recommendations
- The investment necessary to achieve the objectives
- A return on investment analysis
- Answers to frequently asked questions regarding undercover
- A discussion regarding required licensing and insurance
- My organization's qualifications
- Our professional affiliations
- Trade and professional references

Please refer to the sample proposal provided in the Appendix A for more detail. All professional agencies that specialize in undercover rely on proposals in one form or another. Because there is no other way for the client to know the services that are available and how those services will be delivered, a detailed written proposal is absolutely essential. If a written proposal like my sample is not provided, consider the agency too unsophisticated and seek help elsewhere.

Furthermore, If the proposal provided does not adequately calculate a reasonable return on investment, the employer should consider other alternatives. However, even a reasonable return on investment as calculated in a professionally written proposal is only an estimate. The employer should not rely upon it as a guarantee. Workplace investigations are very complex and have many variables, most of which are out of the control of both the client-employer and the agency providing the service. The offering of a guarantee is meaningless. In this business, only amateurs guarantee their work, and only the naïve purchase from them.

Once the proposal is presented, the client-employer should read it thoroughly. Carefully, the proposal should be analyzed to ensure the agency-vendor understands the client's needs and objectives. All references should be checked and, prior to acceptance, a copy of the agency's investigative license (if required by law) and certificate of insurance (naming the client as an additional insured) should be requested and received. As mentioned earlier, some agencies operate outside the boundaries of the law and common sense. Ensure that the agency selected has both the necessary licenses and insurance to do the job and do it properly.

Service Contracts

Once the proposal is accepted a service contract must be drawn. The contract will again detail that which was proposed and describe all of the services to be used. Fees, expenses, and indemnification are also addressed. It is strongly recommended that an attorney review the contract before it is executed. Hold-harmless agreements, indemnifications, and releases of liability often contain complex legal language that if not negotiated may shift too much of the legal exposure to the client-employer. Because both the employer and the investigative agency-vendor are dependent upon one another and share liability, mutual indemnifications and other legal protections are very appropriate. All professional corporate investigation firms use contracts and refuse to do business without them. Don't engage any investigative agency without one.

Choosing the Most Qualified Agency for the Investigation

Investigative agencies are as different as the people who run them. The Hallcrest Report II claims there are over 18,000 working investigative agencies in the United States.[8] However, far fewer know how to run undercover properly. Of those, I would consider no more than five as actual national competitors. But please don't misunderstand me: of the 18,000 or more agencies out there, many are very fine firms run by very fine people. However, only a small few know how to run undercover competently with consistent results.

In order to make your own determination, consider the following factors when selecting an undercover agency (See Appendix B).

Licensing

In all but five states, private investigators and their agencies must be licensed. A failure to have a proper license can result in criminal charges against the investigators and the discrediting of them in court. In rare cases, their investigative results may even be excluded from evidence at trial. To be safe, request a copy of the agency's license and required permits.

Training

The agency selected should provide professional training and rigorously screen its investigators. All of the better undercover agencies have a formalized training program. The training varies in length and content, but the better programs teach everything from drug recognition to employment law. Strict standards and a demanding curriculum are the hallmarks of a quality training program.

Our undercover training program is rigorous and demanding. Those who do not receive this training either have prior law enforcement experience or other qualifications that meet our strict standards. Most of our better competitors have similar training programs and requirements.

---

[8] William C. Cunningham, "The Hallcrest Report II," Hallcrest Systems, Inc., 1990.

Experience

Ensure that the agency as well as the employees they assign to the investigation have the experience necessary to do the job properly. Interview them and demand answers to difficult questions regarding their knowledge and experience with investigations of the type they propose.

Reputation

Reputations vary widely in the industry. The best agencies are well known in the business community and are active in their trade associations. Ask for references and check them thoroughly. Find out about the firm's litigation and claims experience. If the agency has recently been sued, find out why and the outcome. Litigation is part of the business and no matter how cautious, agencies will be sued from time to time. A claim or two should not disqualify an otherwise capable firm. However, a reputation of sloppy work, high-profile lawsuits, and big settlements could spell trouble. Avoid such firms and hire only those with the best reputations.

Willingness to Testify

All investigators must be willing to testify and see their cases through to their final conclusions. Sometimes that means testifying in court or before an arbitrator. An unwillingness to testify could be nothing more than fear. However, more often than not, an unwillingness to stand behind one's investigation and testify suggests inexperience. Some agencies claim they don't want to compromise the identity of their undercover investigators. Others claim it is too dangerous. Both claims demonstrate a lack of experience and professional sophistication. Don't hire these firms. Seek out and engage only those who understand that willingness to testify is an important part of the investigative process.

Reports

Reports are an important part of every investigation, not just undercover. As such, detailed reports should follow all investigative efforts. The information provided in a report should be complete, concise, and correct (more on reports in the next chapter). Every report should be professional looking and delivered on time. Ask for samples and examine them thoroughly before making your selection.

Insurance

All quality agencies carry general liability and errors and omissions insurance. In fact most states that have licensing require insurance. Bonding is not enough protection; in order to be safe require the agency under consideration to provide a Certificate of Insurance naming your organization as an additional insured. Also ensure the coverage is *occurrence* not *claims-made*. Claims-made coverage concludes upon expiration of the policy. Should the agency's policy lapse, and a claim subsequently filed, there will likely be no insurance protection. Only with occurrence coverage is the policyholder and the additional insured properly protected. Because occurrence policies are far more expensive (as much as ten times more expensive) than claims-made, most agencies have the latter. Very few can afford the coverage they need to protect themselves and their clients.

Willingness to Involve the Police

Employee prosecution is not always necessary. As I have already mentioned, it is complicated and often expensive. As such, the decision to prosecute should be made for business reasons only. However, a good agency knows its limitations and can recognize when to involve the authorities. Investigations involving illegal drugs, for example, cannot be done without the assistance of the police. Ask the agency you are considering to provide police references and when they do, thoroughly check them.

Also ask the agency about their success with prosecution. The answer will provide some idea as to how many cases the agency has run and how complicated they were. For example, I've run several thousand undercover investigations over the last eighteen years and have contributed to the successful prosecution of hundreds of offenders. On average, however, the typical case yields less than three arrests and subsequent prosecutions. Therefore, a low prosecution ratio should not patently disqualify an agency. Instead, examine the organization in its totality before making your selection.

Attorney Involvement

All sophisticated undercover agencies insist on the involvement of at least one of their client's attorneys. As previously discussed, the attorney's role is an important one and she should be an active participant during most of the investigation. Sophisticated undercover firms know the attorney will contribute to the smooth running of the investigation and coincidentally protect its interests as she protects the interests of her client.

What's more, experienced agencies know the client's attorney is one of the best marketing tools they have. A successful investigation will produce good word-of-mouth both in the client's circle of influence but also in that of the attorney. To exclude the attorney just doesn't make a lot of sense.

Type of Invoice

Although it may sound peculiar, another way to determine the sophistication of a prospective agency is to examine one of its invoices. I discovered this peculiarity years ago. Like most investigative agencies of any size, we occasionally hire other agencies to assist us or associate with us for licensing purposes. What's interesting is that although the billing and invoicing practices of the firms that have assisted us are as varied as their names, it is common among the better agencies to use professional-looking invoices—for example, computer-generated, three- or four-part preprinted invoices. Such an invoice is easy to read, clearly states the period it covers, and details each participating investigator's rate and his hours. Typed or word-processed invoices on plain bond or letterhead are the mark of amateurs and suggest an unsophisticated agency.

Look to see if the invoice lists the vendor's federal tax number. Smaller outfits use the owner's social security number instead. Also, low invoice numbers suggest that the firm may be new or hasn't a lot of business. No matter, buy smart and select the agency that best suits your needs.

Profile of the Professional Operative

Thus far I have synonymously used the words *investigator* and *undercover investigator* for identifying the individual actually undercover. From this point forward I will additionally use the word *operative*. That word has long been used for this purpose, and according to my version of Micro Soft Bookshelf ® the word is defined as follows:

op·er·a·tive (òp¹er-e-tîv, -e-râ′tîv, òp¹er-) *adjective*

1. Being in effect; having force; operating: *"Two major tendencies are operative in the American political system"* (Heinz Eulau).
2. Functioning effectively; efficient.
3. Engaged in or concerned with physical or mechanical activity.
4. Of, relating to, or resulting from a surgical operation.

noun

1. A skilled worker, especially in industry.
2. a. A secret agent; a spy. b. A private detective.

— op¹er·a·tive·ly *adverb*[9]

Because characterizations like "secret agent" and "spy" tend to conjure up images of international intrigue, underhanded foul play, and dirty double-crossing, I think the popular image of today's undercover operative is less respectable than it should be. For the most part, today's professional corporate undercover investigators are well educated, properly trained, and highly motivated.

The better agencies thoroughly screen, train, and test their operatives on a regular basis. Most have college degrees or have prior law enforcement

---

[9] *The American Heritage® Dictionary of the English Language*, 3rd ed. (Boston: Houghton Mifflin, 1992).

or military experience. In order to be hired, the applicant must not only have the brains but also must demonstrate he can think on his feet and has the street smarts to comfortably mix with the most nefarious of characters. Because the undercover investigator must often work entry-level positions, he must also have the personal fortitude and stamina to work unusual hours and physically demanding jobs. Often doing the work others refuse to do or working excessive hours in extreme conditions, the professional operative must put aside his emotions and personal comfort and remain focused on his objectives.

The better agencies also routinely drug test their operatives. Because the investigator may never know when she will be exposed to workplace drugs and substance abuse, she must constantly be screened to ensure her credibility and discourage carelessness. Short of a life-threatening circumstance, the operative must never use or even sample illegal drugs. To do so threatens her credibility and jeopardizes the entire investigation.

Unlike law enforcement, professional agencies cannot use snitches, informants, and substance abusers with criminal records or drug problems. Although the standard of proof for criminal prosecution is higher, arbitrators, administrative law judges, and other triers of fact are intolerant of sleazy scuzz balls snitching on others in the attempt to save their own skin. The use of such lowlifes by law enforcement is one of the more interesting dichotomies of our criminal justice system.

The professional operative must also have strong communication skills. Not only must he make daily written reports detailing his day's activities, he must be able to effectively communicate verbally with his supervisor and occasionally with the client-employer. The successful operative will also eventually have to testify. His cases will eventually yield criminal prosecutions, terminations, and other employment actions. Compelling testimony is essential for successful prosecution and for winning civil actions, and it is a skill that must be taught. Today's operative must be able and willing to testify effectively and professionally. Never before has the credibility, character, education, skill, and professionalism of the undercover operative been more critical.

Operative Selection

Operatives come in all colors, shapes, and sizes. They vary in age, demeanor, and sexual preference. They are also in very high demand. If the agency selected to conduct the investigation has done its job, each of its operatives has been properly trained, drug screened, and has no criminal record. Because of the high demand for quality investigators, the better agencies (even those with large inventories of qualified investigators) do not have operatives hanging about waiting for their next assignment. In fact the mark of a marginal agency is having two or more undercover investigators without assignments. Thriving agencies do not have enough operatives to meet the demand. So be wary of the vendor who says he has undercover investigators available for immediate assignment.

For best results the undercover operative should match the target workforce in age, race, ethnicity, and apparent socioeconomic background. The investigator should be able to seamlessly blend into the target work-force once hired. Because of this, some of my clients like to be involved in selecting the operative. This usually involves one or more meetings with the client at some convenient time and location. Because our investigators are in such high demand and are rarely free to jet about the country, it also typically involves pulling them from a working assignment for a day or two. In years past I have had clients that would want to meet as many as five investigators before making a choice. Today I rarely offer more than two unless the client agrees to come to our headquarters.

If you sense what may seem to be an attitude on my part, you are right. At the expense of sounding arrogant, these "beauty contests" are little more than time and money wasters. As much as the experienced security or human resource professional has to offer to the investigative process, oper-ative selection is not an area in which they typically have much to offer. Though well intended, the client who tries to assist by selecting the inves-tigator is making a terrible mistake. The agency, not the client, best knows the abilities, skills, and weaknesses of each individual investigator. And while the client can of course provide insight into the ethnic makeup, culture, and work ethic of the target workforce, it is the agency and its man-agers that know the investigators they employ. What's more, the client, who is allowed to make this important decision often selects their investigator for the wrong reasons. I have had clients select an investigator simply because he was witty; others were selected because they were articulate; worst of all, I've had clients select investigators because they were nothing more than knockdown beautiful! All the looks in the world won't help the investigator who cannot perform the cover job and meet the expectations of demanding and at times suspicious supervisors.

If you are the client, leave the operative selection process to the pro-fessionals. Sure, you should take the time to meet the investigators and even participate in their briefings before the assignment begins; but resist the temptation to make the final selection decision. It's too important of a decision to be made by someone that doesn't truly know the people and the business. You'll get a better result in the long run if you leave this impor-tant decision to the experts.

The most important factor in operative selection, however, is the expe-rience and skill of the investigator. More than age, race, or socioeconomic background, the investigator's experience will affect the outcome of the investigation. In most instances, it is experience that overcomes suspicion, discrimination, hazing, and adverse working conditions. In many regards the experienced undercover investigator is priceless. He can see problems before they materialize, maneuver the craftiest of criminals, and recognize when he is in danger. One of the most skillful and experienced undercover investigators I ever supervised (today himself an undercover supervisor for a competing firm) once convinced a largely black workforce during one of our investigations that he was black when in fact he is white *and looks very white!* He convinced the group of thieves, which so happened to be a mixture of black and white warehousemen, that he was the target of race discrimination because he was black. They too claimed victimization (thieves often do . . . it permits the rationalization necessary for them to steal) and instantly a bond of trust was formed. They quickly let our investigator in on their scheme and in no time we popped all of them. When in doubt always select the investigator with the most experience.

Using More Than One Investigator

As a general rule, I recommend one undercover investigator for every 500 employees at a location. For example, if the client employs 1,500 people at the site in question, I will recommend that three undercover investigators be placed into the workforce. I think it is unrealistic to expect a single individual to network a group larger then 500 people. In some environments like hospitals, although they often allow a great deal of mobility, the workforce is highly compartmentalized. The higher the compartmentalization and the less mobile the investigator, the greater the number of investigators required. Another thing to consider is that using multiple investigators tends to make the project move faster. The investment is greater, but typically the speed in which the desired information is obtained more than makes up for the additional cost of the added investigator.

Selecting the Cover Position

Before any particular operative(s) can be selected for the assignment, the proper cover position must first be identified. The *cover position* is the job the operative will assume once hired by the client-employer. Optimally, the cover position should be one that provides the investigator the highest amount of mobility, the least amount of supervision, and is nontask oriented, thus making it possible for the operative to move freely throughout the target location and associate or interact with as many employees as possible.

The best cover positions include expediters, material handlers, mail delivery clerks, maintenance technicians, and, remarkably, *uniformed security officers*. Yes, uniformed security officers. I did not believe it either until I tried it. Over ten years ago the director of security for a large west coast bank approached my firm and asked that we conduct an undercover investigation for him. The only position available was that of a proprietary uniformed security officer, armed no less. After some delay while meeting the state licensing requirements for the position, we quietly placed our investigator. On his first night, his training officer challenged him to a harrowing game of quick-draw in an elevator. Then later, after having completed their rounds, he approached our man and offered to share a marijuana cigarette. From that moment forward our investigator was unstoppable. My biggest challenge was keeping our client-employer from reacting to our information prematurely.

Some months later, in another instance of using a uniformed security officer, our investigator was posted at the employee entrance gate of a large food distribution center. For years inventory shrink, excessive product damage, and allegations of employee substance abuse had frustrated management to the point that threatened the continued existence of the facility. A roving post for our operative would certainly have been better for all the reasons outlined above. However, in no time our stationary undercover investigator at his fixed post had befriended most of the loaders, pickers, and route drivers and gained the trust of most everyone else. Using techniques I will detail in a later chapter, the investigator was able to gain the trust of the suspect employees and soon became their "lookout." Because of the location of his post, he was able to see the facility's main entrance and the exempt employees' parking lot. While on post, he in fact knew exactly when every employee was on site, including the warehouse superintendent and his foremen. Thus, the scheme was extraordinarily simple. The thieves would call the investigator while on post and check to see who was on site before stealing anything. If the investigator reported the coast was clear and no supervision was present, they would simply casually overload the outbound trucks with the product of their choice. The route driver would then later drop the excess inventory off at some predetermined location.

The thieves eventually found *their guard* to be so reliable that they would not risk stealing anything unless he was on duty. Of course, in exchange for his assistance the thieves would provide him a small cut from their take or introduce him to employee drug dealers whenever he asked. The workforce became so trusting of our investigator that they would actually call his post and obtain his approval before overstaying a break or smoking a cigarette in the warehouse (a strictly forbidden activity for all of the obvious reasons).

But when the theft escalated to the point of stealing pallets of frozen shrimp and lobster tails, our investigator really earned his keep. Upon receiving his customary call, our investigator would delay the thieves (and the movement of stolen product) and immediately report the plan to our office. I would then immediately dispatch moving surveillance teams to the site. Once in place, the team leader would signal our investigator, who would then call the thieves and tell them it was safe to move the product. As soon as the target vehicle left the facility, our surveillance teams picked up and followed them. Not only did this arrangement allow us to identify who was stealing products on the inside, but it also importantly allowed us to find out who was receiving it on the outside.

Within several months this highly successful investigation was brought to a dramatic conclusion. Our efforts resulted in over 30 warehouse terminations (nearly one-third of that workforce), half a dozen drivers, and the recovery of thousands of dollars from restaurants that had purchased the stolen product. Interestingly, almost ten years later in another investigation for another employer, I ran into the human resources manager that had been my client contact during that investigation. However, the circumstances this time were quite different. *This time he was the subject of my investigation.* It turned out that he had falsified a large number of expense reports and padded some moving expenses. During my interview of him that followed the investigation and audit, he was most complimentary of my interview technique and said that he was familiar with the process. Without taking his eyes off the confession that he was writing, he said that many years prior, while with another employer, a fellow with the very same name as mine had done a similar investigation for him. He said that investigation also had involved theft and had resulted in the termination of nearly 40 of his employees. Remarkably, he never asked if I had been a part of it!

These fascinating examples and dozens of other cases like them over the years have convinced me that uniformed security officer assignments make excellent cover positions. The manned security post is usually positioned at access and egress points so that it allows the security officer a unique vantage point. Furthermore, as I am sure most readers will agree, over time the security officer gets to know everyone at a facility. It never ceases to amaze me how much about an operation, its people, its customers, or its business uniformed security officers seem to know. For these reasons, I have come to conclude that in most environments protected by a uniformed security force, employee substance abuse, theft, and other forms of workplace misconduct cannot go on without some of the security officers knowing about it. Worse yet, often these same officers are also involved. Some uniformed security professionals may find this claim offensive and, to those who are law abiding, I apologize. But in my own defense, my organization also provides contract security officers, so I know the problem from both sides of the fence.

Some of the jobs that don't make good cover positions include leads, supervisors, or managers. Any time authority is attached to the cover position, the operative is immediately burdened with suspicion. Even checkers, auditors, and quality and safety inspectors are usually not good cover positions. Although I have placed undercover investigators in all of these positions over the years (more recently as ISO 9000 facilitators), they each saddle the undercover investigator, at least initially, with the proverbial "snitch jacket." This unnecessary cloud of suspicion lengthens and invariably increases the cost of the project. Such positions should be avoided if at all possible.

Temporary positions, on the other hand, offer all of the upside with very little permanent downside. Increasingly throughout the American workplace, temporaries have come to make up a larger portion of the workforce. No longer seen as scabs, incompetents, or as the unskilled, temporary labor makes up an important and beneficial portion of America's labor pool. As such, the temporary workforce makes an excellent cover for the undercover investigator. Because organizations that use temporaries are accustomed to high turnover and an ever-changing workforce, the undercover investigator posing as a temporary can quickly infiltrate the workforce and assimilate with little difficulty. In some instances where the turnover is excessively high, the operative who remains in place for as little as several months will soon be perceived as "senior." This perception will make his job exceedingly easy and cause little attention to be drawn to him as he mixes with other employees and actively investigates.

Temporary positions do have a downside. Like regular positions, temporary positions should not be created. The creation of a position for the investigator will only cause suspicion to be drawn upon her. This is particularly true in union environments were jobs are frequently considered negotiable commodities by the union leadership and doled out only with their approval. For these reasons, job creation is not a smart way to go. However, in other environments, temporaries are considered just that, temporary. And because of it, the regular employees will sometimes resist befriending them. Think about it: have you ever intentionally struck up a long-term, meaningful relationship with someone you met while standing in line at the supermarket? This handicap, however, is easily overcome by the skilled and patient investigator.

Of greater challenge is the environment that is dysfunctionally stratified and highly hierarchical. Here again, unionism fosters this type of culture where the new employees are mistreated and hazed while their senior "brothers" and "sisters" torment them. This sort of treatment is not only highly unprofessional but it can also be very dangerous. Environments like this cause the investigation to be longer and more expensive. Because the investigator must both maintain his demeanor and constantly look over his shoulder, moving the investigation into its proactive mode can take many months. Relationship building that would otherwise take only weeks can take six months or more. But, as I counsel my investigators, even this sort of information about a work environment can be invaluable to an employer. As any employer knows, hazing and harassing new hires leads to disgruntlement, reduced productivity, and higher turnover.

Operative Placement

Once the proper investigator(s) is selected for the assignment, he must then be inserted into his cover position. This critical process is called *placing* the investigator and because of its importance, nothing can be left to chance. Practically speaking there are two fundamental methods of placing the operative. The first is via a *cold hire* and the second is by way of a *controlled hire*.

Cold Hire

The cold hire involves nothing more than having the investigator show up at the target business, walk in, and apply for a job. Then by the grace of some higher power, she is hired and placed into the very job desired. Voila! Nothing to it! Just like that the operative walks in and gets hired. Unfortunately, this ideal scenario is not usually the case. More often than not the investigator, no matter how well briefed or prepared, will not be able to get the exact cover position desired. In most cases, too many people, too many influences, and too much politics are involved. And although a cold hire is preferred, too much is at stake to leave the placement of the best investigator for the job to chance. More than nine times out of ten, the experienced agency will opt for a controlled hire.

Controlled Hire

The controlled hire involves massaging or manipulating the hiring process to the degree necessary to achieve the investigator's hire. The manipulation must be handled with the utmost care. If not enough manipulation is used, the hire may not occur. If the situation is too manipulated, red flags will be raised and suspicion will abound. In order to successfully effect the controlled hire, the degree of manipulation must be exact—it must almost be surgical.

The manipulations for this purpose range from selecting the right recruiter for the initial job interview to providing the investigator verifiable job references to providing him the answers to the questions on a skills test. In every instance, knowing every detail of the screening and hiring process is essential. Every element, step, and action must be known to prevent a screw-up or accidental compromise. The investigator, his supervisor, and the client-employer must cooperate and work closely together to ensure every detail is considered and every obstacle is addressed. Only the most inexperienced agencies leave something to chance.

A common debate is whether the investigator should use his actual name and social security number while undercover. Although government undercover agents rarely use their real names, the issue is clearly up in the air for those of us in the private sector. In my earlier years I insisted that my operatives use "cover names." However, over the years my position on this matter has changed. The use of cover names and false social security numbers are problematic. First is the problem of overcoming the client-employer background and screening process. Unless the placement is manipulated such that no background or verifications are attempted, a cover name and any form of false identification are likely to create problems.

Because so many employers are doing a better job screening job applicants, it is increasingly difficult to effectively use a fictitious name without bringing in too many people. Cover names pose another problem: *operatives tend to forget them.* In highly stressful situations it is easy for the investigator to forget her cover name and accidentally respond to someone calling out her real name. For these reasons and others, I now tend to shy away from the use of cover names and false identification unless it is absolutely necessary.

At my agency, our undercover managers use a checklist to guide them and the client-employer through this important and time-consuming process. They leave nothing to chance. Every aspect of the screening and hiring process is covered and rehearsed. We've gone so far as to have the client's human resource office under surveillance so as to know when certain recruiters or interviewers would not be available and by chance interview our investigator-applicant. A poorly orchestrated placement in the end will typically produce a disappointing investigation, *and a very disappointed client.*

Political Hire

To improve the chance of a successful placement, inexperienced agencies sometimes rely on "political hires." These are hires based on contrived relationships that are usually politically or economically based. For example, the cover story might be that the applicant-investigator is a board member's niece or, worse yet, he is the CEO's son or nephew. Another foolhardy ruse is to use the cover in which the applicant-investigator claims to be a friend of a friend of a friend. This invariably raises suspicion and gives rise to too many potential questions.

Another unsophisticated placement technique is for someone in the client's organization of unquestioned authority to "command" that the applicant-investigator be hired. This may in fact get the investigator hired and into the position desired. However once there, no one will likely talk to him. Most employees don't like people who got their job because they knew somebody. People like to think they live and work on a level playing field. When a person, particularly someone we don't know, gets a job in a competitive environment because they know somebody, it bothers us. In most workplaces these sorts of political hires don't work well for placing undercover investigators. They attract too much attention, create suspicion, and tend to cause the investigator to be alienated. Who wants to hang out with and be a friend of the boss's son?

Cover Story

In my opinion, the concern with cover stories and the estimation of their importance is a bit overrated. I've worked with a lot of undercover managers that put way too much time into developing the operative's cover story. Their efforts have ranged from the excruciatingly complex to the absolutely bizarre. I've had managers contrive stories involving sick step-mothers, high-school sweethearts, and communications with ancient Native American ancestors. Nonsense, complete nonsense. The best cover story is a simple one: "I hate New York so I moved to California" or "I couldn't afford to live in Chicago anymore" or simpler yet, "I didn't like the weather in Detroit so I moved to Florida!" Inexperienced undercover investigators tend to overwork their cover story. Remember the acronym KISSS: *K*eep *I*t *S*imple *S*am *S*pade.

Donnie Brasco (actually a FBI undercover agent), the most remarkable undercover agent of modern times, penetrated the New York mob with barely a cover story at all. He simply claimed to deal in stolen gems. That was it. Remember, in the underworld those who ask too many questions are immediately suspect. The workplace is no different. In fact the skilled workplace undercover investigator can actually use suspicion to his advantage. If confronted by a nosey coworker and asked about his past or how he got the job, the quick-thinking investigator may be well served by challenging the individual and asking who needs to know that information and why. Effectively, the investigator can put the "snitch jacket" on the busybodies, feigning his suspicion of them. This technique works particularly well in drug investigations. The employee drug dealer who shies from the investigator and tells others he is suspicious of him can be countered by the investigator's discretely alluding to or telling others the dealer is in fact a "narc" or company informant. I have had investigators do this so effectively that their target dealers eventually approached them and offered to sell dope to them in the presence of witnesses just to prove they were not working for the police.

Cover stories are important, but they should be simple and used sparingly.

Operative Relocation

If it is necessary for the investigator to be relocated in order to work the assignment, it is best that she be relocated several weeks before she starts her cover position. This enables her to "climatize" to her new surroundings and get a feel for the environment. This time also allows her the opportunity to identify where the malls, the schools, and major landmarks are located. It also affords the investigator the time to study the local culture and identify the popular political and social issues for the area. This knowledge combined with a simple yet plausible cover story will enable the investigator to successfully blend into the target workforce (and the community) when she assumes her cover position.

Relocating the investigator, however, can be complicated. The new locale will be unfamiliar and sometimes seem unfriendly to the newly arrived investigator. Necessary care should be taken to ensure that the transition is comfortable and hassle-free. Although I have allowed household moves for some of our investigators, providing a furnished dwelling is my preferred choice. Furnished apartments usually work best, however, on rare occasions I have moved my investigator into some form of temporary corporate housing. The problem with this option is not only the cost—up to $2,400 per month in some parts of the country—but the appearance it creates. Regardless of the precautions taken, eventually coworkers will learn where the investigator lives. If she clearly lives above her means or in the same place that transitioning corporate executives reside, the investigator will be immediately suspect. This unnecessary outcome can be entirely avoided by researching the region and selecting an area and abode more consistent with the socioeconomic profile the investigator is portraying.

At the same time, I avoid moving the investigator into the same neighborhood or apartment complex of employees in the target workforce if at all possible. In some parts of the country this is not possible and the investigator must live "out of town." Care must also be used here as well. If the investigator's commute is too far in relationship to the wages earned or other known employment opportunities in the area, suspicion again may be raised. On the other hand, a commute of 45 miles in some larger metropolitan areas is not uncommon and would not raise eyebrows.

Living too far from the job may create other problems as well. It may to some degree prevent spontaneity and the ability of the operative to easily join impromptu after-hours activities with her coworkers. Although it is advisable to closely regulate after-hours and "off-site" information collection because of privacy and safety concerns, socializing with coworkers after work adds to the investigator's credibility. In some instances, job restrictions prevent the investigator from interacting with or even talking to coworkers during regular hours. In such cases, after-hours interaction may be the only way to collect the desired information. Another consequence of living too far from the job is the appearance that the investigator is not part of the community. Subconsciously, coworkers may see the investigator as an outsider or a foreigner of sorts. This perception can weigh heavily on the investigator during the early and important relationship-building phase of the investigation.

Another problem of living too far from the job is a very practical one: transportation problems. More often than not, when I relocate an undercover investigator any significant distance, I find it cheaper to rent or purchase a local vehicle than have him drive his own. Of course the decision must take into account many variables, but after factoring in the cost of mileage and vehicle re-registration (it is not advisable for the investigator to drive a vehicle with out-of-state license plates to the job—even if his cover story includes some form of relocation), it is often cheaper to rent or buy a local used vehicle. Another problem with the operative using his own vehicle is often the age and condition of the vehicle. Similar to living beyond one's means, driving a well-kept expensive vehicle may not fit the cover story or the socioeconomic class of the cover position. As mentioned, my undercover investigators are very well paid and most of them own expensive new vehicles. An operative driving a new $40,000 sport utility vehicle to a job paying $7.00 per hour would undoubtedly raise questions. What's more, most everywhere in this country the perception exists that you are what you drive. An operative could not possibly hope to be taken seriously if driving a used four-door family car to a job where everyone else drove large four-wheel drive pickup trucks with mud tires and gun racks!

Use of Local Security Professionals and Resources

To help overcome some of the relocation problems described above I use local resources. When we've decided to relocate an operative for an assignment, my case manager or I will immediately secure the services of a local security professional. This individual may be the licensee we have chosen to associate with or, when licensing is not an issue, a reputable security professional or consultant. What I'm looking for is someone who knows the region, has a relationship with local and state law enforcement, and is reliable. Once engaged, I'll have this *consultant* help find suitable housing for the investigator and show her around. The consultant will also provide the investigator background on the community, a quick lesson on local history, and at the appropriate time will make the necessary arrangements for an introduction to law enforcement. I may even have the consultant purchase and register the operative's vehicle, help her move in, and take her grocery shopping for the first time.

I want the operative relocation and placement to go as smoothly as possible. To ensure that happens, a properly selected and well-qualified local resource is invaluable. For a mere several hundred dollars a month, the resource ensures a flawless transition for my investigator and at the same time provides me with needed peace of mind.

Preinvestigation Actions and Final Preparation

Undercover investigations do not occur in a vacuum. While the process is dynamic, it also is structured and focused. But beyond the day-to-day developments and the twists and turns the investigation may take, the client-employer's business must go on. Invisibly, the investigation develops, driving ever closer to its objectives. To ensure that the investigative process does not collide with the client's operations or vice versa, attention must be given to in the final preinvestigation preparation the *environment* in which the investigation is to take place.

As I have already mentioned, using undercover for the purpose of gathering information regarding union activity is unlawful. Thus any undercover investigation in a unionized work setting has the potential to result in the allegation of an unfair labor practice. To bring about such a claim, it needs only to be alleged that an employer or its agent have interfered, restrained, or coerced its employees while they exercised their right to engage in concerted activity (including forming, joining, or assisting a union). This long abused and tiresome allegation must always be addressed whenever it arises and the employer must be prepared to defend itself. Doing so is not necessarily difficult, but it is a distraction (often the primary intent of the allegation) and it takes time and money. Thus care must be taken to avoid even the appearance of improper or questionable activity. It is best in the planning and preparation phase of the investigation that there be no discussion or documentation of any reference regarding a protected activity or organization. This simple advice, by the way, applies throughout the entire investigation as well. But unfortunately thoughtless notes, memoranda, and other preinvestigation correspondence can come back to haunt the uninformed and careless.

Another preinvestigation mistake that is often made also involves communications. This one, however, is often made intentionally: *talking too much*. I've had countless clients make this simple yet easily avoidable mistake. A secret is not a secret if more than two people know about it. An old Hell's Angels' adage says it best: "Three people can keep a secret if two of them are dead." That is a bit extreme. However, I tell my clients and I firmly believe that with each person brought into the loop, the risk of accidental compromise increases exponentially. As a rule of thumb, if more than three of the client-employer's people (excluding counsel) are in on the investigation, *the investigation is no longer confidential*. Against my very strong advice I have had clients disclose the intent to conduct an undercover investigation at a company staff meeting . . . in one case with almost 30 managers present. Many years ago I had a very hotheaded CEO tell his entire organization he had engaged my firm to conduct an undercover drug investigation for him. After the obvious damage had been done, he attempted to justify his lapse of common sense by claiming he wanted everybody to know he meant business and that employee substance abuse would no longer be tolerated. All he succeeded in doing was driving the problem deeper underground and increasing the length and cost of an otherwise simple investigation. If you want to save time and money, keep the investigation confidential and tell only those who absolutely need to know about it.

Another very common mistake is something I call "hardening the target." This involves initiating measures that only serve to sensitize the workforce and alert them that management is aware of an otherwise unknown problem. Things like increasing guard patrols, changing locks, improving perimeter security, or any other security or asset protection enhancement will reduce employee complacency. But more subtle measures, like implementing a random drug testing policy or terminating a suspicious vendor, will send silent tremors throughout the organization's criminal network and send wrongdoers running for cover. Any activity that heightens the security consciousness of the workforce or reduces employee complacency (or reduces the complacency of customers and vendors for that matter) will lengthen the investigation and increase its cost.

There are, however, a few preinvestigative actions that promote positive outcomes. One of the least expensive yet most effective actions is reposting or redistributing critical work rules and policies. If, for example, the matter pending investigation involves a substance abuse problem, reaffirming the organization's policy regarding workplace drug use and the availability of treatment for those who voluntarily seek help would be very appropriate. It would not only be kind, but would serve as a warning and may even cause an abuser to find help . . . before the help finds him. What's more, this sort of policy affirmation tends to neutralize the claim by an employee that they were unaware of the rules until after they were caught.

Some employers go even further. On several rare occasions a few of my clients have offered some form of amnesty prior to initiating a drug investigation. The purpose of such a practice is twofold. First, it satisfies the need to be fair. When properly communicated and not misused by the employer (e.g., later targeting those who come forward), the offer of amnesty plays well to both the substance abuser and nonsubstance abuser. All employees recognize it as a rare form of corporate compassion in its willingness to assist those who want help. Second, the offer of amnesty permits the employer later to demonstrate that it acted in good faith and was fair, that it had done all that it could before undertaking an investigation that resulted in employee discipline. Preinvestigation amnesty sounds fair because it is fair. But before offering any form of amnesty, consult your employment law attorney. She'll be able to help you determine if an amnesty program is right for your organization and, if so, how to properly administrate it.

Who Exactly Should be Involved?

Aside from selecting the right agency and investigator, the client-employer must also select the right attorney. Attorneys play an important role in undercover investigations and no investigation should be attempted without one. In fact, if a prospective undercover vendor does not insist that a labor attorney participate, they should immediately be disqualified. Only the most unsophisticated agencies conduct undercover without the assistance of counsel.

Because undercover is so complex and often produces results that involve the disciplining of employees, the importance of counsel cannot be overstated. Not just any counsel either. What is necessary is employment law expertise. The attorneys that participate should be experienced labor attorneys and be thoroughly familiar with collective bargaining units, labor negotiations, and arbitrations. They should also be experienced in employee discipline, have some understanding of the criminal justice system, and have an appreciation for the complexities of undercover. All in all, the labor attorneys who represent employers undertaking an undercover investigation should be aggressive, well seasoned, and creative.

The attorney's function is not to manage the investigation but to assist the client-employer in deciding what to do with the result. Experienced agencies need little supervision. The good ones have effective processes, recognize their limitations, and know the law. But the undercover agency should not be expected to provide legal advice. That's the attorney's job.

The attorney should be involved from the very beginning. If at all possible, I like to have the attorney participate in the first meeting with my client to offer counsel regarding legal issues I might expose and to answer any of the client's legal questions. Furthermore, the attorney's participation may allow the meeting and whatever is discussed in it to be protected under the doctrine of attorney-client privilege. This fundamental privilege protects the information exchanged between an attorney and her client from the discovery phase of a trial should a legal action follow. Importantly, full protection of this sort is possible if the attorney, not the client-employer, engages the agency. In doing so, that which is produced by the agency and its investigators becomes *attorney work product*. Like discussions between the attorney and her client, attorney work product is also privileged and protected from discovery. Thus, if the attorney is sufficiently involved, the entire investigation and its result can be protected.

This benefit could prove to be more important than it may first appear. Clearly, in most cases the client-employer would not want its entire investigation exposed just because one employee challenged management's choice of discipline. Imagine a complex, six-month investigation in which dozens of employees were exposed and workplace drug use and prostitution was discovered. Now imagine that one of the dealers is prosecuted and his attorney subpoenas the entire case file and all of the investigator's reports. Should that subpoena be honored, it is possible that all of the information provided could become a public record and available to anyone. Not only would such an outcome completely compromise the investigation and the privacy of all of those involved, it would allow the criminal defense attorney the opportunity to identify defects or weaknesses in the investigation. Such defects and weaknesses can be exploited for defense purposes, but more importantly they can become *causes of action* in a civil claim against the employer. The cunning defense attorney not only obtains material and information to better defend his client, he gets a "free look" at the entire investigation to help him determine if a civil action is also viable.

If the discovery produces facts sufficient enough to support even a frivolous claim, the unethical attorney could file a civil suit in hopes of nothing more than a quick settlement. Having of course taken the matter on contingency, his out-of-pocket prelitigation costs have already been covered by his fees for the criminal defense. In a sense, he gets to peek in the circus tent without having to pay. *What a deal!*

An exposed investigation could cause other problems as well. Publicly exposing a workplace drug problem or huge losses due to employee theft can tarnish a business's public image, shake investor or stockholder confidence, and devastate employee morale. No one would fly with an airline whose pilots are publicly known to have drug problems. And investors are not going to be particularly happy to read the morning paper and discover their darling start-up just suffered a million-dollar loss due to employee theft! Employee morale, in particular, can be severely damaged by an exposed investigation. Employees may become outraged that management spied on them and planted snitches among them. Rabble-rousers may use the opportunity to organize and campaign for an employee union. Supervisors and managers can be offended that their departments or areas were targeted or that they were not trusted enough to be looped in and allowed input.

The organization would have to respond to these issues as well as deal with the results of the investigation—instituting employee discipline, taking corrective actions, and providing the government assistance with its prosecution. In short order it can become overwhelming even for the largest organization. All of the benefits of the investigation can be lost simply because everyone learns of it.

An attorney's involvement in an undercover investigation does not necessarily add to the cost of the total project. In many ways the attorney reduces costs. By virtue of having early involvement and continuous oversight, legal problems can be spotted well in advance and usually avoided. If legal problems do arise, legal fees are usually reduced because the attorney is already on board. She already knows the case and its strengths and weakness. She also knows all of the players. What's more, because the attorney has had continuous involvement in the case and fully appreciates its intricacies, she is able to provide better, more insightful counsel to her client.

Another resource essential to most successful undercover investigations is law enforcement. Although law enforcement should not be involved to the extent of counsel, it should play some role in most cases. Obviously, if prosecution is to take place law enforcement must be involved. But it can assist in other ways as well. In the case of drug investigations, law enforcement must participate and in some cases assist in the supervision of the case. Private investigators without exception cannot lawfully possess, buy, or transport illegal drugs without proper permission from law enforcement. In most states, criminal immunity can be granted by law enforcement (the police, sheriff, or district attorney) to private citizens—which private investigators certainly are—while assisting in a criminal investigation. The immunity is not blanket and usually has many strings attached. In most cases, the citizen-investigator must be under the direct supervision of law enforcement and commit no illegal activity without law enforcement having knowledge of it in advance.

These restrictions, though sometimes cumbersome, allow the investigator the ability to purchase drugs from employee-dealers. The restrictions also mean, however, that the investigator has two supervisors and must take directions from both his law enforcement handler and his case supervisor. As long as the directives issued by the two parties don't conflict, few problems arise. But, because the two supervising parties have different agendas, sometimes they do oppose one another. The best example is the case in which the investigation spills out of the workplace into the community. Law enforcement might relish the opportunity to pursue big drug dealers and get to local suppliers; however, using the undercover investigator to do so adds cost to the investigation and often lengthens it. The client under these circumstances is conflicted. On one hand, it wants to focus on its workplace problem and bring about solutions as cost effectively as possible. On the other hand, as a corporate citizen it may feel compelled to assist law enforcement in resolving a community drug problem.

In any event, the business must allocate the resources and invest the time to see the project through and somehow assist the very law enforcement agency that is assisting it. The additional cost can be significant. I've had cases in which our investigator could not be "cut out" and law enforcement's demands of my investigator extended many months beyond that which was required to meet my client's objectives. The extension of the case also delayed my client's ability to take corrective and disciplinary action. In one case involving an outlaw motorcycle gang, my client had to patiently sit on its hands while my undercover investigator and law enforcement carried on the investigation. The delay not only permitted the employee drug problem to continue to evolve, but added an extra $50,000 to the client's tab.

Some would argue that that was a small price to pay for what was ultimately accomplished, and I would have to agree. But also consider the good will such cooperation generated with the local authorities. The client's patience allowed the police to penetrate an ongoing organized criminal enterprise and bring it to its knees. What price could be placed on such a result? Law enforcement by its own admission later claimed it could not have achieved the result it had without the contribution of my client and our investigator. The heart-felt appreciation lasted for years.

The last but not least important member of the team is the client-employer point of contact. For efficiency, one individual should be designated as such, and through this person all information passes into and out of the organization. By restricting the number of individuals in the loop and requiring that all information flow through a single point of contact, confidentiality is protected and the risk of accidental compromise is significantly reduced. Because fewer people have access, the investigation is easier to manage and the result is often better. Management by committee does not work when it comes to undercover.

The point of contact should be sufficiently high enough on the organizational chart as to have the authority to make policy decisions and spend corporate money. The individual should be of strong character and, of course, trustworthy. I also ask my clients to consider whether the individual selected would make a good witness. Remember, even the best cases can go sideways. And when they do, the point of contact will surely be required to testify. I also insist that the individual be accessible. Often, particularly in small, closely held organizations, the owner or owners want to be intimately involved. However, these individuals usually don't have the time or patience necessary to do the job. They have busy schedules and often travel, making continuous communications almost impossible.

Usually the best person for the job is either the security manager or the manager of human resources. These individuals have both the experience and professional acumen necessary to do the job right. They also have the time and are relatively accessible. In many cases, they have filled a similar role in the past and therefore know the drill and can marshall the resources to get the job done. And in most cases, it is corporate security and human resources that are going to engineer the corrective and disciplinary action when the investigation is finally over.

Common Mistakes

Over the years I've run thousands of undercover investigations. I've enjoyed many successes and endured many embarrassing failures. As unfortunate as some of these failures have been, each one offered me the unique opportunity to learn from them. Building upon these opportunities I have done all that I can to improve my approach and inspire those I manage. It is process improvement in its purest form. However, reflecting back upon my failures and those of my colleagues in our industry, five recurring themes appear. Let's look at each of them briefly in order of most likely to occur.

No Clear Objectives

Many an investigation has begun without clear, well-defined objectives. Surprisingly, many client-employers with whom I have worked never considered articulating investigative objectives before they initiated their project. Don't make the same mistake. Before you begin and engage the services of anyone, write out your objectives. Start with a "needs list" from which you derive several clear and easy to measure objectives. Remember that if you have no objectives, you will never be able to measure your results.

Poor Planning and Not Paying Attention to the Details

Any undercover investigation is a huge undertaking. It is always complicated and fraught with opportunities to commit expensive and embarrassing mistakes. Inexperienced agencies and investigators don't know how to plan properly and instead leave much of the process to chance. To exponentially increase your chances of success, plan ahead and pay attention to every detail.

Too Many Hands in the Process

Because undercover investigations are so complex and very often expensive, the tendency is to involve more people than is necessary. By no means is undercover for the fainthearted, but security professionals and executives must resist the temptation to spread the risk and manage their investigation by committee. Nothing will slow an investigation or increase its cost more than involving too many people.

Selecting the Wrong Agency

All investigative agencies are not created equal. Most are small and inadequately equipped. The average agency employs 1.5 full-time people and has been in business less than five years. Before selecting an agency to conduct your undercover investigation, check its references carefully, make sure it is properly licensed and insured, and insist that a proposal be provided before any work is done. If the agency under consideration runs less than 12 undercover investigations a year, it is probably only a sideline. Select an agency that does it for a living.

Selecting the Wrong Investigator

In addition to playing too large of a role in the actual management of the case, client-employers also like to handpick their investigators. This is a mistake. Few client-employers have the experience or ability to properly make this important decision. But more practically they are unwittingly assuming more responsibility than necessary if the investigator fails.

By selecting the investigator, the client-employer becomes an active participant in the investigation and must assume some responsibility if the investigation fails to meet all of its objectives. If you trust the agency enough to hire it, then trust them enough to select the right investigator. To do otherwise may jeopardize your entire investment and even your career.

CHAPTER 3

Case Management and Communications

Successful undercover investigations do not happen by themselves. In order to be successful, the investigation must be worked hard and properly managed. As pointed out in the previous chapter, a simple operational plan and an eager investigator are not enough. In addition to clearly defined objectives, the investigation requires not only the proper pooling of resources and expertise, but also flawless execution. The mechanism that fulfills these requirements and makes this complex process possible is succinctly called *case management*.

From the beginning of any undercover operation, case management plays an important and fundamental role. Whether assisting the perceptive client articulate its investigative objectives or orchestrating the finer details of the case shutdown, effective case management dynamically nurtures the investigation as it unfolds and helps steer it to an ultimately successful conclusion. And like the other elements of the investigation, case management is more art than science. As such, it is probably one of the least appreciated aspects of the entire undercover investigation.

Case Management

The mere utterance of the phrase *case management* causes one to immediately think—*case manager*. But case management involves more than just the case manager. Sophisticated workplace undercover investigations are managed at five distinct but interrelated levels. The management of each level is the responsibility of the following participants:

- Undercover investigator
- Case manager
- Client-employer
- Attorney
- Law enforcement

Like a practiced team, those involved in the management of the case work closely together. Each participant plays a distinctly different role yet coordinates and communicates every effort with his teammates. This active participation and teamwork makes the successful investigation possible. In practice, this case management team becomes the *investigative team*.

Undercover Investigator

Intuitively one would conclude the undercover investigator enjoys the greatest amount of responsibility while maintaining the highest degree of visibility. In most cases this is arguably so. Indeed, without an undercover investigator, no undercover investigation can take place. While the others listed above play important roles, it is the efforts of the undercover investigator that will likely make or break the case. Thus the investigator's proper management of his assignment is paramount.

Many years ago while working in Los Angeles as a young case manager, I witnessed for the first time how important this concept truly was. At the time, one of the cases under my management was a routine workplace drug investigation. The undercover investigator was about my age, and was very well educated and extraordinarily articulate. He was a Native American originally from Oklahoma—a full-blooded Choctaw who spoke fluent Muskogean. He was also one of the most amazing investigators I've ever worked with. Quickly, he penetrated the workforce and deftly identified substance abusers and drug dealers. He even uncovered three employees— a grandmother, her daughter, and her granddaughter—each selling marijuana to one another and a host of others at the facility. Then about two months into the assignment, the investigator told me he had suddenly run into a problem. With some hesitation and a great deal of embarrassment he explained that his sponsor, the person who had vouched for him and introduced him to the dealers, was also his cousin. The problem was that his cousin had now turned out to be a dealer as well. As he sat in my office, head low and deep sorrow on his face, he slowly turned to me and whispered, "Screw him, I'll buy from him tomorrow." He knew full well what that decision meant. If his cousin sold to him, at the very least he'd be fired, at worst he could go to jail. The operative then stood and proudly said, "I've got a job to do and I'm going to see it through."

Until that moment, I don't think I had realized how much the operative manages his own case. My operative clearly had choices. Although it would have been less than honest, he could have chosen to never disclose anything about his cousin. How easy it would have been to simply say nothing. As this example clearly demonstrates, the operative drives the case and its outcome in many fascinating ways.

Case Manager

The case manager or supervisor also plays a significant role in the outcome of an investigation. The case manager is responsible for the day-to-day

administration of the case as well as the daily care and feeding of his operatives. The case manager also has the responsibility of maintaining regular
contact with his client contact as well as the others involved in the case.
In this respect the case manager functions as the vehicle through which all
case information flows and is disseminated.

The effective case manager has certain attributes. He should be a good
communicator, have exceptional writing skills, and a sound background in
investigations and management. Prior law enforcement or military experience, though helpful, is not absolutely necessary. The best case managers
are those that have high ethical standards, understand the intricacies of law
as it applies to the investigative process, and have terrific people skills. I
have heard it said many times that supervising undercover is a lot like
babysitting. The needs of no two children (operatives) are alike, and each
one must be handled (supervised) with kid gloves if there are to be no problems. This adult–child relationship is not an exaggeration. Many operatives
who are recruited out of school or college have never lived away from home.
For others, their undercover assignment may be the first real full-time job
they've ever had. Therefore the relationship with their case manager is
very important. Indeed, if the case manager and operative do not get along,
the outcome of the case will usually be in question. In this regard, the client
is well served to meet the operative and case manager together. It is very
appropriate for the client to ask how long they have worked together and
if they have had problems in the past. The answers to these simple but often
unasked questions should significantly influence the client's decision to
move forward with the project as planned.

The undercover manager must also be patient. For the operative, the
cover position can be hard, dirty, and tiring. Cases that drag on for six
months or more can be boring and sometimes frustrating. The operative
needs to be closely monitored and coached in order for the case to remain
focused and move forward with purpose. The case manager must supervise
and motivate the operative and keep the assignment on track. The case
manager must also ensure that the client and law enforcement are continuously updated and kept abreast of the operative's progress. This daily
coaching, motivating, and communicating can be tiring for the case
manager as well. Consequently, I try to limit the workload of my case managers to not more than six operatives at any one time. Because some assignments have multiple operatives, a case manager conceivably might only be
managing one or two assignments but actually have responsibility for up to
six operatives. There are exceptions, however. Because some of our larger
clients frequently run several cases simultaneously, I have had instances in
which one case manager alone supervised 12 operatives spread among three
locations. That was unusual and a practice that I ordinarily would not recommend. Limiting the number of operatives a case manager supervises to
six allows the manager the time she needs to properly administrate each
case, to keep the appropriate parties informed, and to still live somewhat

of a normal life. Experienced clients recognize this and typically ask how many cases the case manager assigned to them is running. Conversely, if the case manager is not regularly running undercover, she probably lacks the experience to effectively manage a complex assignment. A lack of experience and inadequate training and support combined with an already full schedule spells trouble. Ensure the case manager assigned to your case not only has the ability to do the job properly, but also *the time*.

Client-Employer

I mentioned in the previous chapter that the client-employer's role in the selection of the operative should be limited. Unless the client contact (who is responsible for routine communication with the case manager) regularly runs undercover or has extensive experience supervising operatives, his role in case management should also be limited. I believe this for several practical reasons. The first is that unless the client contact has the time and experience to play an active role, their time is best spent elsewhere. Supervising an undercover investigation is extraordinarily time consuming. A single operative can consume the full attention of a manager for an entire day. So unless that manager has no other responsibilities, case management might not be a worthy pursuit. Second, getting too close to the case can blur one's vision. In this regard, the client contact best serves his client (usually his employer) by keeping the investigation at arm's length— monitoring but not supervising. By getting too close to the investigation the client contact becomes an active participant. Although this may seem appropriate, it is actually problematic. The greater the active participation, the greater the responsibility for what transpires. Therefore, unless the client contact is prepared to assume some of the collateral liability associated with case management, he is safer only monitoring it. The following is a good example why.

Last year the security director of a large east-coast electronics manufacturer asked that I place an undercover investigator into one of his distribution centers. Not only did he ask that he be allowed to select the operative but he insisted on having daily contact with him once placed. Having worked for the director before and knowing something about him, I hesitantly acquiesced and granted his request. Within days of the case's beginning, he began actively directing my operative and in effect assumed the role of case manager. My case manager was none too pleased and begged I intervene and put the director in his place. I told my manager to be patient and allow the matter to run its course. Shortly thereafter, the investigator was offered marijuana by a coworker. After several days the operative reported that he had confirmed the individual was in fact an active dealer and requested permission to purchase from him. Permission was granted; however, the security director insisted he alone coordinate the effort with law enforcement. Shortly thereafter he was pulled away to tend to a matter in Europe, which resulted in the deal's being put off. After more than a week of postponements, the dealer decided our operative was a flake and began to actively avoid him. Upon the security director's return from overseas, he still did not have the time to coordinate with the local authorities and more valuable opportunities were lost. Eventually, when he finally acknowledged he did not have the time to actively participate in the case, the operative's credibility with the dealers was so ruined that no drug purchases were ever made. After the case was closed, no corrective action was taken and not a single individual was disciplined. The entire effort was a complete waste of time and money simply because of the director's need to control.

Don't manage your own undercover investigations unless you have to.

Attorney

Of all of the team members involved in case management, the attorney is the least utilized and least understood. I am surprised by how many of my colleagues don't have a full appreciation for this important participant. Many agencies and their clients never even consider involving an attorney in their undercover investigations. This remarkable lapse in judgment is evidenced by the lawsuits such ill-considered investigations precipitate. The security professional who relies on himself and his vendor-investigator for legal counsel during an investigation as complex as the typical workplace undercover risks his job and his career. I am so convinced that an attorney must participate that I refuse to accept an assignment unless my client engages one. Not just any attorney either. The counsel selected must be an employment law specialist. She must be experienced in the finer aspects of employment law, have defended employers in cases involving employment claims, and have an appreciation for the complexities of criminal prosecution and its impact on employer liability.

For the participating attorney to be effective, it is best she join the team during the investigation's planning phase. As explained in the previous chapter, by her participating early and taking responsibility for information management and dissemination, the work product of the investigators may be protected from later discovery should the production of documents ever be demanded of the client-employer or its investigators. This form of sophisticated prelitigation preparation is unique to the investigative community. Prosecutions pursued by law enforcement rarely must be concerned with planning for future discovery motions and demands. In fact, in most criminal cases the prosecution usually wants more evidence allowed in than does the defendant. Thus, it may seem illogical to protect information and evidence during a workplace investigation even when prosecution is anticipated. However, a workplace investigation can uncover information that the client-employer may not wish to reveal. What's more, the client-employer may have a duty to protect the identity and the contribution of some individuals involved in the investigation. For example, suppose the primary objective of the investigation was to get to the bottom of a suspected workplace substance abuse problem. Then, during the undercover investigation, the investigators discover that several of the employees involved in the substance abuse problem are buying and selling trade secrets. If the employees in question are indeed proven to have violated their employer's substance abuse policy to the extent that they may be effectively dealt with, what sense is it for the employer to reveal it has also lost valuable trade secret information. Sometimes there are things a company simply doesn't what to make public. Civil and criminal actions by their very nature allow discovery. If the business has not protected itself and its investigation, some or all of the investigative results could be made public.

Several years ago my organization placed several undercover investigators into a large food processing facility at a client's request. The facility was huge and employed nearly 3,000 people. During the investigation our investigators discovered not only widespread substance abuse and theft, but also sabotage and product tampering as well. Because of sophisticated quality control measures, none of the "nonstandard" product ever left the facility. However, imagine the public relations problem if the full details of our findings were made public. In fact, during the union negotiations that followed the termination of several of the more significant offenders, the union attempted get its hands on our entire file for this very purpose. By demanding the release of sensitive and damaging documents, the union attempted nothing more than simple extortion by forcing management to settle rather than expose the results of its entire investigation. The effort worked and management ultimately agreed to reinstate most of the terminated employees, and not another word was said.

In addition to the work product protections provided by the participating attorney, she may also be able to provide some useful advice. Unlike the other members of the case management team, the attorney is uniquely qualified to address employment, contract, and prosecutorial questions as they arise. It is not wise for the client-employer to rely upon its vendor or the police for legal advice. Not only are neither of them legally able to do so, but the simple fact of the matter is that they are not lawyers. All lawyering should be left to the lawyers. And although it is frequently claimed lawyers only slow the process down and unnecessarily restrict the cunning factfinder, they also share some of the political liability when they help make decisions. The value of this infrequently considered benefit should not be underestimated. If by chance the project goes sideways, defending oneself and one's own career is far easier if you have in fact simply "followed the advice of counsel."

The participating attorney can also help manage personality conflicts and help sort through opposing personal agendas. As counselor, the participating attorney can add balance and offer needed options when others aren't sure what to do. The attorney is capable of settling labor disagreements and sparring with an aggressive and inexperienced district attorney whenever necessary. As a team member, she can serve either as the voice of reason or the obstinate provocateur. As far as I am concerned, no undercover investigation should ever be considered without the guiding assistance of competent counsel.

Law Enforcement

Law enforcement plays an important role in most workplace undercover investigations. In cases involving illegal drugs, no drug purchases can take place without the approval of law enforcement. In other types of cases, law enforcement may provide resources, manpower, and intelligence, and in some instances actively participate in the supervision of the operative.

For reasons already mentioned, however, law enforcement's role should be limited. As the line between private corporate investigation and public law enforcement begins to blur, legal responsibilities and liabilities begin to shift. As I pointed out in the previous chapter, the more law enforcement becomes involved in the undercover investigation, the more "agent-like" the operative becomes. If agent status is in fact bestowed upon the investigator, the rights of those he investigates are expanded. Foremost among those rights is that of due process and the *Miranda* warning.[1] Furthermore, if the investigator is deemed to be an agent, the criminal defendant can bring forth the defense of entrapment if appropriate.[2]

With these caveats about the role of law enforcement in mind, representatives from law enforcement should be considered for team membership and recruited to provide assistance with the investigation.

Communication

The investigative team, regardless of its makeup, cannot function without effective communication. No investigative plan or strategy, regardless of its detail and forethought, can be implemented without deliberate and effective communication. For our analysis and discussion of this important element, let's look at the different types and functions of communication and see how they are used.

Written Reports

Aside from the telephone, written reports are the most fundamental form of communication used in undercover. Even before the operative is placed

---

[1] *Miranda v. Arizona*, 384 U.S. 436 (1966).
[2] Contrary to popular belief, entrapment is not a crime but instead is a criminal defense. Only the government or an "agent of the government" can entrap a citizen. As such, agent status as described here may give rise to the claim of entrapment and the use of entrapment as a defense at trial. Typically this defense is not available in cases involving workplace investigations and private investigators.

the generation of reports should begin. Although practices vary from agency to agency, most firms require their operative to make daily reports, which in their most basic form detail the who, what, when, where, how, and why of the investigator's daily observations and experiences. Prepared by the operative at the end of his workday, the reports are then transmitted to his case manager for review and dissemination. The formats for these reports are as varied as the agencies that use them. However, the great majority of them follow some sort of chronological format, starting with the operative's arrival at work and concluding with his return at home. Frankly, in my 18 years in the trade, I've tried just about every format possible. Clearly some work better than others, but personal preference plays a large role in whatever kind is adopted. Regardless of the format, the report must be easy to read and use, and above all must accurately describe the observations and experiences of the operative.

The first phase of report writing is, of course, the gathering of all pertinent facts related to the day's events. According to some, the quality of a daily report may flow directly from the quantity and quality of notes made during the day. This eventual use of notes should be kept in mind by the operative as he creates them. He should keep investigative notes as organized and concise, yet as complete, as possible in order to make the eventual report writing an easier and more orderly undertaking. Moreover, the possibility always exists that the investigator may have to produce his notes as evidence under a successful motion of discovery. This leads to the debate about the value of notes that has gone on for years. I for one tend to discourage the practice of note taking by the undercover investigator. It takes time and significantly increases the risk of an accidental compromise.

Years ago, while sitting in my office, one of my undercover investigators reached into his wallet and extracted a small sheet of paper on which were scribblings he told me were his notes. The investigator had worked undercover for years and had much more experience than I did; however, even then I was instinctively uncomfortable with taking notes during the day while working undercover. He attempted to allay my concerns by explaining he only took notes while in the privacy of a bathroom stall. He said he had done it for years and the method had served him well. As he sat before me with his wallet open, I noticed the business card of a competitor inside. I immediately questioned him about it to which he responded that it was the card of his former supervisor. In an effort to demonstrate his loyalty to our organization, he proudly revealed that my card too was in his wallet. With that I confiscated the cards and asked him to remove everything else from his person that might reveal that he was an investigator. Out of his wallet came more business cards and several scraps of paper with phone numbers jotted on them. I told him to completely "sanitize" himself and his vehicle before he reported to work the next day. He hesitantly agreed and left.

The next day the most remarkable thing happened. Shortly after lunch, my client contact for the case to which my card-carrying investigator was assigned called to report that my investigator's wallet had been found in one of the facility's restrooms shortly after morning break. The client said one of the individuals the investigator had previously purchased marijuana from had claimed to have found it on the floor in one of the stalls. The client quickly assured me, however, that my "experienced" investigator had thoughtfully sanitized the wallet, and upon inspection it revealed to contain nothing even vaguely suggesting he was indeed an investigator. The client momentarily marveled at the forethought of the operative and the thoroughness of his training before discussing how the wallet might be returned to the investigator.

Organization of the report is extremely important. A poorly organized report may contain accurate facts, but if they are entangled with trivia or buried within paragraphs dealing with unrelated subjects, they may be overlooked or their importance misunderstood. A simple timeline or chronological format is probably the most basic form of operative report. Box 3-1 illustrates a report prepared in this simple, easy-to-write format. Used for decades, this format is still popular among some of the less sophisticated agencies. Typically written in the first person, the operative chronicles his daily activities. Brief and to the point, this report format tends to preclude the operative from providing a great deal of detail. Consequently, those who prefer this type of report insist their investigators periodically augment them with some form of supplemental report.

The process, however, should not necessarily be bound to a rigid chronological rendering if another form seems more appropriate. The essential point is that the information contained in the report must be organized in such a way that the facts follow one another in logical sequence and that the material related to a particular incident or event can be easily located and understood. In writing his report, the investigator should assume that the reader knows absolutely nothing about the case other than what will be read in the report provided. Partially stated facts that assume a certain degree of familiarity on the part of the reader are vulnerable to misinterpretations. They can also be a source of embarrassment, particularly when there is a need to recall supporting details months after an incident has occurred and no report or reliable record exists. Additionally, ambiguous words or phrases may force the reader of the report to rely on his judgment to interpret the report. For example, descriptions such as "short," "small amounts of drugs," "late day," or "early hour" are relative terms that force the reader to guess what the writer is trying to say. The use of simple, direct language will enhance the accuracy and clarity of the report. The operative's reports should be clear, concise, and complete.

One of the most popular formats used is the structured narrative. This simple yet sophisticated format still allows the information to be presented in chronological order, but it permits more detail to be included. Box 3-2

AGENT:	A1234B	ASSIGNMENT:	000-000-000
DAY:	THURSDAY	DATE:	08/26/99

0600 - I ARRIVED AT 000-000-000 AND CLOCKED IN.

0745 - I TOOK BREAK AND OBSERVED TROY WILLIAMS (EMPLOYEE, SUSPECT #1) AND

        SONNY HERMAN (EMPLOYEE, SUSPECT #2) MEET IN A SUSPICIOUS MANNER.

1000 - I WENT ON BREAK (UNSCHEDULED) AND TALKED ABOUT NOT BEING

        ABLE TO SLACK OFF AT WORK ANYMORE BECAUSE THE SUPERVISOR, CHRIS

        WATTS (EMPLOYEE, SUSPECT #3)HAD RETURNED FROM VACATION ON WEDNESDAY,

        08/25/99. WATTS SAID FRIDAY WOULD BE A 12 HOUR SHIFT.

1200 - I CLOCKED OUT AND DEPARTED FOR LUNCH WITH MIKE KILNER (EMPLOYEE).

1310 - I LEFT MY WORK AREA TO TALK TO JOHN (LNU, JANITOR).

1315 - I RETURNED TO MY WORK AREA. THIS WAS NOT A SCHEDULED BREAK TIME.

        NORMAL BREAK TIME IS 1345-1355 HRS.

1315 - I PURCHASED MARIJUANA FROM RONNY SANDERS (EMPLOYEE, SUSPECT #7).

        SEE INCIDENT REPORT #7.

1450 - I CLEANED UP MY WORK AREA.

1500 - I CLOCKED OUT AND DEPARTED 000-000-000.

1530 - I WENT J.J.'S BAR & GRILL AND DRANK BEER WITH SEVERAL EMPLOYEES.

1600 - I DEPARTED J.J.'S.

END OF REPORT

BOX 3-1   The XYZ investigation company/daily report.

illustrates this modern report format. Notice the simplicity and readability. Respectful of the typical reader, military time is not used, giving the report a much more professional and business-like appearance. Also eliminated are words like *agent, suspect,* and *perpetrator.* As illustrated, I prefer to code name all of my cases. This helps prevent an accidental compromise and allows the case to be discussed in our office without constantly mentioning the name of our client. For further security, the identity of the oper-

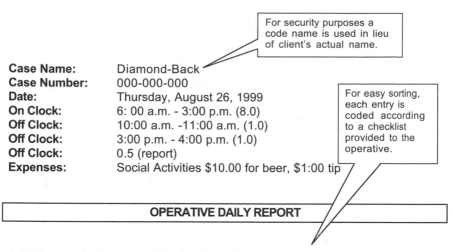

For security purposes a code name is used in lieu of client's actual name.

Case Name: Diamond-Back
Case Number: 000-000-000
Date: Thursday, August 26, 1999
On Clock: 6: 00 a.m. - 3:00 p.m. (8.0)
Off Clock: 10:00 a.m. -11:00 a.m. (1.0)
Off Clock: 3:00 p.m. - 4:00 p.m. (1.0)
Off Clock: 0.5 (report)
Expenses: Social Activities $10.00 for beer, $1:00 tip

For easy sorting, each entry is coded according to a checklist provided to the operative.

OPERATIVE DAILY REPORT

A-13 Suspected Drug activity On Thursday, August 26, 1999 at approximately 7:45 a.m., while in the production area, the operative observed **Troy Williams** (insert operator/temporary) leave his assigned machine accompanied with **Sonny Herman** (production supervisor). **Williams** and **Herman** then entered the supplies closet and closed the door behind them. Both employees remained in the closet for approximately 3 minutes. **Williams** returned to his machine. **Herman** departed from the department. The operative intends to followup and talk to **Williams** about this incident tomorrow.

E-23 Message from Management On Thursday, August 26, 1999 at approximately 10:00 a.m., while in the production area, **Chris Watts** (floor supervisor) informed the production department that Friday, August 27, 1999 was going to be a 12 hour mandatory shift due to excessive customer orders. Watts warned all the production employees not to be absent or tardy. Approximately 15 production employees complained about the overtime to **Watts. Watts** stated to everyone that it was normal to work long hours the first quarter of the year. The meeting ended and production resumed work.

B-2 False Time Records On Thursday, August 26, 1999 at approximately 1:10 p.m., while in the production area, **John** (last name unknown/janitor/temporary) was observed clocking in three time cards. The operative asked **John,** to whom the time cards belonged. **John** explained they belonged to other janitors (names unknown) who were late. No further questions were asked due to **John's** behavior. **John** departed from the area and discontinued the conversation. **John** is described as a white male, approximately 22 years of age, 6'1", 200 pounds, brown short hair, brown eyes and wore a blue janitorial jumpsuit uniform and white tennis shoes.

Footers are used to identify the classification of the report.

BOX 3-2 Operative daily report.

A-4 Marijuana Sale On Thursday, August 26, 1999 at approximately 1:15 p.m., while in the receiving department, **Ronny Sanders** (receiving clerk) handed what **Sanders** identified to be a 1/16 of an ounce of bud (marijuana) to **Mike Lance** (forklift operator) in exchange for $20.00 (two ten dollar bills).   **Lance** placed the marijuana in his right side pants pocket.   **Lance** thanked **Sanders** and exited the department through dock door 11.   **Sanders** stated that **Lance** buys marijuana from him at least once a week at work.   **Sanders** was paged over the intercom by **Tony Lucas** (receiving manager) to receive an order at dock door 14.   **Sanders** responded to the page and discontinued the conversation.   **Sanders** provided no further information concerning the marijuana transaction.

B-1 Absenteeism On Thursday, August 26, 1999 at approximately 2:10 p.m., while in the production area, **John** (last name unknown/janitor/temporary) stated that he planned on calling in sick on Saturday (August 28, 1999).   **John** further stated that he was going hunting for elk with several friends (non-employees/names unknown).   **John** concluded the conversation by saying he often misses work.   No further details were disclosed.   **John** is described as a white male, approximately 22 years of age, 6'1", 200 pounds, brown short hair, brown eyes and wore a blue janitorial jumpsuit uniform and white tennis shoes.

C-17 Sabotage On Thursday, August 26, 1999 at approximately 3:30 p.m., while at J. J.'s Bar & Grill (Cedar Springs, Colorado), **Kenny Sanchez** (truck driver) stated that he and two other drivers (names unknown) frequently puncture their work truck tires to avoid driving to certain delivery locations (locations unknown).   **Sanchez** further stated that he has punctured the tires on his assigned truck on 3 occasions in a 12-month period. **Sanchez** changed the topic of conversation because **Randy Clark** (shipping lead) sat at the table with the operative and **Sanchez**.   The conversation was changed to current affairs and sports. No further information was obtained.

Submitted by: A1234B

End of Report

> Because the report is submitted electronically and can not be signed, this unique code authenticates it and the operative that submitted it.

BOX 3-2   *Continued.*

ative is also protected. Because our operatives submit their reports electronically (they are uploaded to our network by each investigator daily), they are not signed. The use of a unique and confidential code allows the report to be authenticated.

Also notice that the narrative report in Box 3-2 is written in the third person.

Although this practice is often the subject of heated debate among many of my colleagues, I prefer it for two reasons. The first is a very practical one: if the report is written in the first person it technically cannot be edited by anyone other than its writer until it is converted to the third person. That is, if it is written in the first person (the practice of most agencies, see Box 3-1) and then edited for presentation to the client or for some other use, the report would have to be reauthenticated (proofed) by the operative before it could be used. To do otherwise would be to represent a report as written by one person (the operative) when actually it is the product of another (the case manager). This dilemma is easily overcome by simply generating all reports in the third person. Thus the edited report of the case manager is technically correct in where it reads, "the operative observed Troy Williams leave his assigned machine." This practice also precludes the necessity of massive rewrites and edits, saving time and effort.

The second reason I prefer the use of third person reports is a fairly technical one. Suppose the results of the case are challenged after its completion and the case manager (the one who edited the operative's reports prior to their submission to the client) is deposed or otherwise caused to testify in some way. While under oath, if he is shown a report that was originally prepared and submitted by the operative in the first person but later edited by him and is asked to identify the document's writer, he'd find himself in a difficult dilemma. Because he would have to admit the operative's report was altered (edited), he might then be asked to identify all of the alterations he had made. Denied the opportunity to compare his edited version to that originally submitted by the operative, in reviewing a document of any significant size he'd certainly miss something or make a mistake. The error could easily be exploited in an attempt to show that the undercover results that were submitted to the client (and accordingly acted upon) were not accurate and *that the case manager could no longer even recognize that which was altered . . . BAM!* The questioning might go something like this:

Opposing counsel:	So you now admit you altered your investigator's reports before submitting them to your client . . . isn't that so?
The case manager:	Yes. But . . .
Opposing counsel:	And now, even after reviewing your own reports you cannot accurately identify the changes you made, isn't that so?
The case manager:	Yes. But . . .
Opposing counsel:	Then how is it, Mr. Case Manager, you now expect us to believe that your alterations accurately reflect events that actually occurred and that which you represented regarding my client is true?

Although the case manager might wiggle out of this jam with the help of an objection or two, he would not walk away with his credibility intact. At the very least he'd look like a fool. By creating his reports in the third person, the case manager can explain that the report he generated was *his report*, not an edited version of someone else's, that from the operative's reports he created his *own* report. Thus he can attest to its accuracy and explain away any differences from his report and the operative's originals. He could safely claim he took some literary license in creating his report, editing and altering it only to improve its readability, but being careful not to alter it substantively. The version he authored would not look like a doctored operative report pawned off as an original. To better appreciate the importance of this distinction, compare the operative reports in Boxes 3-1 and 3-2 with the case manager report in Box 3-3. Wouldn't it be difficult to get from the first report (Box 3-1) to the report provided to the client (Box 3-3) without using a great deal of literary license and heavy editing?

When any report is written in the first person by one party and then edited by another party, identifying the author is difficult if not impossible. Sophisticated agencies know this and insist their operatives and case managers write in the third person. Which format do you now prefer?

Also note that each entry in the daily report as shown in Box 3-2 is a stand-alone paragraph preceded by an alphanumeric code. These codes allow the case manager to later merge the operative's daily reports and then sort them by topic. Electronically, the case manager can quickly prepare a report for his client in which the information is sorted chronologically and by topic. I have come to call that client report the "Investigative Summary Report." Investigative summaries are provided to the client in the place of daily reports and are written in the third person. Box 3-3 is an example of a typical investigative summary report.

My case managers prepare investigative summaries periodically depending upon the needs and desire of our clients. Typically, however, summary reports are prepared every ten days the operative has worked. This allows the accumulation of enough information to make the report valuable and ensures some sense of continuity. To prepare the report more frequently does not allow enough content to provide adequate context and makes analysis of what's actually taken place more difficult.

Also notice how seamlessly the information from the operative's daily report melds into the investigative summary report. Compare paragraph **A-13** of the daily report in Box 3-2 with the last paragraph of the summary report in Box 3-3. Because the operative's report was written in the third person, it easily merges into the report prepared for the client. Although in this case the daily reports created by the operative would serve just about any purpose, reorganizing the information by topic makes the investigative summary more readable and much easier to use by the client.

Also for the reader's benefit, the investigative summary report begins with a capsulization of the entire investigative effort. The reader is afforded

CONFIDENTIAL

The Very Big XYZ Company
Any Street
Any Town, USA 55555

Because this report is
to be provided to the
client, the client's name
and address is here.

Re: Diamond-Back
000-000-0000

INVESTIGATIVE SUMMARY REPORT

The following Investigative Summary reflects the results of our investigative efforts at the Cedar Springs facility. The dates included are from Monday, August 16, 1999 through Friday, August 27, 1999. The operative developed information concerning the sale of cocaine and the talk of marijuana use/sales. Additionally, information was documented involving security/safety issues, employee misconduct, and employer/employee relations.

To date our efforts have yielded:

12	Cocaine purchases on company time and property
6	Cocaine purchases on company time off company property
7	Marijuana purchases on company time and property

Additionally, we have identified:

16	Employees using cocaine on company time and property
12	Employees using marijuana on company time and property

COCAINE SALE

On Tuesday, August 17, 1999 at approximately 11:35 a.m. while in the rail assembly area of the facility, **Troy Williams** (insert operator/temporary) motioned to the operative to step out the exit located behind the rail blaster. The operative walked out the exit at which time **Williams** reached into his left shirt pocket and pulled out a cigarette wrapper and dumped from it a large white rock wrapped in cellophane, and handed it to the operative. **Williams** explained that the operative could break off a piece, put it in a pipe and smoke it the way it is because it was so pure and better than the last "stuff" (cocaine), that he had sold the operative on Friday, August 13, 1999.

BOX 3-3   Investigative summary report.

At approximately 11:40 a.m. the operative took possession of the cocaine **Troy Williams** (insert operator/temporary) had given him.

At approximately 11:45 a.m. the operative put the cocaine obtained from **Troy Williams** (insert operator/temporary) into an evidence bag that **Special Agent Kenny Berger** left with the him, and then locked it in the evidence box in the trunk of his vehicle. The operative then proceeded to the First State bank to rendezvous with **Special Agent Berger**.

At approximately 12:00 p.m. the operative met Special Agent Berger and surrendered the locked evidence box. Special Agent Berger opened the box and removed the evidence bag. Upon satisfactory inspection of the bag and the evidence within it, Special Agent Berger provided the operative a receipt (see Exhibit A) and returned the unlocked evidence box. **Burger** allowed the operative to photograph the package after examining it himself (see Exhibit C). The operative placed the unlocked box in the trunk of his vehicle. Special Agent Berger retained the only key to the box. At approximately 12:10 p.m. the operative left the bank parking lot and returned to the facility.

At approximately 12:35 p.m. while in the rail assembly area of the facility, the operative gave **Troy** Williams (insert operator/temporary) $300.00 completing the cocaine transaction. The operative handed **Williams** three one hundred-dollar bills provided by the **Colorado State Police Narcotics Task Force**. The serial numbers of the bills are; AB67547008I, AL04508146D, and AJ35735194A (see Exhibit B).

SUSPECTED DRUG ACTIVITY

On Thursday, August 19, 1999 at approximately 11:00 a.m. while in the rail assembly area of the facility, the operative was engaged in conversation with **Troy Williams** (insert operator/temporary).   **Williams** told the operative that **Chris Watts** (floor supervisor) likes to use crystal methamphetamine, because it leaves the body's system in two to three days. **Williams** further told the operative that when **Watts'** hand was cut open at work and for which he received stitches, he was not tested for drugs like other employees who are injured at work.

On Thursday, August 26, 1999 at approximately 7:45 a.m., while in the production area, the operative observed **Troy Williams** (insert operator/temporary) leave his assigned machine accompanied with **Sonny Herman** (production supervisor). **Williams** and **Herman** then entered the supplies closet and closed the door behind them. Both employees remained in the closet for approximately 3 minutes. **Williams** returned to his machine. **Herman** departed from the department.

> Note that this paragraph came directly from the operative's daily report (Box 3-2).

BOX 3-3   *Continued.*

a quick summary of what has taken place and what has been learned. Also notice that the writer has not qualified the activity or results in any way. He has deliberately avoided labeling any of the events as policy violations or violations of the law. Assuming the role of information gatherer only, the writer does not pass judgment on anything or anyone. Instead, he has left such determinations to the client. This allows him to assert his lack of bias and claim he made no effort to influence the reader or the user of the information. Literally, he reports only that which took place. In essence, this forces the client to determine if a policy or law has been broken.

Another report that is typically produced during the investigation is generically called the *special report*. These are nothing more than reports that document a special event or something other than that done in the normal course of the investigation by the operative. A good example is when surveillance is used to supplement the undercover or document someone's activity relative to the investigation, but without necessarily directly involving the operative. Another example of the special report is what are commonly called *incident* or *buy reports*. These supplemental reports document significant events that may be actionable in and of themselves. For example, a district attorney may require a separate special report for each drug purchase the operative makes. As a matter of evidentiary clarity, she may not want everything the operative reported on a particular day introduced. She may therefore insist that in addition to the operative's daily reports prepared for his employer, he prepare a special report detailing solely the drug purchase in question and what led up to it. The prosecution would then rely on this special report, the physical evidence, and the operative's testimony in bringing its case. This approach limits the aspects of the investigation that the defense could challenge in hopes of ultimately attacking the credibility of the operative. For this reason, smart prosecutors stipulate that each prosecutable drug purchase be supported by a special report and do all that they can to keep the rest of the case file out of evidence.

Although there is no established format for these special reports, I prefer those that are easy to read and generate. Box 3-4 is a good example of such a report. Notice that it was created easily from the investigative summary report illustrated in Box 3-3. Using first person or third person is simply a matter of preference. Because my other reports are written in the third person, I prefer to generate my special reports also in the third person. But if the district attorney or prosecutor wanted them in the first person, the change would be simple and fast. In any event, if the document is to be used as criminal evidence it should to be reviewed and signed by the operative before submission.

With a little forethought and a good word processor, professional looking reports are a snap. We have competitors that still ask their operatives to write their reports by hand or periodically to call them in to a central dictating machine of some sort. The reports are then transcribed,

The Very Big XYZ Company
Any Street
Any Town, USA 55555

Re: **Diamond-Back**
       000-000-0000

> Full physical description
> provided to ensure positive
> identification.

SPECIAL REPORT # 16

On Tuesday, August 17, 1999 at approximately 11:35 a.m. while in the rail assembly area of the facility, **Troy Williams** (insert operator/temporary, male Caucasian, 5' 11", 200 pounds, brown shoulder-length hair, blue eyes and large blue dragon tattoo on left forearm) motioned to **Confidential Informant #1** to step out the exit located behind the rail blaster. **Confidential Informant #1** walked out the exit at which time **Williams** reached into his left shirt pocked and pulled out a cigarette wrapper and dumped from it a large white rock wrapped in cellophane, and handed it to **Confidential Informant #1**. **Williams** explained that **Confidential Informant #1** could break off a piece, put it in a pipe and smoke it the way it is because it was so pure and better than the last "stuff" (cocaine), that he had sold **Confidential Informant #1** on Friday, August 13, 1999. At approximately 11:40 a.m. **Confidential Informant #1** took possession of the cocaine **Troy Williams** (insert operator/temporary) had given him.

At approximately 11:45 a.m. **Confidential Informant #1** put the cocaine obtained from **Troy Williams** (insert operator/temporary) into an evidence bag that **Special Agent Kenny Berger** left with him, and then locked it in the evidence box in the trunk of his vehicle. **Confidential Informant #1** then proceeded to the First State bank to rendezvous with **Special Agent Berger**.

At approximately 12:00 p.m. **Confidential Informant #1** met Special Agent Berger and surrendered the locked evidence box. Special Agent Berger opened the box and removed the evidence bag. Upon satisfactory inspection of the bag and the evidence within it, Special Agent Berger provided Confidential Informant #1 a receipt (see Exhibit A) and returned the unlocked evidence box. **Burger** allowed **Confidential Informant #1** to photograph the package after examining it himself (see Exhibit C). **Confidential Informant #1** placed the unlocked box in the trunk of his vehicle. Special Agent Berger retained the only key to the box. At approximately 12:10 p.m. **Confidential Informant #1** left the bank parking lot and returned to the facility.

> Depending upon the needs of the
> prosecutor, the operative's name
> may or may not be used.

BOX 3-4   Special report #16.

At approximately 12:35 p.m. while in the rail assembly area of the facility, **Confidential Informant #1** gave **Troy** Williams (insert operator/temporary) $300.00 completing the cocaine transaction. **Confidential Informant #1** handed **Williams** three one hundred-dollar bills provided by the **Colorado State Police Narcotics Task Force**. The serial numbers of the bills are; AB675470081, AL04508146D, and AJ35735194A (see Exhibit B).

End of Report

Confidential Informant #1   Date

Because the document may be used as evidence, the operative may be required to sign it.

BOX 3-4   *Continued.*

edited, re-edited, and eventually presented to the client. This seems primitive and inefficient to us. Without our high-speed workstations, servers, and notebooks we too would feel as if we were in the Stone Age. Before selecting an undercover vendor, have them show you how they do their reports. I think you'll be surprised.

Electronic Communication

In today's digital age, electronic communication has in many ways replaced traditional methods of communication. Email and now vmail (digitally transmitted video via the Internet) to a large degree have replaced the use of the postal mail system and other physical means of moving information. Because email is fast and inexpensive, it is the preferred method of communications for much of the business world. Today corporate investigation firms of all sizes have access to this electronic marvel. The smart ones use it religiously.

Users of email can move information fast and efficiently. Operative reports uploaded to the employer's network at the end of the day can be downloaded, edited, and within minutes of receipt zapped to an awaiting client. Using digital video and vmail, the technologically sophisticated operative can transmit the video of a workplace drug transaction to virtually anyone anywhere. Today's investigator is really only limited by his or her imagination.

As mentioned above, all of our operatives have notebook computers. At the end of their day they key their reports and upload to one of several secure servers. Passwords, firewalls, and stand-alone systems insulate our confidential internal networks from the peering eyes of the outside. Once received, the operative report files are *physically* removed from the server and given to the case manager. The case manager then uploads the file to an internal network where the report is reviewed, edited if necessary, and in some cases immediately transmitted to the client. Using today's technology and tools like email, a client could receive his reports any place in the world at any time.

The question of email security and confidentiality should not go unmentioned, however. Since its inception, the security of email has been a valid concern. Users know that no system is completely secure and free from unwanted penetration. And although most email users fear some sort of Internet interception of their confidential traffic, the real vulnerabilities are within their local area networks (LANs) and wide-area networks (WANs). Hackers have correctly claimed the only network that is truly secure is one that is powered down. For these and other obvious reasons, email and the other forms of electronic communications (including facsimiles) should be used only when appropriate security is available. Encryption software is simple and inexpensive. Take the necessary precautions and don't let your confidential traffic get intercepted.

Telephone Communication

Telephones have been with us for almost 125 years yet they are still one of our most important means of communication. Telephone communication, whether conventional or wireless, is a necessary component of today's modern investigations. In addition to providing a daily written report, the operative should talk to her case manager every day. This link to the real world allows the undercover operative to expound upon her written report and efficiently consult with the case manager. Communicating by telephone every day ensures that the operative and her investigation are kept on track and closely monitored by management. Then, using the telephone or email, the case manager can communicate with the other members of the investigative team. Daily communication is necessary for the case to run smoothly and be properly managed.

I've interviewed operatives who've worked for some of my competitors that told me that on their previous assignments they called in as infrequently as once a week. A few have told me they called in once a month! How is that possible? What sort of supervision or guidance under those circumstances could the operative possibly receive? And what about safety? How on earth did the employer know his investigators were still alive? Daily reports, you answer. Not necessaily; there are still several agencies out there that require that their operatives *mail in their reports once a week!* My investigators are required to call their case managers every day they work within four hours of coming off the client-employer's clock. Consistent failure to call in on time is grounds for disciplinary action and even termination. Without frequent and consistent communication, successful undercover is not possible.

Team Meetings

Another important means of communication are meetings. Because most of our cases are out of town, my case managers cannot meet their operatives whenever they wish. As such, depending upon budget, the client, and necessity, my case managers try to meet with their operatives at least once a month. Either we go to the operative or the operative comes to us. Regardless, in one form or another I insist that my case managers periodically meet with their operatives.

Operative meetings, as they are sometimes called, are also excellent opportunities to bring together the other members of the team. Counsel, law enforcement, and of course the client contact are all welcome participants in these regular meetings. For confidentiality purposes, these meetings should always be held off site and far enough from the target facility that employees or managers from the site will not happen by. For that reason alone, restaurants, bars, and other public places do not make good meeting places. I prefer to rent a hotel guest room or conference room. Making sure to rent the room in a name other that of my client or my firm, the investigative team can secretly meet and discuss the investigation.

After the meeting, all of the reports, notes, and handout materials that were used are collected and disposed of with a shredder. The room and all trash containers are thoroughly sanitized before adjournment. A good practice is to have the operative arrive last and leave first. Although it is a common courtesy, no one should ever walk the operative out. While in the public cyc, no one on the investigative team should acknowledge or converse with the operative. Operation security is a must at all times.

Meetings with law enforcement for the purpose of booking evidence should be handled equally carefully. Imagine how awkward it would be for the operative to run into a bunch of employees from his assignment in the local police station while booking evidence purchased from one of his coworkers? More on this later, but in the mean time remember that in this business—if it can happen, *it will happen.*

Case Files

Ah, the lowly case file. The electronic age was hailed as the creator of the paperless office. Nothing could be further from the truth. A recent study reported that offices with email access use 30 percent more paper than those without. The study found that email messages larger than a single page on the screen were almost always printed. Upon reflection, that's my practice as well.

Case files are a necessary evil in the trade. Although one can construct marvelous computer filing hierarchies for the management of electronic reports, memos, and miscellaneous documents, there is really no substitute for the good old paper case file. Case file management and format are largely a matter of preference. However, I prefer a system that is simple and neat. Because undercover investigations tend to generate a lot of paper, large three-ring binders work well as document holders. At a minimum, the file should have five sections to accommodate each of the following:

- Operative daily reports
- Investigative summary reports
- Special reports
- Correspondence
- Billing information

The case binder or folder should be marked "Confidential." However, no reference to the operative or the investigation should be on the outside cover. Even a code name or case number on the outside of the file could arouse suspicion and invite someone with accidental access to peek inside. Again the best practice is keep it simple and easy.

At the completion of the project, all case files and evidence should be retained. Original notes, reports, and investigative summaries should not be destroyed. Electronic folders and files should be pulled down and safely stored. For this purpose, Zip Disks® are best. More stable than 3½-inch floppies, Zip Disks® also hold more. Each disk holds about 100 megabytes of information, which is enough space to store the case file of even the largest of investigations. Digital images, spread sheets, and data bases can also be downloaded to disk and stored for safekeeping. Although duplicate information and files can be deleted in order to save space, original documents and files should always be retained.

It is important, however, to store all of the case information in one place if at all possible. This practice will make responding to subpoenas and the demand for the production of documents easier if necessary later. Inventory the material once compiled and retain it in a safe place. A copy of the inventory should also be kept with the case file. Retain all files for a minimum of five years, longer if circumstances dictate. If storage space and cost is not an issue, why not keep your files forever? My former firm kept some of its case files for more than 30 years. Some firms never destroy their files.

However long you retain case files, ensure that someone is the "custodian of record." This important function is carried out by an entity or individual responsible for the safekeeping and production of all case-related

documents if necessary later. As a matter of practice, because client contacts change jobs, law enforcement officers retire, and things just tend to
get lost, I have insisted for years that my firm remain the custodian of record
for our investigations. More than once, many years after the fact, a client
has called me looking for a document or a report it could not locate. A good
filing system and the safekeeping of records is an important function. It
should not be left to chance.

CHAPTER 4

Drug Investigations

There is no workplace problem more complex or dangerous than employee substance abuse. Unfortunately, illegal drugs are everywhere today. They are in our schools, communities, factories, and offices. Drug abuse affects our productivity and competitiveness. It robs us of our spirit, our trust, and our freedom. It destroys people, families, jobs, and careers. It causes birth defects, industrial accidents, bankruptcies, and highway fatalities. It affects everyone. No one is immune.

According to the U.S. Drug Enforcement Agency (DEA), the international illicit drug trade is a $300 billion industry. The illegal manufacture and distribution of drugs is an industry that knows no national borders. Its deals almost exclusively in cash, and enforces its policies and doctrines with violence. What's more, the DEA estimates that 60 percent of all illicit drugs produced in the world are consumed in the United States. Of those illegal drugs consumed here, 75 percent or more are consumed by people with jobs, resulting in an estimated domestic economic impact of over $150 billion annually.

For the employer, the price is paid many ways, as employee substance abuse

- Decreases productivity and morale
- Increases turnover and absenteeism
- Increases the likelihood of accidents
- Increases insurance costs
- Increases the likelihood of theft and dishonesty
- Increases the unnecessary consumption of benefits
- Decreases profits

Employee substance abuse robs the organization of its talent, vitality, and enthusiasm. It destroys teamwork and cooperation. It competes with the business entity for time, capital, and human resources. It may well be the single most formidable competitor we face today.

The Human Cost of Substance Abuse

Substance abusers do not check their drug abuse problem at the door when they enter the workplace. Employees involved in drugs tend to be absent more often, use more medical benefits, and file more workers' compensation claims than do nonabusers. They are also more likely to be fired. But substance abuse affects the abuser's family as well. Studies show that a non-alcoholic member of an alcoholic's family uses ten times more sick leave than others. Family members are more likely to drop out of school, divorce, get in trouble with the law, and use drugs themselves. They are also more prone to suffer accidents and long-term illness. The children of alcoholics are five times more likely to become alcoholics than are the children of nonalcoholics.

Substance abuse also breeds dysfunctional relationships. Abusers have difficulty getting along with others. They tend to withdraw from friends and coworkers and to be secretive. They spend less time at home and work. They contribute less time to their families and avoid opportunities to social-ize. They will go out of their way avoid nonabusers and are less likely to develop long-term, meaningful relationships with others.

At work, they become less productive and creative, and frequently become disciplinary problems. They deny responsibility and quickly blame others for their shortcomings. They become the 20 percent who consume 80 percent of our time.

The Role of the Employer

Unfortunately, solutions are not easy. Concerned employers must take decisive action and efficiently use the resources available to them. They have learned that to create a drug-free workplace, at a minimum they must take the following steps:

- Make a commitment
- Set goals and objectives
- Assign responsibility
- Formulate a comprehensive policy
- Communicate the policy
- Equitably enforce the policy
- Provide education and training
- Help those who want it
- Audit the program regularly

Today's employer understands that creating a drug-free workplace involves taking control. The successful employer must consistently manage the quality of its workforce, the quality of supervision, and its culture. It is a process that demands a commitment of time and resources. It also requires a sound understanding of the problem of drug abuse and its progressive nature.

Understanding Employee Substance Abuse

A *drug* is nothing more than a chemical substance that, once in the body, alters the normal physical, behavioral, psychological, or emotional condition of the user. For the most part, the *drugs of abuse* are psychoactive, that is, they alter the user's perception of reality. In fact, that is precisely why they are used. Psychoactive drugs target the central nervous system and impair the user's ability to think and properly perceive reality. They include legal and illegal substances and are often consumed socially. To learn more about the drugs of abuse see Appendix C.

Substance abuse is the use of a drug for something other than its intended medical or social purpose. Continued abuse invokes the deceptive sense of physical, mental, and emotional well being. Abuse can often easily lead to addiction and/or chemical dependency. Abuse also can create personal, family, and financial problems beyond the abuser's control. Several factors contribute to this process.

Rationalization

One of the most destructive human behaviors is *rationalization*, a means to devise a superficial rationale or plausible explanations and excuses for one's actions. Usually this is done without a conscious awareness that these are not real motives or that the long-term consequences of the rationalized behavior may be undesirable and self-destructive. Substance abusers must constantly rationalize in order to maintain their relationship with their drug of choice.

Employee substance abusers rationalize that the use of illegal drugs is a constitutional right, that addiction and chemical dependency only happens to someone else, and that drug use enhances their ability to perform, produce, and create. They rationalize that they can quit anytime, that drug use at work is okay because everybody does it, and that selling drugs to coworkers is a gesture of friendship and camaraderie.

The lies and deception that shroud the abuser blinds them to the reality of their own actions. Their blindness allows them to rationalize away their values and personal responsibility, as well as respect for other people and their property. This insidious process permits them to lie to their spouse and family, steal from their friends and employer, and continue to use drugs at the expense of themselves and all those around them without guilt. Rationalization is one of the most powerful survival mechanisms the drug abuser has and every drug abuser eventually learns to master it.

Naiveté and Doper Logic

To my continued amazement, employee substance abusers that have been caught often tell me they were unaware that their involvement with drugs at work could result in the loss of their jobs. I know many of these employees are simply lying. Pathetically, they are trying to deflect responsibility and project blame elsewhere. However, some of these people are sincere. I believe, as remarkable as it may sound, they simply don't understand that their involvement with drugs or alcohol at work is inappropriate. This says something about their cultural background and how it conflicts with that of their employers.

For most drug abusers, substance abuse is a way of life. It is not something that is turned on or off, comes in and out of season, or is simply done for fun or some other recreational purpose. For the typical substance abusers, their relationship with their drug of choice eventually becomes a way of life. It influences their thinking, their values, and their morals. In fact, the relationship with their drug defines them as individuals and forms the basis for their culture. The resultant drug culture that is created has its own style, rituals, customs, and language. And like all cultures, its imprint on the individual is deep and very often permanent. Cultural influence is one of the reasons why threats, saber rattling, and antidrug posters are not effective in a workplace contaminated by substance abuse. The employee drug culture can be so strong that it finds such management tactics and efforts laughable.

The drug culture has another side as well, and that is violence. Although the incidence of drug-related violence in the workplace is relatively low, it cannot be overlooked. During one of my investigations several years ago, a drug dealer attempted to take the life of one of my undercover investigators. Here's what happened.

After several months of hard work and a number of disappointments, our undercover investigator had finally infiltrated a well-known network of drug dealers in a large factory. The dealers had a reputation for using force to collect debts and frequently bragged of violent escapades outside the workplace. They had created an environment where even management feared them. Using an employee sponsor, our investigator gained the confidence of one of the dealers. After several small purchases of cocaine at work, the dealer invited our investigator to his home, telling our operative he would like to make him a distributor and would front him the dope to do so. Our law enforcement handlers immediately recognized the opportunity and put a plan into motion. They instructed our investigator to pursue the dealer's offer and arrange a meeting, which was quickly set.

Wearing a hidden microphone and transmitter, our investigator went to the home of the dealer under the watchful eye of the police. He was immediately greeted by the dealer who jokingly said to him, "Just to be sure you're not a cop, I think I should pat you down. You know, maybe you're wired or something." As he approached, the investigator told him he was welcome to do whatever he wished, but if he laid a hand on him it would be the last human being his hand would ever touch. As tough as he thought he was, the dealer was taken back by his new comrade's subtle aggressiveness. He stopped in his tracks and, with an awkward smile and rolling wave of his right arm, told the investigator, "Come on in *narc*, join the party!" (After his arrest, he later told the police he knew right then and there our guy was a cop. He said that "dopers don't say shit like that, they're nothin' but a bunch of pussies.").

Once inside the house, our investigator found a group of five or six in a back room drinking whiskey and joking loudly. He recognized several of the men as coworkers from the factory. Following brief introductions the party began. The dealer broke out a bag of "weed" and while gabbing away, expertly rolled two fat marijuana cigarettes. Just as he was about to light the first cigarette, the doorbell rang. The dealer got up and went to the door. A moment later he returned, accompanied by a large, rough looking man in his late thirties. The dealer, with a somewhat twisted and uncomfortable look put his hand on the shoulder of the man and said to the group, "This is the dude I was telling you guys about." With that, the "dude" grabbed my investigator by the neck with his left hand, yanked him to his feet, and drove him into a wall. Almost as if magic, a cocked .45 appeared in his right hand which he drove forcibly under the chin of my operative. The "dude" turned to the dealer and in a calm, icy voice said he wanted his money. The eyes of the dealer, as well as those of everyone else in the room were on the gun. The dealer said nothing. The "dude" pushed the gun deeper into the neck of the investigator and again demanded his money. Although the investigator does not recall it, his wire transmitted the voice of someone else in the room telling the dealer to give the man his money. After a 15-second exchange of mindless expletives, the "dude" tells the dealer he is going to kill the man he is holding to make a point. Relating the clearest of doper logic I have yet to hear, he tells the dealer that if he kills him (the dealer), he'll never see his money. But if he kills his "customers," the dealer will soon run out of friends and have no choice but to pay his debt. Before the dealer could respond, the police were already in the house and without incident the "dude," the dealer, and several of the others were taken into custody. The dealer later revealed that he owed the man less than a thousand dollars.

The fact that employees claim to be unaware of the consequences of on-the-job substance abuse also says something about the employer. To me it suggests that the employer has not said enough about substance abuse nor has it adequately communicated its expectations. And that is exactly what I often find. Employers by and large don't communicate enough with their employees. When it comes to substance abuse, employers often say nothing. How can we expect anything but ignorance if we don't share our expectations regarding behavior and communicate our policies with our people? Employers must clearly and frequently communicate with their employees. They must do all that they can to create and maintain the workplace culture they desire. For if they don't, they will find they have a culture created by others, perhaps even by substance abusers.

Addiction and Chemical Dependence

Addiction is the disease of compulsion. An individual may be addicted to or by anything. Most often, however, we think of addiction as the uncontrollable repeated use of a substance or behavior. In the case of substance abuse, the addict often not only becomes addicted to the effects of the drug but to the social behaviors surrounding its procurement and rituals involving its preparation and use.

In many ways the addict becomes a "dues payer." The drug addict or alcoholic pays with:

- Drunk driving arrests and convictions
- Hangovers and blackouts
- Dysfunctional relationships
- Confrontations with family, friends, and employers
- Lost opportunities and disciplinary actions on the job
- Demotions
- Terminations
- Imprisonment and sometimes even loss of his life

No one ever aspires to be a drug addict. Involvement with drugs usually begins with experimentation, frequently with introduction to the drug by a friend or family member. If the drug produces an enjoyable effect, experimentation is usually followed by a pattern of irregular use, most often in social settings.

If the progression is uninterrupted, the user begins to select and develop relationships with friends and coworkers who are also involved with the drug(s). As these relationships solidify, former friends and coworkers are increasingly shut out. The user's appearance, behavior, interests, and relationships all begin to change. As he withdraws, his social circles shrink even further. The user becomes more secretive, suspicious, and paranoid.

The user's relationship with the drug also changes. He becomes protective of it, defending its benefits, value to society, and the constitutional right to its use. The user frequently thinks about it, sometimes even studies it, but always talks about it.

Other things change, too. On-the-job performance deteriorates. Users develop attendance problems, usually with recognizable patterns. They seem less focused and begin to have more personal problems. They use drugs more frequently and irresponsibly. They may drink and drive, smoke marijuana while hunting or while handling firearms, and consume drugs in public places with people they don't even know.

Eventually they begin to use drugs or alcohol while on the job. At first their use is very discreet, but gradually becomes flagrant. Employee abusers will drink in the employee parking lot at lunch and during breaks. They will smoke marijuana in restrooms and locker rooms. They will consume cocaine or other drugs at their desks or workstations. They will use drugs in company-owned vehicles or while out of town on business. Given the opportunity, such abusers will even use drugs with customers and vendors. They will keep drugs in their desks, lockers, and toolboxes. They will use the company mailroom or shipping department to distribute drugs and use interoffice mail, company pouches, and overnight delivery services to move and receive them. They will hide drugs in safes, furniture, trash containers, hazardous material containers, beverage containers, lunch boxes, briefcases, purses, shoes, coats, raw materials, and finished goods.

Employee drug abusers are resourceful, cunning, and deceitful. Many become what are known as *functional abusers*. The functional abuser in many ways seems to be able to manage their addiction. These individuals require the effects of the drug just to be "normal." In many ways, functional abusers look like anyone else. They keep steady jobs, work regular hours, have families, and appear happy. The functional abuser, however, leads two distinct lives. One we can see, and one we can only imagine. These abusers usually use drugs everyday but, because they seem to contribute and be productive and behave normally, they are particularly difficult to identify. But when they are deprived of their drug, they are entirely different people. These abusers are usually the ones we never knew abused until they stop.

Dealers are altogether different. The can be extremely aggressive and brazen, and at other times passive and timid. However, most are risk takers and will not hesitate to secretly sell right in front of nonabusers, supervisors, and managers. Dealers tend to socialize more than others. They are constantly networking while feverishly trying to avoid detection. They are frequently not where they belong or absent while on the job. They tend not to make trouble and generally avoid interaction with management whenever possible. If accused of misconduct, they quickly grow belligerent. Employee drug dealers support employee causes and enjoy creating strife between management and labor. They resist team building, pursue secret agendas, and despise authority. And they are an essential component of workplace substance abuse.

Chemical dependency differs from addiction in a number of important ways. Although it is an integral component of addiction, it is a condition involving significant yet seemingly subtle chemical changes in the body. These changes are both psychological and physiological. In this condition, the abuser uncontrollably craves the drug and is relieved only by the consumption of it. The chemically dependent may lose all rationality and do anything to obtain the drug. Usually when abusers arrive at this stage, no level of discipline, concern, or love will reach them. The drug controls them and all that they do.

Employee Drug Users and the Opportunities of the Workplace

For the substance abuser, the workplace abounds with unusual opportunity. For them it is like no other place. There are a number of reasons why this is so.

Better Quality

In most cases, abusers would have to go to the source to obtain drugs of better quality than typically found in the workplace. Workplace dealers want repeat customers and they recognize that high quality drugs keep them coming back.

Fairer Quantity

Illegal drugs are expensive. Often sold in quantities as small as a one-fourth of a gram, accuracy in weight is important to the employee user/buyer. Again workplace dealers recognize the importance of repeat business and consequently tend to not only sell high quality drugs to their coworkers but to distribute them in fair and accurate quantities as well.

Low Risk

The typical employee-abuser and dealer perceive the workplace to be a safe place to use and sell drugs. Abusers perceive supervisors and managers as uninformed, untrained, and afraid to confront problems. Rarely do they see a drug abuse issue addressed or even talked about. In many cases the security policies and practices of an employer that are intended to protect assets and people also protect the abusers and dealers. Walls, fences, and locked doors not only keep out unwanted outsiders but also protect employees from the peering eyes of management and law enforcement. In prior investigations, employee dealers have told me that they had specifically targeted their former employer because of its reputation of being soft on drugs and providing a safe place for dealers to ply their trade. See Appendix D for more details regarding the criminal penalties under the controlled substance act.

High Return on Investment

Employees who choose to sell drugs at work often do so as a means to obtain drugs for themselves. Others clearly do it for profit. For example, an ounce of high-quality cocaine, cut (diluted by adding an impurity), and repackaged in one-gram quantities can yield a dealer about a $4,600 profit. In a work-force of 100 employees or more, a single employee-dealer can move an ounce of cocaine a week through direct sales to coworkers and by net-working. Profits can sometimes be enormous. We've caught employee-dealers (earning less than $10 per hour from their employer) who never carried less than $10,000 cash to work! One such employee admitted to having earned $20,000 per month selling drugs at the hospital where he worked. With his earnings he purchased a beachside condominium. A week after he moved in, he paid over $60,000 cash to have *the kitchen remod-eled.* Although he spent most of his workday managing his drug business, his employer paid him $7.50 per hour as a purchasing agent. He was 21 years old at the time of his arrest.

The Ability to Buy and Sell Drugs on Credit

In the workplace it's called a *front.* The drugs are sold to the employee-user under the agreement that they'll pay for them later. Usually that means payday. For this service, employee-dealers generally charge a small premium. Usually keeping a small amount of the drug exchanged exacts that premium. However, abusers win too. Fronting allows them to obtain and use drugs even when they don't have the cash to buy them. I've seen cases in which the employee-user was so desperate to obtain the drugs that she was willing to pay twice the asking price if the dealer allowed her to pay him the next day!

The Progressive Nature of Substance Abuse in the Workplace

As the abuser's relationship with his drug(s) of choice progresses, he finds that paying for it becomes increasingly difficult. Once the abuser has exhausted his discretionary income, he usually resorts to buying his drugs on credit. However, once his credit lines are exhausted and no one will any longer front him, he is generally forced to either deal or steal to sustain his habit. If the choice is made to become a dealer, he will most often sell to coworkers at work. If the abuser chooses to steal, the first victims will usually be his employer and coworkers.

Employee theft that is related to substance abuse often begins with stealing food from coworkers. It took me years to recognize the significance of this all-too-frequent phenomenon. The food items most often taken are soft drinks, fruit, sandwiches, and snacks. Be it cognitive consistency or simple doper logic, the workplace abuser consciously or unconsciously rec-ognizes that the criminality of taking someone else's cookies and their pos-session or use of an illegal drug cannot be compared. Like the getaway driver following a bank robbery who does not obey the speed limit or signal when turning, the employee substance abuser that regularly possesses or uses at work finds it easy to rationalize the commission of other offenses. Moreover, because the abuser has likely lost respect for himself, it is only logical that they not respect coworkers or their property.

As the progression of substance abuse continues, next we typically see the theft of petty cash, postage stamps, cash receipts, office equipment, and the personal effects of coworkers. Invariably training equipment (VCRs, televisions, and video cameras) and other relatively accessible company property will disappear. Soon missing will be company maintenance tools (hoses, lawnmowers, and even small tractors), aluminum ladders, small hand tools, power tools, pneumatics, and precision instruments. In the office, software, peripherals, computer memory, and computers (particularly portables) will disappear. Left unchecked, the substance abuser will eventually steal to the extent the system will allow. Eventually stealing scrap, raw materials, and finished goods, abusers may also steal client lists, confidential information, and trade secrets. To the desperate abuser, nothing is sacred.

The process continues with a decline in morale and productivity. Management begins to distrust the workforce, and the workforce begins to lose confidence in management. A culture of fear, anger, and distrust begins to evolve at the workplace. As confidence declines, so does loyalty, teamwork, and profitability. Effectively the organization corrodes from within. I have seen this problem progress to the point where female employees sat on their purses the entire day so that an office thief could have no access to their wallets and at the end of their shift completely clear off the tops of their desks of everything including personal photographs.

Employee substance abusers also steal from customers and vendors. They may short a shipment to an important customer, keeping and selling the difference. They may accept kickbacks for miscounting, allowing overages, double shipping, approving improper or unauthorized credits, or diverting a vendor's delivery. The impact on the employer can be devastating. Relationships can be destroyed, and valuable vendors can withhold service or necessary materials. Customers may cancel contracts, refuse payment, or even file suit, and reputations may be ruined. But, unfortunately, the employer's problems don't end there.

Substance abusers are more likely to have accidents and get injured. They file more health claims and consume more than their share of the benefits provided them. Increased claims translate into higher insurance costs and lower profits. The resulting absence of the injured or sick drug abuser may disrupt operations and result in lower productivity for the organization. Furthermore, it may necessitate recruiting, hiring, and training replacements.

While real claims cost real money, fraudulent claims cost money too. Substance abusers are more prone to file false claims and feign on-the-job injuries. As the abuser's burden grows and performance begins to slip, some form of progressive discipline usually begins. Missed deadlines and careless mistakes are rarely terminable offenses. However, repeat offenders are not as readily forgiven, and are usually punished. With each subsequent transgression, the punishment is more severe and figuratively the abuser moves closer to the door.

In many instances, the abuser foresees what may be the inevitable—termination. However, this outcome is unacceptable. For the substance abuser and the non–substance abuser alike, the job often defines how the individual thinks about himself and how he understands others to perceive him. For the abuser the job may even be more important, representing what is perhaps the last thread of hope. It may be the only element of stability, structure, and normality in an otherwise chaotic life. As a result, for many substance abusers the job is the last thing surrendered. Many will give up their car, home, and family—*everything* but their job. When this happens, abusers are left with few choices. Obviously, they can give up drugs, and some do. Or they can get out from under the yoke of progressive discipline by feigning an on-the-job accident; unfortunately, this is the far more frequent choice.

The fraudulent claim of disability frustrates management and escalates the ever-increasing costs of insurance and doing business. Sadly, the cycle of destruction may repeat itself several times before the employee is terminated, seriously injured, or hits rock bottom. At that point, the employer, spouse, family, friends, and the abuser all lose.

Destructive Behaviors

Substance abuse in the workplace does not exist in a vacuum. Not only does the abuser play a significant role, but so does the employer. In order for a substance abuse problem to exist, the participants must engage in an assortment of dysfunctional behaviors. Of these, denial, enabling, and codependency are the most significant. Both the abuser and the employer engage in these destructive behaviors and create an interactive dynamic that is so powerful that many believe substance abuse in the workplace cannot exist without it. Let's look at each of these behaviors individually.

Denial

In the case of the substance abuser, denial is the condition or state of mind in which one refuses to believe or consciously acknowledge that one's behavior has come to adversely affect one's own and others' quality of life. Denial is a destructive behavior and, if allowed, it often fosters continued substance abuse by the abuser. Abusers rationalize that their behavior is acceptable and minimize the adverse impact of their conduct. They deny that their involvement with drugs affects their health, job, and family. They deny the existence of a relationship with their drug of choice and the ever-escalating cost of that relationship. Abusers in denial say things like

- "It doesn't affect my work."
- "What I do on my own time is my own business."
- "I can quit anytime."
- "I don't have a problem."

Friends and coworkers engage in denial as well. They deny the abuser has a problem, or if they do admit it, they claim the problem is temporary or even justified. This cooperation in denial by friends and coworkers can be a very harmful influence on the abuser. They unwittingly encourage the abuser's continued abuse by fostering the illusion that their behavior is normal, acceptable, or even expected. This form of reinforcement allows the abuser to further rationalize that it is not they who have the problem, it is others. In a family situation, the abuser whose denial is encouraged by friends will not accept the advice and pleadings of concerned family members. Instead, they perceive the family as critical, insensitive, or overbearing and that their involvement in drugs is a natural response to the "problem at home." Naive friends (often themselves abusers in denial) support this perverted notion and continue to act as a support system for the abuser. However, instead of encouraging therapy, treatment, or abstinence, they encourage continued abuse. This destructive cycle of reinforcement can go on for years. Eventually the abuser's view of reality becomes very distorted. To the abuser in denial the world is upside down. It becomes a life filled with chaos, disorder, and disappointment.

Supervisors, managers, and even entire companies engage in denial. Supervisors and managers sometimes deny that an employee has a problem even in the face of undeniable proof. They refuse to admit that someone for whom they are responsible could be involved with drugs. However, in denying the existence of a problem, they are also denying the abuser help. The cruelty of this form of denial is perverted further when the supervisor himself is also an abuser. In these cases, both abusers tumble through life cloaked by a dysfunction state both see as normal. The irrational, destructive behaviors and attitudes of one define normalcy for the other, while each contributes emotional justification for the other's continued abuse. Denial of this sort can lead to ruined careers, accidents, and on the job fatalities.

When a company engages in denial, scores of people can be affected. This occurs when companies fail to create sound drug abuse policies, fail to enforce the policies they have, and fail to respond to incidents involving drug abuse when they occur on the job. Companies in denial say things like

- "We don't have a drug problem here."
- "If we had a drug problem we'd know about it."

- "We're only concerned about the dealers, not the users."
- "If we enforced our policies we couldn't get anybody to work here."
- "This industry doesn't have those kinds of problems."
- "Those kinds of people don't work here."

Such institutional denial is not only destructive, it is cruel. Out of a fear and unwillingness to confront the truth, employers deny the abuser the help they need. In doing so, they are active participants in the progression of the abuser's disease and in the very destruction of some of the most important people in their organization.

Enabling

Enabling is nothing more than consciously or unconsciously allowing or encouraging the destructive behavior of others. The backdrop to this destructive behavior is often denial. The enabler's actions shield the abuser from experiencing the full impact and consequences of his drug abuse. The enabler often unwittingly protects the abuser, thus making possible the continued destructive abuse and relationship with the drug. The enabler assists in maintaining everyone's delusion that the abuser is okay and does not have a problem.

Family members enable when they call in sick for the abuser, make excuses to their bosses for them, and lie to protect them from discipline. Such behavior at first often seems kind and protective; however, nothing could be further from the truth. It allows the abuser to continue his rationalizations, denial, and abuse. Eventually the abuser begins to rely upon the support provided by the enabler and does not have to face the reality of his actions. Family members also enable when they forgive. Forgiveness itself is an act of caring and love; however, when forgiveness is given inappropriately, as in the case of the dysfunctional drug abuser, it is only harmful. The resulting promises and commitments that are continuously broken become a pattern of behavior that in time destroys his family's trust and love. Enablers, however, always come back for more. In a pathetic attempt to change the abuser and his behavior, the enabler actually contributes to the abuser's self-destruction by fostering a protective environment in which the abuser is shielded from the escalating adverse consequences of his relationship with his drug.

Supervisors and managers enable too. They cover up for the abuser at work. They make excuses for the abuser's attendance problems, his poor or substandard performance, and his general inability to meet the reasonable expectations of others. Supervisors and managers also enable by accepting excuses from the abuser such as

- "I have a lot of problems at home."
- "It will never happen again."
- "I can handle it, just give me more time."

- "I'm not the only one who has problems around here."
- "I promise to do anything to keep my job."

Unfortunately, for most people it is easy to permit the enabling to continue. Dealing with difficult employees and the problems they bring to work is not fun and is certainly not easy. It's also scary. Supervisors and managers sometimes are afraid of being wrong or being tagged "the bad guy." They doubt their judgment and ability to do the right thing. Sometimes they are concerned about what their boss will think and how their actions will affect their career. The abuser will use these emotions to his advantage and play upon a leader's sense of fear, guilt, and inadequacy. When an organization gives in to such tactics, it is enabling.

Supervisors and managers must:

- Know and understand their company's drug policy and how it is to be enforced
- Know the symptoms of drug abuse and when to get help
- Accurately document the performance of their employees
- Recognize enabling behaviors when they occur
- Stop enabling
- Communicate their expectations and hold their employees accountable
- Document their efforts and results
- Communicate with one another and upper management

Breaking the cycle of enabling involves being honest and confronting the problem. It means being willing to stop accepting responsibility for the actions of the abuser and to start holding him accountable instead. It means being a caring and concerned person by being firm, fair, and holding people responsible for themselves and their own behaviors.

Codependency

Codependency, another destructive behavior common in the workplace, is allowing the behavior of others to overshadow and influence one's own values and judgment. It is a behavioral pattern with its own rules about not feeling, talking, or standing up for what is right. The codependent becomes so involved with the abuser's addiction and chemical dependency that his own needs and desires are ignored and largely left unmet. The resulting relationship between abuser and codependent is almost sure to disintegrate. In extreme cases, in a pathetic and sometimes fatal attempt to influence the behavior of the abuser, the codependent will actually resort to using drugs himself. However, only more pain and suffering is usually the outcome.

Codependency is typified by the following:

- Preoccupation with a partner's or coworker's chemical dependency problem
- A feeling of having to do more than one's fair share of the work to keep the relationship going
- A fear of expressing feelings about a friend or coworker
- Acceptance of a partner's or coworker's inability to keep promises and commitments
- A fear of disciplining a key employee for fear that he'll leave and have to be replaced

Codependency most of all involves feelings. While in a codependent relationship, a person often has feelings of anger, isolation, guilt, fear, embarrassment, and despair. He may also feel out of control. For fear of rocking the boat, codependents often enable and allow the abuser the opportunity and support mechanism to continue their drug abuse. Codependents become rescuers, caretakers, and adjusters. They also sometimes respond by becoming an overachiever or hero in an attempt to be a role model for the abuser. Other times they simply give up and become a joiner.

Supervisors and managers need to:

- Focus on performance and not allow the manipulative behavior of the abuser to overshadow them and what they know is right
- Set limits and boundaries for the abuser; tolerate only that which is acceptable and consistently manage employee performance
- Talk and get help; use internal resources such as the human resources department and the company's employee assistance program
- Refer the problem employee to resources that can help
- Document their efforts and results; communicate with upper management

In order to be effective, supervisors and managers must understand the intricacies of addiction and chemical dependency. They must also understand and be able to recognize the destructive behaviors of denial, enabling, and codependency. Finally, good supervisors and managers must be prepared to deal with these behaviors when they confront them.

Intervention

Intervention is the calculated interruption of the destructive behaviors of drug abusers and those around them. Intervention is not discipline. It is a caring behavior in which one plans, prepares, and takes action. Intervention is a process that brings the immediate and long-term consequences of the abusers actions and behaviors to their full attention. Its purpose is to correct, not punish. In its purest form, intervention is an attempt to salvage the troubled employee through coaching, counseling, and consistent feedback. In many cases, management intervention is the abuser's only hope prior to discipline and corrective action. The measures taken in effective intervention include the following:

Observe and Document Performance

Consistently observe and document performance. Be objective and fair. Ensure that the employee (all employees for that matter) understand what is expected of them. Observe and document inappropriate behavior. Obtain the opinions of others in management if there is any doubt as to the appropriateness of an employee's behavior. Take immediate action if it is necessary to prevent an accident or serious mistake.

Interview and Discuss Expectations

First, isolate the employee. Remove the troubled employee from his or her immediate work area and confront him or her in private. Never confront the employee in front of his peers or subordinates. Do not do anything or say anything that might embarrass or shame the employee. Have a witness present if at all possible. Include a union representative if appropriate or required. If an investigation has preceded your interview, share with the employee what you can. State only specifics, never generalize or moralize. Provide the employee documentary proof of their substandard performance (e.g., attendance records or timecards) or behavior. Describe in detail what is expected of them, referring to written policy whenever possible. If witnesses assisted in the investigation do not identify them unless absolutely necessary. Discuss with the employee only the facts you can support, not suppositions or generalized conclusions. Do not accuse, diagnose, or attempt to rationalize the employee's behavior.

Next offer the employee the opportunity to provide an explanation and/or mitigation. Be open-minded but remember the employee may be steeped in denial and might easily rationalize away responsibility. Document the employee's responses and comments. Then ask the employee what the company might reasonably do to accommodate him in order that the employee could meet company expectations. Do not make a commitment, only listen and attempt to understand his request. Communicate empathy but by no means agree to quick fixes or obviously short-term solutions. Suggest instead the employee seek professional assistance such as that offered through the company's employee assistance program or other resources. Be prepared to provide the employee the appropriate telephone numbers and/or literature if available.

Again specifically detail for the employee his shortcomings and your expectations. Clearly define boundaries and the specific consequences if those boundaries are violated (e.g., "Your next absence will result in a written warning."). Indicate that the employee's performance and/or behavior will continue to be monitored and state when his efforts will formally be reviewed and discussed again (e.g., "In 30 days from today, we'll meet again here in my office to review your progress.").

Conclude your discussion on a positive note. Indicate that you anticipate the employee will improve his performance (or change his behavior) and that your expectations will be met. Ensure that the employee knows you support him and no one is out to get him. Make clear that his success will also be your success. Excuse the employee and let them return to work.

Document Results

Following your meeting with the employee, document all that took place. Detail what was said by you and the employee. Document his demeanor and response to the demand for improved performance and a change in behavior. Calendar your intended follow-up meeting and ensure in writing, if necessary, that the employee knows the date it's scheduled.

Communicate

Thoroughly brief upper management and human resources. Provide human resources copies of the supporting documents used in your meeting and copies of your notes. If appropriate, suggest that a human resources representative participate in your next meeting with the employee and that he too calendar the date.

Follow Up

As scheduled, again meet with the employee. The meeting should be short and to the point. Those who attended the first meeting ought again to be in attendance. Quickly review the employee's progress. If he has met prescribed expectations, state your appreciation and congratulate him. If he has not, impose the corrective action or discipline discussed in your first meeting. Again set goals and establish a follow-up date.

Intervention is an important management tool. It is designed to correct, not discipline. Used properly, it will enable supervisors and managers to improve performance and change behavior. In many cases, consistent intervention will improve the quality of life in the workplace for both employees and management. In the long run, it can prevent unnecessary discipline and employee turnover, and may even save a life.

Progressive Discipline and Corrective Action

Sometimes intervention is not enough. Troubled employees and drug abusers do not always respond the way we wish. The effects of addiction and chemical dependency are often too much for the abuser to overcome alone. No matter how understanding or accommodating we may be, the abuser is simply unable to respond. At this acute stage the abuser is often resentful, seemingly uncaring, and almost spiteful. In some cases the individual may have actually surrendered to the disease. At this hopeless stage, progressive discipline may be the only answer.

Progressive discipline is the incremental escalation of discipline in response to continued performance shortcomings. It frequently begins with verbal warnings. Next are written warnings, followed by suspensions and ultimately termination. The escalation of discipline clearly sends the message to the abuser that their relationship with their drug(s) of choice has its cost. Progressively (and quite apparently) they begin trading things of value for that relationship. As the abuser slips down this slippery slope, the last thing they surrender is their job. Usually they have already given up their family, friends (except those also involved in drugs), home, primary means of transportation, savings, and health. Desperately they cling to the only constant in their life, their *job*.

In these circumstances, the job is more than a source of income. It is the last place of normalcy and order in the chaos of the abuser's life. For this reason, they cling to it with a vengeance. The abuser rationalizes that they are not sick, addicted, or chemically dependent as long as they are able to maintain a job. The abuser at this stage is capable of most anything . . . except giving up drugs. They will lie, cheat, and steal in order to keep their job and may even resort to violence if it is taken away from them.

Progressive discipline is a process that must be tightly managed and closely monitored. It can only be done properly under the watchful eye of human resources. However, short of discharge, there may be another option. That option is a management referral to the employee assistance program.

Employee Assistance Programs

Today's employee assistance programs (EAPs) address a broad range of issues, including alcohol and drug abuse, family problems, marital problems, and other personal problems. The services of the employer-provided EAP are free and are usually available to family members as well as the employee. The relationship between the employee or family member (both are called *clients*) and EAP professional is strictly confidential.

In effect, the EAP is a clearinghouse for employee help services that is provided free of charge by the employer. EAPs do not conduct investigations or drug tests. They do not enter into long-term relationships with their clients. By design they provide hassle-free, high quality, professional help to people in need. EAP services are professional and confidential and an essential component of a drug-free workplace.

Employees can voluntarily seek help through their EAP or management can refer them. With a *management referral* as a condition of employment, the participating employee agrees to be professionally supervised and monitored, and management is kept fully informed of his or her progress.

Over time the employee is provided the assistance and treatment they need and is eventually reintegrated into the workforce.

Prevention

No examination of workplace substance abuse would be complete without some discussion of prevention. Although no employer can absolutely guarantee a drug-free workplace or provide impenetrable islands of safety for its employees, there is much an employer can do. A successful prevention program should include the following:

- Management commitment
- Clear and meaningful objectives
- Assignment of responsibility
- Formulation of a comprehensive policy
- Distribution and communication of the policy
- Education and training
- Consistent and equitable enforcement
- Program and progress audit

Once a commitment is made, employers must set goals and objectives. Accountability must be established and specialized policies developed (see Appendix E for sample policy). Those policies should prohibit the use, sale, and possession of all controlled substances and alcohol on company time or property. Drug testing and fitness-for-duty applications should also be incorporated. The policy should not include terms such as *under the influence* that imply some legal standard. Instead, use terms such as *impaired* or *the presence of any detectable quantity*. Have all policies and procedures reviewed by legal counsel before implementing them.

Employers should also better screen applicants. By testing for drugs, conducting in-depth background investigations, and using trained interviewers, employers can avoid hiring mistakes and create a safer workplace.

Background investigations are easy to obtain and inexpensive. However, if time or resources is a concern, the employer should consider outsourcing this task. Organizations that specialize in employment screening can conduct quick and inexpensive searches of criminal conviction records, driving histories, and other pertinent public records.

References should always be checked and past employment verified. Consistent with the amended Fair Credit Reporting Act (FCRA) of 1997 (See Appendix I) applicants should sign a release of liability and provide written authorization before inquiries are made. The applicant should also be required to provide copies of past performance reviews or other records.

Applicants should also be carefully interviewed by well-trained and experienced interviewers, professionals who can detect immaturity and emotional instability. Each applicant should be interviewed individually by several different interviewers. Questions should be carefully worded so as not to violate the law or infringe on the rights of the applicant. The interviewer should attempt to learn how the applicant would deal with workplace problems and resolve disputes. An interviewer's gut feeling should not be trivialized; if he or she feels any unease about the applicant, additional interviews or investigation should be considered.

Next, employers need to communicate and equitably enforce their substance abuse policy. All employees must clearly know what is expected of them and know the consequences of any transgression. Each employee should be provided a copy of the policy and acknowledge in writing that they have received it and understand it. Posters, payroll stuffers, company newsletters, and staff meetings are effective ways to remind employees of corporate policy and expectations. As mentioned earlier, many employees simply don't know the rules.

Training and education are also important in creating a safe and drug-free workplace. Every employee must receive training. The foundation of policy understanding and compliance is education. The typical workplace cannot remain drug-free without it.

Finally, employers must devise audit and review procedures to ensure company-wide commitment and policy compliance. Self-audit and bench-marking is the first step. For larger organizations, outside help is often necessary. However, local law enforcement and EAP providers may not have the experience or sophistication to provide the assistance needed. In these cases, employers must seek out qualified resources that understand the problem and appreciate the corporate culture. Such resources include security and management consultants, employment law attorneys, and other organizations that specialize in workplace substance abuse issues.

The Process of Investigation

Unfortunately, prevention and intervention do not always work where drug abuse is concerned. Employees are human and they make mistakes. When they do, management must respond swiftly and effectively. In order to do so, investigation of the circumstance and individuals allegedly involved is often necessary. As already mentioned, allegations, circumstantial evidence, and suspicion are not enough to warrant corrective and/or disciplinary action. And as we have already learned, a workplace investigation is simply a factfinding process involving one or more persons in the objective collection of information.

The simplicity ends there, however. Workplace substance abuse investigations are often complicated, time consuming, and expensive. Employers also need to be aware of the enormous liabilities that are associated with the decision to confront workplace substance abuse. An improperly conducted or otherwise defective investigation can result in civil actions against the employer and those who conducted the investigation. Such proceedings carry with them the potential for adverse publicity, huge attorney fees, and expensive judgments. However, as explained in Chapter 2, many of these problems can be eliminated and the risks significantly reduced when the investigation is properly engineered.

No investigation of any complexity is possible without strategic engineering of that investigation. This is particularly true with respect to investigating workplace substance abuse, making it possible to systematically collect information for the purpose of obtaining specific goals. For our purposes, we will call this organized effort *the process of investigation*. In order to properly function and fulfill expectations, the process must be well scripted and unfold precisely and incrementally. Workplace undercover investigations are no exception. Because of their complexity, such undercover operations are not possible without a high degree of order and carefully planned process. As such, they tend to unfold in five distinct but interdependent phases. I call them the five *phases of investigation*:

- Planning and preparation
- Problem identification and information gathering
- Verification and analysis
- Disbursement of disciplinary and corrective action
- Prevention and education

Interestingly, not just undercover but all workplace investigations can be engineered to unfold in this fashion. But to better appreciate that, and to better understand the process itself, let's briefly examine each element.

Planning and Preparation Phase

In Chapter 2, I explained in some detail the planning and preparation of the workplace undercover investigation. You were probably surprised how much effort really went into setting up an investigation even before it began. But by now you should appreciate that the planning and preparation phase creates the foundation on which the entire undercover investigation will rest. If the investigation is not properly planned and appropriate preparations are not made, the investigation will be riddled with problems and in the long run consume more time and money. Therefore, the outcome of your undercover investigation is controlled to a great degree by the amount of planning and preparation you put into it.

Problem Identification and Information Gathering Phase

For many of those in my profession, this phase of the process constitutes their *entire investigation*. For them, their investigations start and end here.

They do not subscribe to the necessity of a process as outlined above or of any sort of formal organization. They just *investigate*. Unfortunately their results reveal this haphazard approach. Lacking objectives and having no chart to direct their course, their investigations simply unfold as chance would dictate. Such an investigator only randomly collects information and naïvely hopes his findings somehow meet the needs of his customer. The competent professional investigator is far more sophisticated. He engineers each investigation to meet the unique business needs of his customer. This professional understands that information gathering is only a small part of a successful investigation. The professional investigative team must therefore determine the investigative tools available and combine them to achieve its predetermined objectives. There are six basic methods of factfinding and information gathering:

- Physical surveillance
- Electronic surveillance
- Research and audit
- Forensic analysis
- Undercover
- Interviewing

In order to be successful, the investigative team must use these different forms of investigation in such a fashion that objectives are pursued logically, legally, and ethically. In the case of undercover it is the case manager that usually oversees this responsibility. The other members of the team offer assistance and support to drive the investigative process ever forward. Let's look briefly at each of the methods of investigation.

Physical surveillance is nothing more than watching or observing people, places, and things. When this activity is outdoors, it is usually augmented with the use of cars, vans, or other specially designed vehicles used for cover. Outdoors or in, the savvy investigator will usually record what he observes with a camera or video. In summary, physical surveillance:

- Is relatively easy
- Is comparatively inexpensive
- Has limited applications
- Has limited evidentiary value
- Should be considered only as corroborative evidence

Electronic surveillance is much like physical surveillance; however, the investigator enhances his capabilities using electronic technology. This technology may be in the form of closed-circuit television (CCTV) or a computer program that records the keystrokes of a word processor. In summary, electronic surveillance

- Is relatively easy
- Is comparatively inexpensive
- Is fraught with legal risks
- Has limited evidentiary value
- Should be considered only as corroborative evidence

Research and audit actually is nothing more than the review and examination of documents and records. *Audit* in this context refers to documents and records held by the client-employer and not normally in the public view. Examples of such documents include personnel files, drug test results, production and quality records, and incident reports. *Research* refers to documents and records that are publicly available. Examples include state driving records, land titles, and criminal conviction records. In summary, research and audit

- Is relatively easy
- Is comparatively inexpensive
- Requires access to the information sought
- Usually has significant evidentiary value
- May be considered both as compelling and corroborative evidence

Forensic analysis is the application of modern science and scientific technology. Examples of this method of investigation would include polygraph, ion scan (as bomb detection), and gas chromatography-mass spectrometry (such as in human drug testing). In summary, forensic analysis

- Requires scientific ability
- Is relatively expensive
- Is not possible in all environments
- Has significant evidentiary value
- May be considered as both compelling and corroborative evidence

Undercover investigation is nothing more than the surreptitious placement of a properly trained and skilled investigator, posing as an employee, into an unsuspecting workforce for the purpose of gathering information. Undercover of course is interactive and thus allows the collection of physical evidence and testimony. In summary, undercover

- Is interactive
- Allows the collection of physical evidence and witness testimony
- Is not possible in all environments
- Requires close supervision
- Is often lengthy and costly

Interviewing is also an interactive form of information gathering. Requiring little more than an interviewer and interviewee, it is simultaneously one of the most basic yet most complex forms of investigation available. In summary, interviewing

- Is logistically simple
- Is interactive
- Has high evidentiary value
- Has high corroborative value
- Provides some element of due process

It is the investigative team's responsibility to use these fundamental methods of investigation in combination such that they permit the gathering of the information desired.

Verification and Analysis Phase

Although this phase of an investigation is often unappreciated, it is likely one of the most important. For our purposes, it should be understood to involve interviewing of the most serious transgressors and obtaining statements from them. For example, following the workplace undercover drug investigation (the problem identification and information gathering phase), the employee-dealers and users are interviewed regarding their behavior. If done properly, the process should yield both more information about the workplace substance abuse problem as well as voluntary admissions of personal involvement.

What's more each employee who is interviewed is extended some measure of due process. The interviewee is allowed to explain himself and his behavior. At the same time the employee is allowed a peek at the evidence against him. Effectively he is put on notice and told that the employer has learned of his misconduct and before taking action the employer is prepared to hear the employee's side of things. This sort of interview with the employee before disciplinary actions are taken not only seems fair—it is fair. Moreover, it makes good business sense.

Disbursement of Disciplinary and Corrective Action Phase

The fourth phase of the investigation is the disbursement of disciplinary and corrective action. If the investigation has been properly engineered and carried out according to plan, following the employee interviews described above, the employer would next render decisions regarding discipline and corrective action. If the interviews with the transgressors were successful, theoretically the employer could make its decisions based upon employee admissions alone. Tactically this is genius. For if the employer were to use only the employee's admission (given it was obtained properly) and the employee were to challenge the employer's disciplinary decision, he would have to overcome his own admission without the opportunity of simultaneously attacking the investigation. The investigation itself would be immaterial. Although arguably relevant to the disciplinary action, the employee would likely find it difficult to challenge the investigation because of lack of materiality. In other words, because the employer did not rely on any aspect of the investigation's factfinding process, the employee could not challenge its process or outcome. The employee would be forced to stick with his admission and ask for leniency or recant the admission and impeach himself.

Affirming his admission and asking for leniency would probably not work because the employer would already have made its decision. Under the circumstances, it is unlikely that even the most compassionate employer would find any reason to reverse itself. Alternatively, if the employee decided to recant, he'd be forced to explain under which circumstances he lied—when he first made his incriminating admission or after the employer dispensed its discipline? This double bind leaves even the most aggressive employee with no viable options. He either affirms an incriminating admission or admits to lying.

Prevention and Education Phase

Of all aspects of a workplace investigation, this phase is least regarded. Following the disbursement of discipline and corrective action, it is time for the employer to look back and analyze its mistakes. How did the problem occur and why? Objectively examining its mistakes, the employer can rethink and re-engineer its processes. Augmenting its process improvement effort with education, the employer can bring about long-term, cost-effective change.

It may seem that I've gone fairly far afield here and perhaps you've already wondered what all this has to do with undercover. The answer is that it has everything to do with undercover. For if the investigation has no process and it has not been properly engineered, it is destined for failure. Regardless of the collective skill and experience of the investigative team, if each member does not have an adequate appreciation for the process of investigation and for all that is involved in executing an investigation as complex as a workplace undercover, the results will be disappointing. Yet even in my profession today, I have respected colleagues who have no real understanding of the process of investigation and how the failure to appreciate it affects every investigation they conduct.

Investigating Employee Substance Abuse

Having completed all of the necessary preinvestigation planning, let's fast forward now into the first several weeks of the investigation. Although no two investigations are alike, all workplace undercover drug investigations share several common characteristics. Contrary to popular belief, drug investigations for the most part are relatively easy, they are not dangerous, and are most often successful.

Substance abuse is common and discriminates against no one, and because most employers have not done all they can to test and screen their workforce for illegal drugs, substance abuse almost always finds its way into the workplace. Complacency, denial, and other destructive behaviors are contributory, but the heart of the problem is people. And wherever you find people, you'll find drugs.

Relationship Building

Once positioned in the workplace, the undercover investigator must immediately do two things. First, she must learn her job; second, she must earn the respect of her supervisor. The failure to do either of these things will likely result in her termination. Because new hires are most often considered to be on probation, the investigator's failure to quickly learn her job and gain the trust of her supervisor will cause her to be more closely scrutinized than normal. This results in a vigilant supervisor constantly looking over the shoulder of the operative. Under such a watchful eye, socializing and the collection of information will be very difficult. In order to be effective, then, the undercover investigator must quickly become a productive contributor and begin to gather allies. This transitional period is called the *relationship building* phase.

During this period of the investigation, the investigator simultaneously learns her job and begins to make friends. In addition to a great deal of will and determination, the operative must have a *sponsor*. The sponsor is an employee the operative seeks out to be friends with and who the operative can use to vouch for her and her credibility. This is a process that is carefully orchestrated and manipulated. The operative must first carefully select her target sponsor, who usually has the following traits or characteristics:

- Has tenured seniority, that is, employed long enough to be considered one of them. This is critical because how much workplace history he knows and the number of employees with whom he is familiar to a large part determine the sponsor's value.
- Is friendly, but somewhat introverted. The best sponsor is someone looking for a friend. A person who is outwardly capable yet somewhat insecure is best.
- Is well respected among his peers and management. The best sponsors are good workers. They know their job or trade and people who work with them also know it.

• Has impeccable credibility with everyone. Of all things, the effective sponsor must have credibility. If no one trusts the sponsor, he will not be able to vouch for the operative.

Once a target sponsor is selected, the operative must make her approach. Befriending the would-be sponsor must be done slowly and carefully. However, over a period of several weeks, the trained investigator will gain the trust and friendship of this person and slowly bring the sponsor into her "confidence." By this I do not mean that the investigator tells the employee her true identity or purpose. That mistake is fatal to the investigation and is the mistake of only the untrained and unskilled. What I mean is that the sponsor should be told something about the investigator that no one else knows. This should be something the investigator and case manager have fabricated together, something that gives the situation play, something unusual or romantic.

Only after the *sponsor* feels trusted, will he trust the operative. Over time and with care the operative must cultivate the relationship so that eventually the sponsor will trust the operative enough to introduce her to his friends and others within the facility. This is the part of the process—called *sponsorship*—in which the sponsor effectively vouches for her and her trustworthiness.

During sponsorship the skilled investigator networks her way through the organization. Using the credibility of her sponsor, she interacts and socializes with the intent of putting herself in the right place at the right time. Carefully working her expanding network, the operative slowly begins to identify the *players*—those employees actively involved in the substance abuse problem, culturally outside the rest of the workforce. As the players begin to grow comfortable with the operative, the investigation transitions from the relationship building phase to the proactive, involvement phase.

Information Development Made Easy

Once successfully sponsored and accepted by the substance abusers, the operative's work has only just begun. With the guiding assistance of the case manager, systematically the operative must pursue each substance abuser as they are identified. Separating the users from the dealers, the operative must eventually buy drugs from those willing to sell them. Because dealers need customers, they are usually not hard to find. In most workplaces, the substance abusers know exactly where to go for their drugs. But because illegal drugs are expensive, many users eventually become dealers in order to provide for their own drugs. By purchasing a quantity of drug exceeding his own immediate need, the user can easily sell a portion of the purchase to a friend. The transaction is called a *split* or *split purchase*. Usually the amount sold to the friend is sold at cost. However, because a larger quantity was originally purchased, the combined price of the splits is lower than if each individual had made his purchase alone. Pathetically, the user unwittingly becomes a drug dealer. This cycle continuously repeats itself in the workplace and over a period of time, every user eventually becomes a dealer.

This workplace user–dealer dynamic becomes particularly problematic for the employer. In enforcing its policies, the employer must differentiate offenses. The employer must decide whether selling drugs at no profit or simply "as a favor" is, in fact, drug dealing. Interestingly, the criminal law in most states makes no differentiation. What's more, in most states neither the drugs nor money need to be exchanged; the offense of selling is committed upon the offer. However, in order to properly make this determination, the employer should look at its policy manual. Most substance abuse policies I've read don't contemplate this issue. Take a look at yours and see if it's addressed. If not, make a recommendation that it be changed.

Because drugs are so easy to purchase from dealers and users, the operative must exercise care. It serves no purpose to dupe an unwitting user into becoming a dealer. Because the operative enters the workplace with purpose, training, and money, drug purchases are not particularly difficult to make. As such, guidelines should be established to direct the operative during this important stage of the investigation.

Guidelines for Workplace Drug Purchases

The guidelines established for workplace drug purchases are not a matter of public policy or the law. Effectively they are self-imposed by the investigative team. With the investigation's objectives clearly in mind, collectively the team should decide the rules of the game. The investigative agency will certainly have policies and guidelines for its operatives, but surprisingly, law enforcement will likely have none. With the exception of those agencies that routinely assist in private sector drug investigations, most agencies haven't a real clue as to what should or should not be done. Certainly, such an agency will have a good sense of how to put together a criminal drug case, but it may fall surprisingly short in its ability to assist the employer in deciding what to do and how to do it. And because each case is unique, there are no hard and fast rules. The following guidelines should help make the process a bit easier.

Qualify the Dealer

In order to overcome an allegation of entrapment (actually not a crime, but a criminal defense), I suggest the operative *qualify* each person whom he intends to purchase from. Qualifying is simple. First the operative should establish that the behavior or activity in question was preexisting, that is, it was taking place before the operative came on scene. To do this, for example, the operative simply asks others if they previously purchased drugs from the dealer now offering to sell to the operative. Establishing that the suspect dealer had dealt prior to the operative's approach will negate the dealer's later claim that he was induced to engage in an activity in which he was not previously involved.

Next the operative should establish why the dealer wants to sell to him. The perfect motive would be financial gain. But by establishing any proper motive the dealer is denied the recourse of claiming that he was improperly induced to engage in an activity that he knew was wrong. The outcome of this carefully choreographed test removes any chance of a defendant-employee raising the defense of entrapment. If done properly, the operative will avoid buying from first-time dealers.

All Drug Buys Should be Controlled

All workplace drug buys should be done under the control and supervision of law enforcement. Although this is not always possible, every attempt should be made to ensure law enforcement is aware of and approves every drug purchase. Without the appropriate approval and immunity, the operative exposes himself and his organization to criminal prosecution for the simple possession, transport, or purchase of any controlled substance. To avoid this potentially embarrassing legal predicament, all workplace drug purchases must be coordinated with the appropriate authorities in advance. The local sheriff, chief of police, or local drug taskforce should be contacted before the investigation begins to obtain proper immunity if appropriate.

Buy Down, Not Up

As a matter of practice, law enforcement typically buys increasingly larger quantities of drugs from the dealers it pursues. In an effort to find the source, law enforcement agents purchase their way up the distribution chain hoping to eventually eliminate the supply at its source. However, in workplace drug investigations, the operative should purchase the smallest quantity the dealer is willing to sell. The employer must only demonstrate that the dealer committed a policy violation; the quantity sold is not an issue. Furthermore, by buying small quantities the operative can buy more often. The operative should appear to be a small-time user. *Buying up* makes the operative appear agent-like. The operative should always *buy down*.

Avoid Purchases Off Premises

Under most circumstances, an employer cannot control what an employee does on his or her own time. As long as the activity does not adversely affect the employee's ability to perform while on the job, an employer should neither attempt to control nor monitor the activities of an employee away from work. This fundamental right to privacy precludes an employer's intrusion into the private lives of its employees. Thus, under most circumstances the employer should not permit its investigation to stray into the private affairs of its employees, even if the activity in question is substance abuse and drug dealing. The focus of the workplace investigation should be workplace issues and misconduct—not the enforcement of public law. All drug purchases should be made on company premises to the extent they can be.

The Operative Must Not Use Drugs

Short of a life-threatening situation, the operative should not use illegal drugs. To do so affects her health, impairs her credibility, and threatens the success of the entire investigation. A professional undercover investigator does not use illegal drugs *ever*. To help preserve the operative's credibility, routine drug testing should be done. Using a combination of periodic hair and urine testing, it can be demonstrated that the investigator is not a substance abuser and has not used an illegal drug. The testing laboratory as well as the agency should maintain the test results as a permanent record. Should the investigator's credibility later be challenged, the test results can be produced in her defense.

As a matter of practice I test my investigators before, during, and after the investigation. It is not enough to test every six or twelve months. For credibility purposes, I cause my operatives to be tested every time they are exposed to an illegal drug during their investigation. Testing immediately after a drug purchase, for example, could demonstrate that the investigator did not sample or test the drug before or after the purchase. Because the window of detection varies from drug to drug, it is important to test the operative as soon after exposure to a drug as possible. Testing outside the window of detection serves no purpose and could even harm the operative's (and the investigation's) credibility.

Importance of Drug Purchases

I am sometimes asked why bother to make drug purchases at all—isn't the word of the operative enough? The short answer is that drug purchases give drug investigations credibility. More than once an unfriendly arbitrator has asked me, "Where's the dope?" Without the benefit of a drug purchase, it can be hard to demonstrate the scope and severity of the problem. The question will be asked, "If the problem were so severe, and so many employees dealing drugs, why weren't some of the drugs obtained as evidence?" Clearly, without the ability to put *dope on the table*, the investigative result is more easily challenged. And as frequently argued in criminal drug cases, the best evidence is the dope.

However, never should the lack of a drug purchase be considered fatal to a workplace drug investigation. Many factors and situations may arise precluding a drug purchase. For example, a qualified dealer might insist that all drug purchases take place off company premises at locations he alone would take the investigator. This scenario is simply too dangerous and the dealer who insists on these terms might never be purchased from. In other cases the dealers might insist that the operative use the drug before the purchase. Under these circumstances, the investigator again may be forced to forgo a chance to make a purchase. Regardless, the properly engineered investigation contemplates these situations during the planning phase and identifies alternative strategies. Experienced investigators (and arbitrators) know that drug purchases are not necessary to make good drug cases. *Good investigations make good drug cases.*

Supporting Investigation

As mentioned above, the properly engineered investigation contemplates the totality of the problem and its circumstances. In not all drug investigations are drug purchases possible. In some workplaces, primary drug dealers deal only to established subordinate dealers, thus making purchases from them impossible. In other instances, dealers refuse to be seen possessing either dope or money. They employ elaborate schemes in which they hide the drugs in some secret location at the workplace to which they direct their customers after receiving payment. In yet other schemes the careful and conniving dealer can make it almost impossible to tie him to his crime. For these reasons and others, the investigation must allow for more than just undercover. It is unreasonable that the operative alone can make the case. More often than not, some form of supporting investigation is needed to assist the investigator and his team.

Of all of the additional aids available, physical or electronic surveillance is the simplest and most useful way to augment the operative's efforts. For example, properly orchestrated drug purchases can take place openly in an employee parking lot and be documented on video by well-placed surveillance teams. In states permitting voice recording, the operative can be wired in advance so that both video and voice can be obtained. When this is possible, the case can be made on the investigator's testimony, the testimony of eye witnesses (the surveillance team), and the video. If later the dealer is interviewed and admits to his transgressions, the totality of the evidence is virtually overwhelming and so compelling that even the most creative defense counsel will be unable to save the dealer's job or keep him out of jail.

While on the subject of video surveillance, another important point comes to mind. As is too often the case, the video evidence obtained is sometimes of poor quality. Shot from too far away, in too little light, or compromised by any of the other difficult conditions often facing the videographer, the video is just not good enough for use as evidence. These situations are at first disappointing if not outright defeating; however, all is not lost. What remains is the eyewitness testimony of the surveillance team members. Though their video may not be up to evidentiary quality, their personal observations very well may be. This often-overlooked strategy allows testimony that in and of itself may be more compelling than the video evidence would have been. What's more, the human eye often sees more than the camera. In many cases not all that takes place during a drug transaction can be captured on video. If more than one scene is unfolding in view and only one camera is on scene, much of what takes place is not recorded. Yet the videographer himself may see and remember it all. It is for this reason that I am not a strong advocate of surveillance vans. Unless designed properly, a paneled van restricts easy wide-angle viewing. Even those with expensive periscopes do not permit viewing close to the van. Using the right vehicle can make or break a case.

During one of our more memorable undercover cases of 1997, my case manager decided he needed to corroborate his operative's reports of extensive employee marijuana use while at work. The operative reported that the employees in question would routinely exit the facility through a back door and congregate in and around their vehicles during lunch. There they would eat and, almost every day, smoke marijuana. My case manager (not one to leave important matters to others) flew to Seattle, rented an ordinary multi-passenger family van, and drove off to the client's facility. Upon arrival he patiently waited for the perfect parking space to come open. When it did, he quickly pulled the van into place, climbed into the back, and "covered-up" with nothing more than a bed sheet. Likewise covering his camera and equipment, he patiently waited.

Ten minutes before the scheduled lunch break, employees began to stream out the back door. In short order, our subjects emerged and gathered around a small pickup truck parked directly across from my case manager's position, not more than 30 feet away. One of the subjects, a supervisor, remained outside the vehicle and as he talked to the driver he cautiously looked around, almost sensing someone was watching. Without warning, he jumped to his feet and aggressively approached my man. Frozen in his place with camera trained on the pickup, my manager held his breath. The supervisor walked right up to the van and looked inside. Apparently not concerned with what little he saw, he unwittingly placed his left hand on the rear window, almost covering the lens of the camera inside. Slowly he bent over and went out of view of the camera. Without moving, the still-startled case manager peeked out the large side window of the van. Seeing that the supervisor was now bent completely over and peering under the car beside him, he slowly shifted his position to be closer to the window. Obviously completely unaware his every move was watched, the supervisor pulled from beneath the adjacent car a small, clear plastic bag containing what appeared to be marijuana. Then standing erect he carefully examined his treasure inches from the eyes of my manager. What a sight!

What took place next is no surprise. He walked back to the pickup and in plain view of our camera proceeded to smoke the marijuana he had just obtained with his confederates. Subsequently he was interviewed and admitted his misdeeds. He told us that he routinely stored his marijuana under the bumper of his car (just as we had seen). However, when asked if he had any awareness of our surveillance of him, he admitted he never saw a thing.

The investigative team should not overlook other methods of investigation either. Workplace drug investigations lend themselves to an assortment of investigative tools and the creative team will use every one that is available. From chemical testing to ion scan technology, the process of investigation should employ every information-gathering tool, all of which serve to later facilitate the interviews of those most involved.

Another interesting tool often overlooked is the dog. Today, trained narcotics dogs play a greater role than ever in maintaining a drug-free workplace. When used properly, dogs can augment the undercover effort by discretely identifying locations or "hot spots" within the target facility where controlled substances have been or are present. Caution should be exercised, however, not to alert the target workforce of management's concerns or actions. If employees learn of the use of drug dogs, employee complacency will be reduced and the length of the investigation and its cost will be increased. Nothing should ever be done that exposes management's concerns or intentions during an undercover investigation.

Employee Prosecution

The use, sale, possession, and manufacture of most of the drugs of abuse is strictly regulated in every state in this country and in most of the world. It is logical that those who are caught violating the law be punished. In fact, it is the mission of law enforcement to enforce public law and bring to justice those who violate it. However, I have yet to see a corporate mission statement that even suggests employee prosecution as a goal. And therein lies the dilemma. What should the employer who catches its employees violating the law do?

The final answer to this question of course is not simple. But it is true to say *that it depends*. It depends on the law that is broken, the law as it pertains to those who should report the crime, and most importantly the objectives of the investigation. If those objectives include the elimination of workplace substance abuse, the investigative team must then articulate how employee prosecution will help achieve that objective. In most places, only dealers can be prosecuted. The criminal justice system in most parts of this country doesn't have the capacity to prosecute every user. In workplace drug investigations, the users are almost never prosecuted. But how, then, does dealer prosecution reduce workplace substance abuse and impairment? Perhaps the most contentious point of this book, I'm afraid, *is that it does not.* There is absolutely no empirical evidence to even suggest that the elimination of workplace drug dealers solves workplace substance abuse. In fact, my experience suggests something quite different. In my cases in which the employer solely pursued the dealers (and sought their prosecution) yet did nothing about the users, nothing was achieved beyond temporarily driving the problem underground and out of sight. In some of these cases, our undercover investigators reported that after the dealers were removed, often much to the joy of some customers who owed them large sums of money, eager users quickly replaced them and became aggressive dealers. The prosecution of the dealers created a vacuum and new dealers quickly filled the void. What's more, the new dealers were less experienced and more careless. Eager to establish a reputation, they replaced the sophistication and diplomacy of their predecessors with the use of weapons and violence.

Employee prosecution is also expensive. Although it is counterintuitive, prosecuting employees is more expensive than any of the other alternatives available to the employer. Successful prosecution requires time, resources, and patience. Documents, evidence, and witnesses will have to be produced. Court appearances and testimony are often required. Then, after lengthy delays and extensive plea bargaining, our imperfect system often renders nothing more than a mere slap on the wrist. Even if the employer only sought some sort of deterrent value in its pursuit of prosecution, what's the real value of such an outcome?

Just imagine. Twelve months after your dealer was fired, he's finally found guilty and is sentenced to three years probation. *Who cares?* What a waste of time and resources! Yet there are those who still insist on employee prosecution. Go figure.

If your objectives include prosecution, be sure its necessary. Most importantly, make sure the value of employee prosecution is carefully calculated when determining the investigation's overall return on investment. Surprisingly, employee prosecution rarely provides any real return. In the final analysis if you still have trouble deciding a course of action, take a look at your corporate mission statement. I'll be surprised if it suggests prosecution.

CHAPTER 5

Theft Investigations

Statistics gathered by the U.S. Chamber of Commerce indicate that employee theft costs American businesses something on the order of $40 billion a year. In 1995 the Association of Certified Fraud Examiners reported that fraud and abuse was costing employers an average of $9 a day per employee, or roughly $400 billion a year.[1] That same report also revealed that small businesses with less than 100 employees were most at risk. Among the victims, the median loss per occurrence was roughly $120,000. Companies of more than 10,000 employees had a median loss of $126,000.[2] The U.S. General Accounting Office estimated that, in that same year, internal fraud and abuse had consumed about 10 percent ($100 billion) of the $1 trillion spent on health care. Clearly, employee theft and fraud is a problem that faces us all.

Employee theft not only reduces productivity and profitability but it also lowers morale, increases insurance costs, and reduces our competitiveness. And like workplace substance abuse, it is almost inescapable. While nearly one-third of all business failures are the result of internal theft or criminal wrongdoing, few employers protect themselves. Ineffectual policies, procedures, and practices create the gateway through which the dishonest employee is allowed to fleece his employer.

Why Employees Steal

In today's society, values that were once pillars of strength have begun to crumble. A variety of factors have influenced a new moral compass, including the dynamic displacement of the traditional employee and his perceived sense of economic security, the redefining of family values, and an

---

[1] "Report to the Nation, Occupational Fraud and Abuse," The Association of Certified Fraud Examiners, 1995.
[2] Ibid.

unexplained growth in personal greed. These factors, combined with what is widely accepted as the erosion of the American work ethic, have created a workplace like no other in our history. Shamefully, the mutual loyalty between employers and employees has seemingly been replaced with anger, greed, and self-gratification. Within this turbid brew, workplace theft and dishonesty is born.

Studies have shown that:

- The greater the opportunity for theft, the greater the likelihood it will occur
- Employees who steal will do so to the extent the system will allow
- Employee theft left unchecked is contagious
- Workers who steal are also frequently involved in other counterproductive workplace behaviors

But we also know that:

- The greater the chance of detection, the less likely employees are to steal
- Employee theft is not necessarily correlated with external factors or forces
- Employees who are satisfied with their jobs are less likely to steal
- A strong commitment to deter theft will reduce losses

Thus there are motivators and deterrents of theft in the workplace; and employers must work to eliminate these motivators and leverage the deterrents. But employees do steal. They steal raw materials, finished goods, services, ideas, money, and time. It was said to me perfectly many years ago by a very frustrated manager as we toured his facility, "Everything you see here is stolen, it just hasn't left the premises yet."

The motivations that drive theft in the workplace are manifold. Some employees steal because they feel underpaid and unappreciated, others do it in order to fulfill a perceived need. Categorically, the motivation of employees who steal usually falls into one of three simple groups—the *greedy*, the *needy*, or the *foolish*.

The Greedy

The greedy employee typically begins to steal when his lifestyle has exceeded his ability to maintain it. Carelessly managing his financial affairs, this type of individual "gets in over his head." Unable to make ends meet he must make increasingly difficult decisions and choices. Often combined with a sense of entitlement and fundamental disrespect for others, the subject is able to make these difficult decisions by rationalizing away some of his own values and morals. Adhering to a pseudo sense of self-preservation, the greedy employee is able to rationalize stealing from others. And as I detailed earlier in the book, his first victim is usually his employer.

The Needy

The needy perpetrator usually feels like a victim. She understands herself to be facing one or more insoluble personal problems. And like her greedy counterpart, she is able to rationalize away respect for other people and their property. In many instances the need is so great that it is perceived as entitlement. In turn, this sense of entitlement can become so powerful that the urge to steal is stronger than the perceived risk of detection. When caught the needy always play victim.

The Foolish

Theft is also committed by the foolish. Every security professional knows from experience that thefts often are really nothing more than crimes of opportunity. Many times after my investigations have peeled back the layers of workplace theft, the seemingly sophisticated, well-planned crime was revealed to be nothing more than the handiwork of a rag-tag group of opportunists. These foolish souls often pay a high price for their indiscretions. Some combination of termination, prosecution, and restitution are usually their reward.

Theft as a Process

Those who steal typically start small. I would imagine there are few emotionally balanced, happy people who have never stolen before who wake up one morning and say to themselves, "Today's the day. I'm going into work and steal my employer blind!" On the contrary, most people who steal start small and their thievery progresses over time through several recognizable phases. Although most perpetrators progress incrementally through each phase, some "fast track." We see this phenomenon particularly in children and teens.

In the workplace, the phases are usually fairly well defined and observable. What's interesting, however, is that, similar to workplace violence and aggression, the progression is continued from job to job. In other words, changing jobs does not seem to break the progression—it makes it only more difficult to detect.[3]

The phases through which the thieving employee progresses are the following:

---

[3] Eugene F. Ferraro, "What Every Employer Should Know About Workplace Violence," Group Dynamics, 1995; Business Controls, Inc. 1999.

- A need is perceived
- The act is rationalized
- Opportunity is identified
- The crime is carried out
- Some form of conversion takes place

Perceived Need

The need to steal may be predicated on the basis of a variety of needs: an excessive lifestyle or living beyond one's means; unmanageable or seemingly oppressive debt; an inability to pay medical expenses; a gambling problem; and, of course, a substance abuse problem. In some cases the need is psychological. That is to say, the act of stealing and taking other people's property satisfies some deep or repressed psychological need. When this behavior is compulsive, the disease is called *kleptomania*.

Rationalization

One of the most destructive human behaviors is rationalization. By definition, to rationalize is to devise a superficial rationale or plausible explanations and excuses for one's actions. Usually this is done without the conscious awareness that these are not real motives and that the long-term consequences may be undesirable and self-destructive. Those who steal rationalize that their behavior is justified or somehow acceptable. They often rationalize that their need entitles them to the property and possessions of others. In some cases, this sense of entitlement is strong enough to allow the thief even to deceive himself psychologically. Many individuals consequently convince themselves that their motives are justifiable and reasonable without giving adequate thought to the long-term consequences of their intended actions. Their blindness allows them to rationalize away their values and personal responsibilities. They come to believe that what is ours should be theirs.

Opportunity

Once the individual has sufficiently rationalized his motive, he then seeks out opportunity. Unfortunately for most businesses, they abound with opportunity. What takes place in these organizations is that the dishonest employees seek out and identify targets of opportunity. Empowered by a perceived need and a sufficient amount of rationalization, these individuals exploit the opportunities that are available to them. Those organizations that have not properly protected their assets will be the first victims.

Commission of the Crime

Once the opportunity is identified, the crime will be carried out. In most cases of workplace theft, the perpetrators act alone. Contrary to popular belief, most thieves generally operate without the assistance of anyone. What is true, however, is that most thieves are known to be thieves. Their malfeasance is generally widely known among the people they trust. In most workplaces, those individuals include other thieves and the substance abusers. I call the relationship among these employees the *unholy marriage*. For it is rarely the case that there is theft in the workplace without substance abuse as well.

Conversion

Conversion is simply the act of converting the company's assets into one's own. Once removed, the property or asset is converted into an asset or something of value the thief himself can use. It should be noted that it is during conversion that most thieves make their mistakes. All too often the perpetrators, in their haste to convert their booty, expose themselves and their crimes. In many cases the conversion creates a trail that the corporate investigator may trace, often exposing not only the thief but the recipient of the stolen goods as well. This creates the opportunity to recover from both the dishonest employee and the receiver, a process called *third-party recovery*; it often allows restitution from even the second and third receivers of the stolen property.

Not long ago I had a case in which this valuable tool was put to use. The matter involved the massive diversion of backup tape drives like those commonly used in personal computers. The manufacturer for years had maintained shoddy product return records and as such had accumulated a huge unrecorded inventory of returns. Most of the devices were serviceable or needed only minor repairs. However, as the manufacturer lacked sufficient procedures for handling these returns, the devices were simply cast aside and stored haphazardly in large bins. Eventually the inventory reached such proportions that the bins were stored off-site in a large leased (and unsecured) warehouse quite some distance from the manufacturing facility.

The supervisor in charge of the returns, though trusted, was a very disgruntled employee. He had been demoted several times for poor performance, yet the company in its infinite wisdom had insisted he train his replacements (a sad and thoughtless mistake made by many organizations). He was a loner and had few friends at work. He also had what he believed to be insoluble personal financial problems and had not adequately prepared for his retirement, which was only several years away. In the midst of his despair and self-pity, he came upon an opportunity. Realizing the inventory in his control was not recorded he decided he would personally sell some of it. He rationalized that the company had no need for the returned items— that the company did not care about him or the inventory. In his desperate state, he decided to steal.

And steal he did. In a matter of about 18 months, the supervisor had diverted and converted over 100,000 drives. The principal receiver was a west-coast "re-manufacturer" that refurbished the drives and sold them at steep discounts to resellers. The stolen drives passed through at least six hands before reaching the consumer. The scheme was elaborate and profitable.

Our undercover investigators eventually penetrated both our client's organization and the distribution network. Working what had become a criminal enterprise from both ends we closed in on the ringleaders. Our investigators made purchases at all levels. In some cases, we secretly video-taped the transactions, others we made in the presence of undercover police officers. In some instances we even made purchases with checks so that we could trace the money. In the end, we not only obtained the necessary incriminating evidence on the supervisor but on all of the central figures between him and the consumer. All told, 12 foreign and domestic organizations and over 30 individuals were directly incriminated.

When we finally closed in, our client's corporate attorneys were at our side to bring civil actions against each party. Consequently, in addition to criminal charges, each faced civil damage claims equivalent to their share of the take. Not only were the defendants eager to stay out of jail, each had a business at stake, in some cases significant and otherwise legitimate businesses—businesses with deep pockets. In the end, my client not only recovered its losses but its expenses as well. Because the investigation was properly engineered and the client adequately patient, third-party recoveries were made from every defendant. All told, some 150,000 drives were accounted for and over $1 million recovered.

Undercover Theft Investigations

Undercover theft investigations begin like any other undercover investigation. However, special care should be taken during the planning phase. Because not all investigators are created equal, particular attention must be given to the operative selection process. Although important in any investigation, the selection of the right operative in theft cases is critical. Theft investigations are difficult and demanding. In most instances, they require an investigator who is both talented and experienced. Not just any operative will do.

Operative Selection

Operatives come in all shapes, sizes, and colors. Each has a different ability and level of experience. Of course the best operatives for theft investigations are those with theft experience. And because there are different kinds of theft, there are different kinds of theft experience. However, the type of theft experience most suitable for undercover is that involving the theft of tangible assets: goods, inventory, raw material, scrap, and company property. The theft of such assets usually involves removing or displacing physical objects. It is this *physical activity* that makes undercover the most appropriate investigative choice.

As I mentioned earlier, undercover is one of the few forms of investigation that is interactive. That is, not only does undercover allow the discovery of what has taken place, but it also uncovers why it took place. The undercover investigator is both the eyes and ears of the investigative team. It is she who will see what is taking place behind closed doors and out of the public view. It is also she who will learn how and why the crime is taking place. In crimes involving the movement of physical assets, the undercover investigator is particularly suited to position herself *in the action*. For example, unlike cases of embezzlement involving a lone bookkeeper, in which there is no opportunity to "participate," theft of physical assets allows the investigator to become an active participant. As such, the investigator selected must have the social skills and personality necessary to befriend the malfeasant and even become a trusted associate.

Another thing the operative must be able to do is control her fear. For some reason, most operatives are more afraid of thieves than other types of workplace transgressors. I don't fully understand why this so. I suppose it is because theft is universally seen as a crime, not just as a disease or social ill like substance abuse, and thus it tends to be seen as something more serious. Theft also doesn't have the social acceptance of other crimes we see in the workplace. A thief any way you look at him is a criminal and most people, including a lot of very good operatives, are surprisingly afraid of criminals.

Most readers would assume drug investigations to be the most dangerous. They certainly can be risky. But theft investigations can be too. I've had investigators who have been stalked, chased, and threatened. I know of operatives who have even been kidnapped during an assignment. But theft investigations can also be a lot of fun.

Someone we'll call Easy Money was an outside sales representative for a large electronics firm. Easy was also a thief and my undercover investigator soon befriended him. His employer leased computers, printers, and all sorts of electronic gadgetry to large businesses. After a month or so, my operative Glenn was able to convince Easy that he had connections that would gladly fence anything he might get out the door. Lacking any better resource, I decided to pose as the fence.

My first meeting with Easy was in his employer's warehouse during business hours. My undercover insisted that Easy give "his fence" a tour and demonstrate that he in fact had access to the merchandise he claimed he did (this simple action combined with Easy's later tape-recorded conversations defeated any entrapment claim he ever hoped to use). Dressed like a wise guy, I arrived in a brand new Cadillac and boldly swung into the first available reserved parking space behind the warehouse. My arrival had been timed perfectly so that several warehouse workers were taking lunch, yet my operative was nowhere to be seen. As if I owned the place, and leaving the car obviously unlocked with windows open (something never done in the part of town I was in), I leaped upon the dock and rudely asked the workers, "Where's Glenn?" Silently, one of the men pointed into the warehouse. I strode in and proceeded past a shipping clerk as he stuffed a sandwich in his mouth. On his desk was a sign that read SIGN IN HERE.

Deep inside the warehouse I found Glenn and Easy doing some sort of busy work but in a place that others could easily overhear any conversation that might take place. Glenn introduced me as "this guy I was telling you about" and the conversation quickly lead to theft and Easy's alleged access to inventory. Easy boasted of his many past crimes and how easily he had stolen from his employer previously. After our conversation and a fast tour of the facility, I abruptly left.

Our next meeting was at the Beverly Hills Hotel (known affectionately by the rich and famous as *The Pink Palace*) in the historic Polo Lounge. Taking up a quiet booth, undoubtedly once used by Clark Gable, we ordered drinks and began to talk. This time, however, I was wearing a wire. The Beverly Hills Police Department graciously provided both the transmitter and manpower. As a well-respected department known for its no-nonsense approach to crime, the BHPD was anxious to join in our effort. Easy spilled his guts. He told us everything. In fact he told us so much, some of it was hard to believe. Clearly he wanted to impress his new fence and do business.

Gathering in a guestroom after the meeting, however, our balloon was popped. Not a single word had been recorded. In turned out that someone was jamming us. Unintentionally, other bad guys working close by who were jamming their prey had coincidentally jammed us. The BHPD detectives told us it was not an uncommon occurrence when working in Beverly Hills and that another meeting would have to be set up.

Glenn again made the arrangements. This time, however, he told Easy to bring a sample. Because our investigation had met all of its objectives, we decided that this time it would be a "buy bust." This effective police tactic involves arresting the unsuspecting criminal in the act of selling his wares. Used frequently in drug cases, this tactic works equally well in theft cases because it allows the money, the booty, and bad guys to be taken in one fell swoop.

Our plan was simple. After meeting in the bar and some more qualifying conversation we'd move into the parking lot. There I'd "flash the cash" and Easy would show the goods. Upon my asking Easy "Where's the serial numbers?" (not very original I admit), the hiding police would leap out and arrest us.

All went fine until we left the bar and got outside. Easy did not park where instructed but had instead parked on a dark side street. Moving slowly, and without communicating Glenn and I both knew the police were out of position and my flash money was nothing more than cut waste paper stuffed in a gray envelope. If it came down to it, our bluff could be called. We did all we could do to stall and give the police the time they needed to set up.

When we arrived at Easy's car, he slowly opened the trunk while constantly looking over his shoulder. As promised, there were the computer components I had ordered. He immediately demanded the money and began to lower the trunk to cover the booty from view. Behind us the bushes began to rustle and one could faintly hear the voices of men talking. Then the distinct crackle of a radio, *a police radio*, came from behind a nearby tree. Easy panicked and nervously said the deal was off and abruptly closed the trunk. Glenn firmly told him there would be no such thing; he wanted his fee for making the arrangements and curtly told me to show him the money. I removed the phony money packet from my breast pocket and flashed the cash.

Overcome by greed, Easy again opened the trunk of his car. I quickly grabbed an exposed keyboard, held it over my head as if to put some light on it and loudly asked, "Where's the serial numbers?" But nothing happened, except Easy got more nervous. Louder yet, I repeated the signal. Then again, yet louder. This time all hell broke loose and what seemed like two dozen police officers flew out of bushes and trees. Playing his role to the hilt, Glenn broke and ran for it. Easy and I stood fast at gunpoint with hands above our heads. Then, bent over the roof of Easy's car face-to-face, as we were being handcuffed, Easy began to cry. With tears streaming down his face, pathetically he begged me, "Tell me what to do . . . you've been through this before." In a tone of great confidence I told him to cooperate and tell the police anything they wanted to know and that I would take care of everything else.

He did, and not long after was convicted for his crimes. Before sentencing, however, we passed each other inside the courthouse. As Easy solemnly walked by he whispered to me, "Nice work . . . asshole."

Operative Placement

Once the operative has been selected, she must then be placed. Using either a cold hire or controlled hire, the investigator must be placed discretely and cautiously. And like any undercover investigation, as few people as possible should be involved. Only those with an absolute need to know should be included in the hiring process. Even the most experienced investigator will have difficulty if she is not properly placed.

Cover position is important also. Care should be given to select the position that allows the investigator the greatest amount of mobility and the least amount of supervision, and that involves something that is not task oriented. In theft investigations, it is important to place the investigator in an area where she has exposure and access to the property that is being stolen or diverted. Clearly an office position would not be suitable when the losses are in shipping and receiving. Conversely, if the problem is in the front office, the investigator is not going to be effective if placed in the warehouse.

The investigator need not handle the property, however. She need only be in an area where she can monitor the property or those who handle it. This raises an important point. Not all thefts involve the actual movement of property or inventory. The most common type of workplace theft involves some form of shipping and receiving fraud. Fraudulently, at the hands of the dishonest employee, the employer either receives less than it has been billed for or ships more than it charges for. These simple crimes are facilitated by shipping and receiving personnel and don't actually require removing or fencing any goods. The perpetrator is either paid in cash or in some cases is given drugs in exchange for the simple doctoring of paperwork. Unfortunately, without adequate inventory controls and monitoring, this sort of crime can go on for considerable lengths of time. One client of mine who suffered this type of loss didn't realize it until he could no longer ship product. To his dismay, and contrary to inventory documentation, he simply had no inventory. The crime had gone on for so long, he virtually had nothing in his warehouse.

Tactics

Like the drug investigations discussed previously, strategy and tactics play important roles in almost every successful theft investigation. Once the operative is properly placed and is sufficiently acclimated to her new environment, her factfinding efforts can become more aggressive. Because most theft is a private matter, unlike substance abuse, which is very social by nature, the investigator must creatively place herself in a position to be noticed. By this I mean that the investigator must become visible and accessible to those who are stealing. Because the identity of the perpetrators is not always known at the beginning of the investigation, this could be a particularly difficult and time-consuming thing to accomplish. Consequently, the tactic I teach my operatives is to attract the thieves to them. To my constant surprise, this simple and innovative approach is rarely used by my competitors. Instead, their operatives spend weeks or even months desperately trying to be in the right place at the right time. The cost of this approach to the client is enormous. What's more, the longer the investigation, the more losses the client suffers. We know from our experience that the rate of theft accelerates over time. The more it is tolerated, the more it will occur. Not only will the incidence of theft increase, the amount of each loss will increase. Rarely, unless influenced by outside factors, does workplace theft decline over time.

The Wedge

One of the most basic tactics used to investigate theft is something I call the *wedge*. A wedge is nothing more than using the appearance of some other form of criminal activity to give the operative credibility. The most common of these is an apparent involvement in illegal drugs. Because substance abuse is such a social activity, those involved are usually easily penetrated. Once the operative has gained the trust of those selling and using illegal drugs, it will be easy for her to ask questions about other forms of workplace misconduct. It is common that those who break the law in one way should break it in other ways as well. Psychologists call this unique human behavior *cognitive consistency*. This behavior allows the lawbreaker (and most rulebreakers for that matter) to easily rationalize the breaking of other laws (and rules).

A good example is the "get-away driver" who, in leaving the scene, recklessly speeds and violates other driving regulations *when not even chased!* Why? Because the punishment for running a stop sign pales compared to that for armed robbery. Those who regularly investigate fraud come across this phenomenon all the time. Rarely during a fraud investigation do we see a fraudster who perpetrates only one kind of fraud. Usually the subject is not only "cooking the books" in some fashion but is also engaged in a variety of other lesser schemes. I've investigated instances in which the fraudster's scheme was netting him over $100,000 a month, yet he was consistently falsifying his expense reports and claiming extra reimbursable mileage. If you are investigating fraud and have uncovered one scheme, do yourself and the organization a favor and look for other schemes as well. What's more, be aware that often the first crime uncovered is not the most serious. It is highly embarrassing and possibly damaging to one's career to uncover the really serious crime long after your perpetrator has been let go or punished.

It is an undercover axiom that where one finds substance abuse one will also find theft. That being the case, the prudent undercover investigator looking to solve a theft problem should first look for a substance abuse problem. Once fully aligned with the substance-abusing element, the investigator can then go after those involved in theft. Relying on the wedge, it will not seem peculiar for the operative who has been accepted by her marijuana-smoking coworkers to talk about theft. Cautiously, and without raising suspicion, the investigator can ask penetrating questions about theft, who may be involved, and with whom the prospective thief could team. To the workplace substance abuser, these seem to be perfectly normal questions and they are unlikely to subject the skilled investigator to any heightened scrutiny. Moreover, for the workplace substance abuser, such conversation is unlikely to cause any alarm, for the employee substance abuser himself is violating company policy and the law. Why should he be worried over conversing about other criminal or dishonest activity? Thus by seemingly placing herself in the middle of the client-employer's substance abuse problem, the operative can gain direct access to those involved in theft. Using the wedge of her apparent involvement in drugs, the cunning investigator can leverage her way into other criminal circles. The camaraderie surrounding the use of illegal drugs is used to position her next to those involved in other criminal activity in the workplace.

Use of Associates and Other Third Parties

As in the operation reported above involving Easy Money, undercover theft investigations can sometimes be very nicely enhanced by using an *ostensible fence*, which for these purposes is nothing more than another investigator who poses as a shady associate of the operative with criminal connections. Depending on the need, this *associate* or *third party* could be the purchaser of stolen property; in other cases he could be the purveyor of stolen property. And like so many criminals, the associate can be made to appear to have involvement in whatever criminal activity makes money. It is not too difficult to have this additional investigator maneuver onto the scene and assist the undercover when needed. Without a great deal of lead-time or preparation, the associate can be brought into and out of play. For this reason, in most of our theft investigations we use an associate or third party of one form or another.

The supplemental investigator is best cast as a trusted criminal associate of the operative. Brought up in conversation during the relationship-building phase of the investigation, the associate may or may not ever be produced. However, the operative carefully weaves him into conversation as opportunities arise. Never actually calling her invisible associate a fence, a thief, or drug dealer, the operative carefully casts him as a highly trusted friend, relative, or gang affiliate. For purposes I will explain in just a moment, it is best that he be criminally cast a rung or two above the operative. The associate should be spoken of with reverence and respect so that if actually brought into play, others will naturally be respectful of him. He should be created to seem distant, almost mysterious. The effect is to create suspense and anticipation. Later in the investigation, should this individual be introduced and become an active participant as cast by the operative, there should be no doubt of his role or his interest.

It is most important that the associate be given a place in the criminal hierarchy that is above the operative or her workplace criminal peers. As such, he will be allowed to make decisions and call the shots. This ability is critical to the success of the investigation and the safety of the investigator. For if the fence is seen as a superior influence, few will question or challenge him. As a leader he will be able to control when and where his subordinates commit their crimes. He will be able to control which crimes take place and which do not. He can fashion himself as a sophisticated leader or an occasional player. As a third party he will be able to move in and out of the scene as he pleases. If the criminal activity moves out of the workplace or the villains decide to get rough, the leader can appropriately challenge them.

I have used this powerful influence to control some truly nasty players with a real thirst for violence. On more than one occasion, as the unchallenged ringleader, I told the bad guys that violence or the use of guns would not be tolerated during the commission of their crimes. Eager to do the deal, they hesitantly complied. As the one in charge, "our deals" were done my way or not done at all. And as all narcotics detectives know, the fastest way to get hurt is to let the bad guy gain control and call the shots. Workplace undercover theft investigations are no different. Safety is paramount.

The skilled operative will use this deference given to the third party to her advantage as well. If the players spontaneously decide to commit a theft, the operative can suggest the crime be put off so that it may be coordinated through her associate. This will allow the investigative team time to possibly mark the targeted property with invisible markers, record serial numbers, or put surveillance teams in place. In cases involving particularly valuable goods, it may be unwise to simply let it walk. Instead, surveillance teams can be set up to follow the property from the scene of the crime to its destination, often permitting receivers and other criminal parties to be identified.

The first time I used this technique with real success was a case in which my client operated a large cold storage facility. The targeted product was frozen shrimp and lobster tails. In a scheme that on its face was rather unsophisticated, the bad guys would distract a supervisor and quickly set about overloading several preselected outbound delivery trucks. The scheme was complicated, however, by the fact that (1) they needed to know where supervision was at all times, (2) the targeted product had to be in position to be moved quickly and with stealth, and (3) they needed to know the drivers on duty and their routes. Upon analysis we determined that the only people that had all of this information at any given time were the contract security officers. And of them, only the "gate guard" consistently knew which supervisors and managers were on site and when.

With the guard contractor's assistance, we placed our operative in uniform at the front gate. At night it was a roving post that allowed the operative access to the entire facility. After some initial difficulty, the operative eventually befriended several of the suspects. Acting as if he knew nothing of the thefts, he offered his service as a lookout should the service ever be needed. Knowing his new friends often smoked or slept outside the freezers at night, he offered to call the shipping desk whenever a member of management arrived or left after hours. After testing his reliability, the thieves put him to work big-time. Every pallet of stolen product, every smoke break, and every stolen lobster tail was coordinated through our investigator. If the heist was of any significant size, our surveillance teams were dispatched. If the stolen product did not yet have a buyer, our fence was introduced to handle the job. In what seemed like no time we identified every dishonest employee. We also identified a number of wholesalers and restaurants that had been purchasing the stolen seafood. Clamping down hard on the bad guys with the demand for restitution and aggressive criminal prosecution, we solved our client's problem and made a huge statement to the rest of the industry: *Those who steal will be caught!*

This brings to mind a very common question: Can the operative steal from the client-employer during the investigation in order to enhance or maintain his cover? We know in drug cases that the investigator can never use illegal drugs for any reason. And he can certainly not sell drugs. However, in theft investigations it is perfectly acceptable for the operative to steal. But because her credibility is at stake, all of her theft activity should be done with an explicit purpose and be pre-approved. Stealing for the sake of stealing or simply proving it can be done is inappropriate and risky. If the operative is caught stealing, for example, he may be fired, thus jeopardizing the entire project. Even if not caught outright, other thieves in an attempt to rid the workplace of a "competitor" may report him. Furthermore, stealing without the client-employer's knowledge simply looks bad. But, again, when it is necessary to help the operative's credibility, controlled stealing is permissible and creates no technical or legal problems for either the investigator or the assignment.

Other Techniques and Approaches

Over the years I've tried a lot of different things to lure the leery and suspicious thief into trusting my investigators and me. Of those that seemed to have worked best were schemes in which the target thought he'd get something for nothing. Everybody likes the idea of getting something for nothing and criminals are no different. Offering small appliances at seemingly ridiculous prices is one such ruse. How this works is simple.

The investigator is provided a carload of small home appliances (toasters, blenders, food processors, etc.) all in their original boxes. Such items can be inexpensively purchased at any of the large box stores or discounters. The investigator then simply takes them to his assignment and offers them for sale to his coworkers at prices no one can refuse. The investigator tells no one where he obtained the merchandise or that it may have been stolen, but insists his source offers no refunds . . . all sales are final. But who can resist? The opportunity to purchase a $25 appliance for only two or three dollars is usually too good to pass up. If asked if the items are stolen, the operative answers with an indignant "Of course not." He tells his customers with a greasy smile that he'd never sell stolen merchandise and that he is insulted that anyone would think such a thing. The next week we send the operative in with several cases of cigarettes. These, too, he sells at ridiculous prices.[4] In several weeks the investigator will have developed the reputation of a low-level fence with ties to some larger criminal element. It will be only natural for him to next ask his customers what he can do for them.

Although it should go without saying, introducing guns or contraband is dangerous and may be unlawful. Although many a bad guy has asked one of my seemingly well-connected operatives to obtain weapons or contraband, I have never allowed it. Safety is job number one. Intentionally introducing weapons of any form is unnecessarily dangerous and most likely unlawful. Don't allow your investigator to do anything that will diminish his safety or that of the workplace, or do anything else that is unlawful or otherwise inappropriate. There are simply too many ways to work a case without placing people at risk. Be smart and be safe.

Buy-Busts and Sting Operations

Law enforcement pioneered the buy-bust and sting operation during the Prohibition Era. Today these tried and true techniques are used by sophisticated undercover agencies and others as well. The buy-bust is nothing more than arresting the perpetrator at the moment he is either buying or selling the property in question. Usually the other party to the transaction is a member of law enforcement or a designated agent. Upon some prearranged signal, the bad guy(s) is confronted and arrested on the spot. In theft cases, like most drug cases, the technique works best toward the end of the investigation. Usually by design, the true identities of undercover operatives and law enforcement agents are subsequently revealed. Although this is not always the case nor is it always necessary, buy-busts usually culminate the investigation. Arresting the offender(s) at this stage of the investigation precludes the loss or destruction of valuable evidence or the need to later chase down dangerous and possibly armed offenders.

Sting operations, on the other hand, are similar but generally involve a longer, more complicated investigative effort. They also usually require more elaborate set-ups than do buy-busts. Sometimes these involve the actual set up and operation of a business as a front or place where stolen goods are sold or traded. Because of their complexity, good sting operations are usually expensive and time consuming, and are not usually practical for most privately conducted investigations. For these reasons, I have only conducted several true sting operations over the course of my career. Other agencies may do them more often, but I suspect not.

---

[4] It should be noted that in some states the selling of cigarettes is a regulated activity. Before this technique is employed check with the local authorities to ensure it is legal.

Evidence Markers

Invisible evidence markers have been around for years. These interesting products allow the user to invisibly mark property so that if stolen and recovered later, its rightful owner can be identified. Years ago about the only thing available was a very messy product generically called *theft powder*. Touted as an invisible powder designed to be easily applied to targeted property, when later handled the powder would dissolve from the moisture in one's hand and release an indelible purple dye. In its application, the powder was not exactly invisible. But did it ever turn purple when handled! The powder easily covered anything and anybody who got near it, including the investigators that used it. Sure it worked, but what a mess! The stuff got all over everything, and I mean everything. And it did not wash off. In fact, the worst mistake one could make was to try to wash it away. The poor sap that tried would find himself dyed purple head to toe.

Today, fortunately, the market offers a multitude of new and easier to use products. Some of these markers are applied with pen-like applicators; others are aerosols and are sprayed on. One manufacturer provides uniquely formulated chemicals that are "user specific" and can be applied any number of ways. Each formula is unique to a specific user so that no two are alike. Thus, the marked property can be easily identified if later necessary. For more information about these unusual products, go to the Web and search *invisible markers* or look in any law enforcement supply catalogue.

I recommend you use invisible markers to augment your investigation whenever possible. In order to make good cases, it may be necessary to positively identify stolen property and establish ownership. By giving the application process some thought, the use of invisible markers will allow not only ownership to be established but the date and time the property was stolen as well. By marking selected inventories differently, and knowing who had access to which inventory, recovered property can help identify the actual thief. The use and application of these useful products is limited only by the creativity of the investigator.

Corroborating Evidence

In most theft cases, corroborating evidence beyond that provided by the undercover investigator is often invaluable. As I will explain in a later chapter, I routinely conclude my investigations by interviewing the transgressors who were most involved. Usually these highly structured interviews yield admissions, and it is on those admissions that my clients base their decisions regarding discipline and prosecution. However, not in all cases are we able to interview or obtain incriminating admissions. In anticipation of this possibility, I cause my case managers to augment their undercover theft investigations with other forms of investigations for the purpose of obtaining additional, and very often, corroborating evidence.

Covert Surveillance

The most common and most economical form of corroborating evidence is videotape. If the crimes under investigation can be recorded on videotape, we usually do it. In most theft investigations this is surprisingly easy. If the property in question is being stolen and resold by the thief we usually try to buy some of it. Because a key element of the crime is physical removal of the property, we ask the thief to deliver his wares to us outdoors. Specifically we instruct him to meet us outside the facility, warehouse, or physical structure containing the business. Company-controlled parking lots are in fact preferred because they are usually controlled enough to make it safe for our purposes by restricting access to intruders and at the same time allowing us to control the play. By planning ahead, we will arrange to park our surveillance teams next to or near the operative's vehicle, where the investigator will arrange to meet the thief. By carefully choreographing the action, the operative and the thief can be placed in perfect position to be videotaped. The stolen property, the money and entire play can be documented. What's more, after the purchased stolen property is secured in the operative's vehicle in our presence and on tape, a solid chain of evidence has been initiated. We can later prove if necessary what was sold to us, who sold it, and what became of it immediately following the transaction. For added credibility, we will sometimes invite our clients or law enforcement to come along with us. Imagine the combined evidentiary impact of the operative's testimony, corroborated by two eyewitnesses (one a law enforcement officer), a videotape of what took place, and production of the invisibly marked stolen property!

Only one thing could improve this already solid case and that is tape-recording the dialogue of the operative and the thief at the time of the transaction. Federal law permits the tape-recording of any conversation as long as one party to the conversation is aware it is being recorded. However, the law varies from state to state. Most states are more restrictive and require all parties to be aware the conversation is being recorded. Remember that just because someone has committed what is suspected to be a crime, it does not obviate any rights he might otherwise enjoy. However, the law enforcement authorities assisting in the case can give approval to record. If there is any doubt, obtain such authorization ahead of time.

Multiple Buys

As in drug investigations, multiple buys from the thief make stronger cases. As a matter of practice, we always try to make more than one buy from each player. Multiple buys help eliminate the claim that the activity was spontaneous or some sort of anomaly. They help prove the perpetrator is a true offender and not just someone who made a one-time mistake. Multiple buys also help destroy the claim of entrapment. As mentioned previously, entrapment is not a crime or some illegal act but instead is a criminal defense that can be raised at trial. Interestingly, however, to raise the defense of entrapment, *the defendant must first admit he committed the crime.* Remember that the next time you hear the claim of entrapment raised during arbitration—most arbitrators don't readily volunteer this important fact. Multiple buys overcome the defense of entrapment by establishing that the activity has been ongoing.

Multiple buys also make the case look better. Putting aside the claim of entrapment, multiple buys give all parties concerned (except the thief, of course) the confidence they need to justify prosecuting their case. Be it an employer hoping to just terminate the offender or the criminal justice system attempting to make a convincing prosecutable case, multiple buys enhance the case against the offender. Multiple offenses say a lot about the mindset and intention of the perpetrator. Repeat offenders always seem more criminal-like.

Multiple buys also provide some element of insurance for the investigation. If, for example, one of the buys is ruled defective—that is, for some reason deemed inadmissible—the surviving buys are still available to support the prosecution. Should only a single transaction have taken place and for some reason be thrown out, the entire case could be in jeopardy. Multiple buys will simply make your cases stronger and I strongly recommend them whenever practicable.

Recoveries

Recoveries can be a big part of theft investigations. Because undercover investigations permit a high degree of interactivity with the offenders, they permit the gathering of information not generally otherwise obtainable. Of obvious value is the determination of who is stealing and what it is they are taking. But of equal value is why they are stealing and how the stolen property is being disposed of. If other parties are receiving the property, it is possible some form of civil recovery for damages can be effected. A properly conducted investigation should reveal the identity of any third parties and the degree to which they are involved. Once identified, the investigation can be engineered to allow recovery from them as well as from the principle perpetrators at its completion. Not only can property or consideration for the property be recovered, but also some of the costs of the investigation. Recovering costs is surprisingly rarely done. I know of few agencies that even contemplate it. Ask your vendor next time you are considering undercover if they routinely attempt to recover the cost of the investigation from the offenders. If they don't, suggest they engineer their process in order to do so. A recovery of costs will significantly increase the return on investment of any investigation, not just undercover.

Theft Prevention

Theft prevention is a study unto itself. However, no discussion regarding theft is complete without mentioning prevention. As discussed in the previous chapter, the incidence of workplace crime is a function of three fundamental elements:

- The quality of people we hire
- The environment in which we place those people
- The quality of management supervising that environment and those people

When the outer layers are peeled away to reveal what is at the core of workplace theft, we see people that should have never been hired who are placed in environments with inadequate controls and overseen by untrained and/or incompetent supervisors. If you wish to control employee theft in your workplace, don't rush out and obtain more locks, gates, and guards. Look introspectively. Consider the core of your organization and its people. Most of the thieves we expose had no business enjoying the jobs they did, and they should have never been hired. Stopping the problem at the door only makes sense. Think about the last theft investigation you conducted. If the perpetrator was in fact an employee, would the crime have ever been committed had he not been hired?

CHAPTER 6

Organized Labor and Other Important Management Considerations

> On each landing, opposite the line shaft, the poster with the enormous face gazed from the wall. It was one of those pictures which are so contrived that the eyes follow you about when you move. Big Brother Is Watching You, the caption beneath it ran.
>
> —George Orwell

Orwellian indeed; the fear of being watched is pervasive in our society. With the use of undercover comes the stigma of deceit and deception. The fear of its abuse and misuse is widespread. In some organizations it is counter-cultural. In others it is "simply something that isn't done." For these reasons and those already discussed, there is much to be contemplated before undertaking an undercover investigation. Not only is there potential legal liability, but there is political liability as well. As mentioned in Chapter 1, undercover investigations are not only lawful but also are very often necessary. As a broad investigative application, it offers a legitimate alternative to what seems to be many of today's insoluble complex business problems. Unlike any other form of investigation or factfinding strategy, undercover allows the unique opportunity to peek into the mind of the perpetrator as he commits his crime. Consequently, undercover investigation is uniquely misunderstood and fraught with complexity. Let's now look at these assorted complexities, particularly those associated with organized labor, and remove some of the common myths and misconceptions surrounding undercover.

Common Misconceptions

It is a widely held misconception that undercover investigations cannot be conducted in a unionized environment. Nothing could be further from the truth. Nothing bars an employer from hiring undercover investigators and placing them into its unionized workforce. There are no federal or state laws or regulations to prohibit such activity. There are, however, some very important restrictions of which both the employer and its investigators must be aware. The body of law that imposes these restrictions is the National Labor Relations Act (NLRA).

Under the NLRA, employees have the right to form, join, and assist unions. Any interference with, restraining, or coercing employees in regard to engaging in lawful union activity is a violation of the Act and can subject the offending employer to heavy fines and other sanctions. As an acting agent of the employer, an undercover investigation team must be particularly careful and go so far as to avoid even *the appearance* of interfering in any organized labor activity. Therefore, under no circumstances may the employer conduct surveillance on or otherwise monitor lawful union activities. Such efforts may constitute an unfair labor practice and be actionable.

It is easy to see why it might therefore be assumed that placing an undercover investigator into a unionized workforce would be unlawful. Again, this is not the case. Undercover is lawful and the undercover investigator may even join the union (a necessity in a closed shop). The legal line is crossed when the investigator begins to collect information *about the union* and its business. Let's look a little closer.

An *unfair labor practice* can best be defined as any activity in which the employer (or its agents) interferes, restrains, or coerces employees in the exercise of their collective bargaining rights as created by state and federal labor relations law. Among the prohibited activities established by this body of law is the interference, restraint, surveillance, or investigation of the actions of workers *in exercising such rights*. Hence, union or union member activity outside that which may constitute the *exercising of those protected rights* is not protected. The employer may therefore use undercover in any unionized environment so long as it does not interfere with a protected activity. Investigations for any other lawful purpose are absolutely permissible.

Although less than 25 percent of our undercover investigations are in unionized workplaces, all of our investigators receive the necessary training to work in a union environment protected by a collective bargaining agreement. As a matter of practice we prohibit our operatives from reporting any union activity that may be protected. That would exclude the time and place of union meetings, who attended, and what was discussed. Inside information regarding contract negotiations, demands, and settlement strategies are also excluded. In a work environment that is attempting to organize, we prohibit the identifying of sympathizers as well as company loyalists. We go so far as to even prohibit the use of the word *union* in the body of the operative's reports. However, we do permit the investigator to join the union (again, a requirement in a closed shop), pay union dues and, if necessary, attend union activities. To do otherwise would create suspicion and lengthen the relationship-building phase of the investigation.

Unionized employees enjoy other rights as well. Most important of these from an investigative standpoint are the *Weingarten* rights, which were promulgated in the U.S. Supreme Court decision *NRLB v. Weingarten, Inc.*, 420 U.S. 241 (1975). These rights effectively allow a member of a collective bargaining agreement (a union member) personal representation during an employer's investigatory interview. There are, however, two very interesting and often-overlooked conditions that apply. The first is that the employee must reasonably believe the interview might result in disciplinary action against him. The second is that the employee must request the representation. That is, unless contractually stipulated, the employer has no obligation to offer the representation. The right to representation is triggered at the request of the employee, not the employer's initiation of investigatory interview. Accordingly, disciplining or discharging an employee for refusing to cooperate in such an investigatory interview without union representation is a violation of the §8(a)(1) of the NLRA. Some further analysis is necessary.

In its *Weingarten* decision, the Supreme Court more specifically explained that

1. The right arises "only in situations where the employee requests representation"
2. The employee's right to request representation as a condition to participation in the interview "is limited to situations where the employee reasonably believes the investigation will result in disciplinary action"
3. Exercise of the right may not interfere with "legitimate employer prerogatives"
4. The employer may carry on his inquiry without interviewing the employee, thus leaving to the employee "the choice between having an interview unaccompanied by his representative, or having no interview and foregoing any benefits that might be derived from one"
5. The employer has no duty to bargain with any union representative who may be permitted to attend the investigatory interview

Furthermore, the Supreme Court and the National Labor Relations Board (NLRB) have held that under *Weingarten*, an employee has "no Section 7 right to the presence of his union representative at a meeting with his employer held solely for the purpose of informing the employee of, and acting upon, a previously made disciplinary decision." However, the full effect of *Weingarten* protection might become applicable even at a disciplinary interview if the employer engages in any conduct "beyond merely informing the employee of a previously made disciplinary decision."

Simply fascinating, isn't it? There is more, however. In the next chapter we'll explore *Weingarten* further and discuss how it affects the closure and shutdown of our cases. In the meantime, let's examine another common misconception.

It is widely held that law enforcement must be notified of any known violation of the law. The logic follows that in the case of undercover, as soon as criminal activity is discovered, law enforcement must be notified. Categorically this is untrue. There are only a few instances in which federal law requires a citizen to report a crime.[1] Only a few states have such laws and those that do, sadly, rarely enforce them.[2] For the most part, the crimes and activities that are uncovered during the typical workplace undercover investigation, require no reporting. The major exception may be violations of the Occupational Safety and Health Act (OSHA). Consult a competent attorney familiar with state and federal law if you are unsure. In any event, the point I want to make remains: most criminal activity uncovered during a workplace undercover investigation does not have to be reported to the authorities.

So why then is there the knee jerk reaction to call the police as soon as something unlawful is uncovered? The answer is simple—because the majority of those who supervise and run undercover are former law enforcement types. It is instinctive for those of that culture to bring criminals to justice. The conflict, of course, is that we as security professionals in private practice are not responsible for the enforcement of public law. Our mission, and let us not forget it, is to serve our customer, whomever it may be.

Don't get me wrong here. I am not suggesting that any criminal activity be covered up or disguised. What I am saying, and now have said several times, is that law enforcement should play a limited role in our workplace investigations, not a central one. The key to success here is achieving the investigation's objectives. If criminal prosecution is not an objective, then why involve the police? Even in cases of illegal drug sales or grand theft, it is not necessary for the crimes to be reported. Unnecessarily involving the police increases the length and the cost of the investigation. Furthermore, some element of confidentiality may be lost. Again, unless it is necessary, why involve outsiders in your investigation and make it more complicated? When you or your organization uncover a tax problem, do you first call the Internal Revenue Service? Hardly. Then why call the police when you discover a couple of two-bit hoodlums smoking dope in the company parking lot or helping themselves to janitorial supplies?

Conversely, there are some very good reasons to involve the authorities even if prosecution is not contemplated. As previously mentioned,

---

[1] These exceptions are found largely in matters having to do with the environment, publicly traded securities, and banking.
[2] Many states have laws or regulations mirroring those of the federal government. To be safe and avoid any missteps, consult a competent attorney.

private citizens cannot lawfully buy, sell, transport, distribute, manufacture, or use illegal drugs. When this activity is uncovered in the workplace and the investigation necessitates the involvement of the undercover, immunity against prosecution must be sought in advance. Only certain authorized individuals within the criminal justice system can grant that immunity. Those individuals include some law enforcement officers (for example, the detectives actually working the case), district attorneys, and judges. And it is because immunity is necessary, not the desire to prosecute, that the decision to involve law enforcement is made.

Another very valid occasion to involve law enforcement is when dealing with a matter in which the decision to prosecute has not yet been made. This is particularly true in large fraud investigations. A good example might be a complex case involving a very sophisticated fraud, potentially involving huge losses and a large number of perpetrators. Given the totality of the circumstances, it might be professionally negligent not to involve law enforcement from the start, or at least seriously contemplate their inclusion in some way. It all boils down to timing. Like a lot of things in life, it's not a matter of doing it, it's a matter of when.

Labor Relations

The entire specter of labor relations must be kept in mind when considering undercover. Its potential impact on morale, productivity, and management's credibility must all be contemplated. The first two questions I am usually asked by the employer of a unionized workforce are: When should the union be notified? And what should it be told?

When Should the Union Be Notified?

Before I answer this question, let me point out that it is not that management decided to undertake an undercover investigation that upsets most unions, it is the *outcome of the investigation* that becomes the issue. On its face, the investigation is like anything else management decides to do. That is, unless it has some adverse impact on organized labor and its members, it is usually considered inconsequential. In short, it's a nonissue. It is only after management has processed the investigation's findings and has decided to discipline a union member that it becomes a matter of interest to the union. From the union's perspective, therefore, the earlier it is apprised of what's going to happen, the better. In other words, the more opportunity there is for the union to monitor the investigation, drive decisions regarding discipline, and defend its members, the better off everyone will be. Unfortunately, things don't always work out so well in the real world.

Unions have a lawful duty to properly represent and protect the interests of their members. To act in any other way may give rise to the legal claim known as the "failure to represent." A civil claim of this type by one of its members is a very serious matter for a union and can be quite expensive if such a suit is successfully brought against it. Because of this duty and a valid fear of civil claims, even a very agreeable union may be placed at legal odds against a management attempting to team with it and share information. It is best therefore not to disclose the investigation with the union until it is lawfully necessary. This can be extremely hard for some organizations. Those that have spent years cultivating a trusting relationship with a formerly hostile union will have great difficulty not disclosing the investigation until it is completed. But by disclosing the investigation before it is necessary, the organization puts both the investigation and the union at risk. Unfortunately, many times I've had very well meaning clients reveal our investigation to a "cooperative and friendly" union only to have that investigation hopelessly compromised and ruined. Do not disclose your investigation to any union until it is absolutely necessary.

What Should the Union Be Told?

Although I will answer this question in more detail in the following chapter, let me simply say it now—*the less you reveal the better*. Should discipline arise from the investigation and a union member disagree with it, he has the lawful right to file a formal grievance and have the matter reviewed. The grievance procedure will allow for some discovery and require management to produce certain documents relative to the case. I encourage you not to produce any information or documents until you are lawfully required to do so or it is tactically advantageous. Although it may seem to be in the spirit of cooperation and trust to share some or all of the investigation's findings with the union or selected members, remember that the union has the lawful duty to represent the interests of its members. By prematurely providing confidential information, management may surrender a significant legal advantage, not to mention risk precipitating additional claims. When it is finally necessary to disclose the investigation, disclose only that information about it that is absolutely necessary.

However, as hinted above, there are instances in which an early disclosure is tactically advantageous. The best example I can think of is the case in which management has obtained written admissions or confessions from the grievants. If the grievants have claimed physical and mental mistreatment (or any assortment of other frivolous claims) in addition to their innocence, the early production of a written confession can go a long way in bringing about a quick resolution. I have suggested the use of this tactic in matters involving very hostile and vocal unions. Often by providing proof of member misconduct early on, the union can convince a guilty transgressor to drop his case and go away quietly, saving everyone a lot of time and money.

Another interesting variation of this effective play is to make very carefully crafted statements to the press. If employee arrests have been made, public relations can be used to disclose the identity of those arrested and the charges against them. Though not yet convicted, the union must decide how aggressively it should take the side of alleged lawbreakers. This highly effective play can be leveraged even further when those arrested earlier made confessions to management prior to their arrest. Under these circumstances, a carefully worded press release could reveal that the arrestees had already admitted their crimes and *even named their accomplices*. Though extreme caution would have to be taken to avoid a defamation claim, this powerful play can stop the most aggressive union in its tracks. See Appendix F (Media Response Kit) for an example of how public relations can be powerfully used for the incremental disclosure of an investigation.

Grievances and Arbitrations

Any organization that has a collective bargaining agreement with a union representing its employees will have undoubtedly agreed to some form of *grievance procedure*, which is a process by which an employee (the grievant) can formally bring forth a dispute with management. The format of this structured process is negotiated and usually described in the labor agreement (the *contract*). Each "step" incrementally escalates in formality and structure. The last step is usually *arbitration*, in which the union and company bring their respective cases before an unbiased third party (an *arbitrator*). At arbitration both sides are permitted to call and question witnesses and make arguments. At its conclusion, the arbitrator issues a decision, which is usually binding, that settles the dispute in favor of one party or the other. If the matter involved a termination, for example, the arbitrator's decision might be to "uphold the termination," or it might be to "reinstate" the terminated employee with no back pay, or it could be reinstatement with back pay. Actually the arbitrator can decide practically anything. And sometimes they do—labor arbitrators are notoriously unpredictable.

Evidence

Central to the arbitrator's decision is evidence. Because the strict rules of evidence do not apply in arbitrations, all sorts of evidence may be "allowed in" or "excluded." Therefore, it is important that the employer get in as much evidence as it possibly can, even if that evidence is only hearsay. Operative's reports, lab reports and other forensics, surveillance tapes, witness statements, and all forms of confessions, written or tape-recorded— all these are potentially valuable to the employer's case. Interestingly,

because the rules of evidence are not strictly applied, documents like statements and confessions can be entered into evidence without their being
authenticated by those who made them. This type of evidence at a trial is
usually considered hearsay if the persons responsible for them are not available for questioning. Arbitrators will give appropriate weight to such documents and typically consider them less convincing than those that are
authenticated. Regardless, the employer and grievant are permitted to
submit all forms of evidence in support of their case, and it is up to the
arbitrator to weigh the evidence and decide its relevance.

In arbitrations stemming from an undercover investigation, usually
both of the opposing parties want to get the investigator's reports into evidence. The employer desires to do so from the standpoint of its incriminating value, the union from the standpoint of hoping to discredit the
investigator, the investigative team, or the investigative process. The union
may attempt to do this by exposing what it claims to be investigative bias,
discrimination, carelessness, unlawfulness, inconsistencies, and just plain
poor investigative technique. As can be commonly observed elsewhere in
our legal system, cornered defendants and wrongdoers attack the investigators and the investigative process when the facts are not in their favor. If
the accused is able to attack hard enough and long enough, somebody may
eventually believe them.

This defense technique was applied to perfection in the O.J. Simpson
case. Defense counsel Johnny Cochran masterfully attacked the investigators and their process. Regardless of what you think of Cochran or his client,
the defense team brilliantly destroyed the prosecution's case. So powerful
was *their* offensive that 12 jurors were eventually convinced that not only
did the "glove not fit" but that the entire investigative process was criminally defective, and they shamelessly acquitted the defendant.

Before you complete your investigation, make sure your reports
and documentation are *tight*. Ensure that one of the first documents in
your case file details your investigative objectives. Proof your reports,
letters, and memoranda to eliminate any inconsistencies or inaccuracies.
Properly maintain your case files and eliminate unnecessary documents and extraneous material. Be professional and run your cases like a
professional.

The introduction of physical evidence is uncommon in arbitrations.
In my experience, other than documents very little real physical evidence
is ever introduced. This puzzles me because physical evidence can be very
compelling, particularly in drug and theft cases. As a matter of practice I
always recommend my client introduce the dope or stolen property from
our case if available. Few arbitrators have ever seen an illegal drug. Imagine
the impact if one were able to produce the actual dope sold to the undercover investigator during the investigation! I've done it and it's powerful.
Imagine also filling the room with cartons stuffed with stolen property
recovered from the grievant. Even if I've only recovered a stolen roll of tape,

I suggest it be entered into evidence. In producing such evidence, no matter how seemingly insignificant, the grievant can not deny that he stole. *The only truthful argument he could make is how much.*

Testimony

Arbitrations are largely decided on testimony. Regardless of how compelling some piece of physical evidence may be, its value can always be affected by testimony. For this reason, witness testimony is the most important element in successful arbitrations. And because testimony is so important, there is no substitute for proper witness preparation, rehearsal, and conditioning.

In preparation, the undercover investigator should review all of his notes, reports, and other documents produced during the investigation. The investigator should familiarize himself with every document he created that may be entered into evidence. Most important of these documents are his daily reports. In Chapter 3, I covered reports in some detail and why I favor certain report formats; I won't repeat myself here. But let me briefly make one additional point: *undercover investigators should not quote themselves in their reports.* This common mistake can produce dreadful results in arbitrations. If the investigator routinely quotes himself in his reports, later while under examination he may be asked to recall what he said at any particular time. No big deal, right? Well, here's the trap. If the investigator in earlier testimony perfectly recalled what the *grievant* had said verbatim (and you can bet the well-coached and motivated investigator most assuredly will), how will it look when that same investigator cannot remember verbatim what *he* said? The trap is sprung after the eager investigator has rattled off snippet after snippet made by the grievant as quoted in his reports (all of which he reviewed and studied in preparation for the arbitration). But, not having so much as looked at what he quoted himself in the reports as having said during the exchange, and therefore not being able to remember them verbatim, his testimony will look embellished and even contrived. In pressing his point home, opposing counsel might close with asking, "How is it you can recall so vividly nearly every word spoken by the grievant nearly six months ago, yet you can't recall even a single sentence spoken from your own mouth?"

The operative should also be prepared to answer other questions as well. Here is a partial list of questions likely to be asked of the operative-witness:

- What professional training have you received that makes you qualified for this type of work? (An attempt to infer that the operative is unqualified or untrained.)
- How long have you been an undercover investigator? (An attempt to infer that the operative is inexperienced.)

- For whom did you work your prior cases? (For confidentiality reasons this question should never be answered.)
- Have you ever used an illegal drug? (An obvious attempt to discredit the operative. Should be objected to by the employer's counsel.)
- Are you licensed to buy drugs in the state of ..? (An attempt to throw the operative off balance by inferring he acted unlawfully and should have been licensed.)
- Have you talked to anyone about this case? (An attempt to infer it is improper to have talked to someone about the case—which, of course, is patently not so.)
- How many times did you have to ask the grievant to sell you drugs before he finally came through? (Inferring the grievant was badgered.)
- Did you know you broke the law when you transported the company property given to you by the grievant? (Another attempt to trip up the operative by suggesting he acted unlawfully.)

By no means is this a complete list. The point here is that the operative and the entire investigative team need to be prepared if they hope to effectively testify. To rely on one's recollection and naively believe that the truth will suffice can be a tragic mistake.

There are other traps for witnesses as well. One of the best of them is to ask the witness to answer a hypothetical question. When asked a hypothetical, the witness should immediately think *Trap!* Why ask a hypothetical where facts exist? The hypothetical is nothing more than an attempt to cause the witness to offer testimony contrary to the facts or the testimony of others. Here's how it works. An obscure passage in one of the operative's reports reveals that during a lunch break in the company break room she was handed what was claimed to be a marijuana cigarette. The person who had given it to her did so only so that she could look at it, it was not a gift. Upon examination it was returned to the owner. For the sake of my example, if these facts are in evidence the questioning might go something like this:

Opposing counsel:	Your supervisor has previously testified that as an undercover investigator you are prohibited from providing or selling illegal drugs to others. Is that your understanding of your company's policy?
The operative:	Yes.
Opposing counsel:	So, *hypothetically*, if an operative . . . like you for example . . . ever gave an employee an illegal drug during the investigation . . . you would never do that would you?
The operative:	No, of course not.

Opposing counsel:	It would be a clear violation of your company policy and *the law*, isn't that so?
The operative:	Ah, yes . . . it certainly would.
Opposing counsel:	Fine. Then please tell the arbitrator why you broke both your company's policy . . . *and the law I might add* . . . by providing a marijuana cigarette to Mr. •• on July 4, 1999, in the company break room?

BAM!

Be careful of hypotheticals. Of course a well-prepared witness would not fall into this trap and I make it a practice to never answer a hypothetical if at all possible. The best technique I've found to counter the hypothetical is to tell the questioner that his question cannot be answered without more facts. For example, the operative could have responded:

The operative:	I'd be happy to answer the question but in order to do so I need more information. First, did the operative in your hypothetical have prior permission from law enforcement before he provided the illegal drugs? Next, had the individual to whom he gave the illegal drugs threatened the operative in any way? Also, was the DEA involved or just local law enforcement? Did the incident take place in California or New Mexico? . . . *and so on and so on.*

This sort of response should stop even the most aggressive opponent. What's more, the arbitrator would quickly see where this is going and insist that opposing counsel question the witness using facts and not waste his time analyzing hypotheticals.

Another trap the witness should look out for is one in which the question demands a conclusion. Normally witnesses (other than expert witnesses) are not permitted to draw conclusions. They are to provide only the facts as *they know them to be*, which excludes even that which they were told by someone else (typically considered hearsay). However, in arbitrations the rules of evidence and strict civil procedure do not apply. A cunning opponent may try to trap a witness by causing him to give testimony that conflicts with testimony already given by someone else. By providing partial facts, using hypotheticals, and asking a witness to draw conclusions, opposing counsel can use one witness to impeach another. If done effectively, the investigative team can be made to look like a gaggle of misguided amateurs attempting to frame a small group of innocent hard-working employees.

Winning Arbitrations through Criminal Prosecution

As discussed in detail in Chapter 2, it is unlawful to threaten criminal pros-ecution to coerce someone to resign, or to force the payment of restitution or the surrender of any right or entitlement. To do so is considered extor-tion and is in many jurisdictions both criminally and civilly actionable.[3] In workplace situations, the employer must be very careful to not even inti-mate in any way that an employee's action (or in some cases inaction) may affect its decision to prosecute or even report the matter to the authorities. When balancing discipline, restitution, and prosecution, therefore, employ-ers need to be very careful. But the juggling act can be significantly simplified merely by prosecuting whenever possible. And although I gener-ally do not advocate employee prosecution, in cases involving offenders belonging to a union, I fully embrace it.

Because unions are obligated to represent their constituents and because unsophisticated union leaders often try to make names for them-selves by taking on groundless cases, management is often faced with defending perfectly justified terminations. In some of these cases, at huge expense to the employer, the discharges are even overturned. These traves-ties of justice are unfair and divisive. A bad decision can artificially boost the morale of a cocky union leadership, damage long-term labor relations, and adversely affect productivity. What's more, if the decision reinstates those with drug problems and attaches no treatment or other condition to their return to work, employee safety also becomes an issue.

The remedy is simple: prosecute all unionized offenders to the fullest extent possible. I have learned from experience that organized labor is not always interested in a safe, productive, and drug-free workplace. More often than not, the leadership at the local level is interested in power, politics, and making management miserable. In dealing on the local level with unions such, I've learned that compassion is often perceived as weakness and that professional respect and human dignity are hollow, meaningless concepts. The culture of some of these organizations does not respond to reason, the appeal for civility, or even the extension of simple common courtesy. A great deal of time and money can be spared by engineering the investigation so that the convicted offenders working in these environ-ments simply go to jail.

---

[3] California Penal Code §§153 and 519 make it a crime to threaten criminal action in order to obtain the settlement of a civil matter.

In order to make that possible, the investigation has to be properly planned and each case rock solid. For starters, law enforcement must be involved from the beginning. Cooperating with the authorities and the district or state attorney's office from the gate will ensure that any criminal cases made are built properly and successful prosecution an almost sure bet. Next, in your drug cases, make multiple buys and buy up whenever possible. Score as much weight as possible from each subject. Multiple large buys will almost ensure jail time for the offenders. If it is necessary to extend the length of the investigation to make larger buys, do so. If possible make one buy in each subject's vehicle and home, which may allow the vehicle to be confiscated and the home searched (or possibly seized). I've even arranged buys in the dealer's wife's car so her vehicle would be confiscated as well. If the case involves theft, also make multiple buys. Corroborate all potentially criminal activity with multiple operatives and surveillance teams. Make solid cases and make them big.

Coordinate the case shutdown with the authorities. Arrange for the offenders to be arrested swiftly and visibly. Assist law enforcement to the fullest extent possible without allowing yourself or any member of the investigative team to be labeled a "police agent." After the arrests, publicly announce management's cooperation with the police and encourage search warrants be served on the business so that lockers, toolboxes, desks, and offices can be searched by law enforcement. If your organization is the victim (as would be in the case of theft of company property), file a complaint as soon as possible and don't negotiate any deals. Make every defendant go the hard way. No sympathy, no compassion, no deals. Everybody gets jail time.

If the union dares to arbitrate (a difficult task since the grievant may be unavailable), use both the investigative result and the criminal result at the hearings. Obtain transcripts from the criminal trial and get them into evidence. Ask the arresting officers, the case detectives, and the prosecutors to all testify. Get everybody involved. Get your PR machine working as well. Provide regular updates on the cases in the company newsletter. Post progress reports on the company bulletin board and keep the union membership informed. Also let the community know that the organization does not lay down to criminal activity in the workplace and that those who break the law are punished. Make it a spectacle. But whatever you do, make it known that *law-breakers lose their jobs and go to jail!*

Hardball aside, the grievance procedure and arbitration process were designed to be efficient and fair. And for the most part both mechanisms are exactly that. However, to win one must have a plan and be prepared. Before your undercover results are challenged make sure you have the right people on your team. Seek competent counsel familiar with employment law and the arbitration process. Take her advice and keep yourself and your organization out of trouble. Be a winner.

Unemployment Hearings

All states provide some form of unemployment benefits to those between jobs. In most cases these benefits are in the form of insurance that has been paid for by the employer. Upon separation, the former employee files an "unemployment insurance claim" and, if entitled, benefits are awarded and eventually paid. Because the employer has the right to deny benefits, the claimant if so inclined has the right to challenge that decision and ask for a hearing.

Because "unemployment hearings" are administrative proceedings, they are often very informal. In fact, in most cases the claimant is not allowed representation. This obvious employer advantage is diminished, however, by very loose rules of evidence and the fact that the hearing, once completed, becomes a public record. Let's briefly examine each of these disadvantages in turn.

The first is evidentiary. Because the rules of evidence are so relaxed that nearly anything may be allowed in, the claimant can offer character witnesses, submit double and triple hearsay, and make all sorts of claims for which there is no support or corroboration. I've had cases in which the claimant produced seven or more character witnesses, attesting to the high morals and sobriety of an admitted drug user/dealer.

The other disadvantage is that in many states the results of an unemployment hearing become a public record. Anyone can view them. If witness statements, confidential or internal company documents, or confessions are entered into evidence, they may eventually become available to the public. If privacy, confidentiality, and public relations are at all important, one should carefully consider each piece of evidence before its submission. Once it's in, you can't get it out!

Public Relations

Earlier I mentioned public relations and suggested the reader look at the material provided in Appendix F. If you haven't done so yet, do so now. I don't want the importance of this matter to be glossed over. Effective public relations today are more important than ever before. Years ago, most companies could (and did) ignore the media and go unscathed. That's not true anymore and increasingly security professionals, human resource managers, and even line managers are finding themselves thrown before the camera.

Nevertheless, it is still a somewhat rare occasion that an investigation is made public and brought to the attention of the media. These disclosures are usually the handiwork of a disgruntled employee or a hostile union. Though sometimes disruptive, these otherwise uncomfortable situations can often be successfully managed so that they inflict little or no damage to the organization. However, to minimize the impact of an unwanted disclosure, preparation is necessary. To that end, I have provided in Appendix F a simple collection of media statements and responses for you. These were custom written by corporate public relations professionals and have been designed to provide incremental disclosure while protecting the privacy and rights of all of those concerned. I strongly encourage you to examine them to determine their suitability for you and your organization.

As an aid, use the following nondisclosure guidelines when communicating with the media. However, for best results and the protection of the organization, I strongly recommend that you consult your attorney and public relations department before making these or any public disclosures.

1. DO NOT DISCLOSE the names of any employees involved in the investigation. If given a name, confirm employment, job title, and date of employment only.[4]
2. DO NOT DISCLOSE any specific details regarding the types of company violations under investigation. Refer instead to the company policy statement regarding the use, sale, and so forth of drugs (or whatever the issue may be).
3. DO NOT DISCLOSE the details regarding the information-gathering process.
4. DO NOT DISCLOSE the exact number of employees involved. Instead indicate: "fewer than ..."
5. DO NOT DISCLOSE the departments, sections, or areas where the employees who are involved worked.
6. DO NOT DISCLOSE the length of the investigation.
7. DO NOT DISCLOSE the cost of the investigation or investment made to date.
8. DO NOT DISCLOSE specifics regarding disciplinary action or prosecution unless advised to do so by counsel.

Remember, if your organization does not manage its public relations and help shape public opinion, someone else will. I would never leave this important detail to chance.

Employee Relations

An important question to those who have never used undercover before is what affect does it have on employee relations? The answer is simple: *it*

---

[4] As mentioned earlier, under some circumstances in which the identity of those arrested has already been disclosed (say, by the police), carefully confirming that information and revealing that confessions have been provided (if in fact so) may help quell union dissension and improve public opinion.

depends. For simplicity, let's look at the most typical detrimental effects and what usually causes them.

Poor Investigative Plan

Nothing will sabotage a well-intended investigation faster than a poor plan. By now you know the importance I give planning and engineering. Without sound objectives, a well-conceived plan, and a sprinkling of luck, your investigation is not going anywhere. What's more, a poorly planned investigation will yield disappointment, frustration, and embarrassment. Plan your work and then work your plan.

Accidental Compromise

Accidental compromises happen. When they do, the emotional and political fallout can be devastating. Not only can a huge investment be jeopardized but also the life of the operative can be at stake. Accidental compromises most often occur because of carelessness. And most often that carelessness is on the part of the client-employer. Yes, I've had my share of operatives "flip" or "go stupid," but most often it is my customer who makes the big mistake. Most carelessness can be avoided. Force yourself and your team to constantly think operations and communications security. Leave nothing to chance and remember, *loose lips sink ships*. Protect your organization, your investment, and employee morale by protecting your investigation.

Hostile Litigation

In most jurisdictions it costs less than $75 to file a lawsuit. Unfortunately, in some parts of our great country suing is considered as a type of lottery. Litigation is expensive and it is time consuming. Of its many forms, frivolous hostile litigation is the worst. Most often this weapon is unleashed by people who feel cheated, abused, and mistreated. The best defense in such a situation is a good offense. Work only good cases and work them right. But most importantly, treat all people with respect and dignity. Regardless of the outcome of the investigation and the severity of the resultant punishment, if the recipients are treated with respect and dignity they will rarely lash back.

Ineffective Postinvestigative Communication

The leading cause of all adverse employee relations is poor communication. Following a highly visible undercover investigation, management communication with employees is critical. People (both offender and nonoffender) want to know what happened. People want to know where they stand, if they are at risk, and what will happen next. The biggest boost to employee morale and long-term employee relations are effective postinvestigation communications. The best are those that are personal and made by the decisionmakers involved in the investigation. Frank, open, and meaningful communications as to why the company undertook the investigation, what its objectives were, and finally what was learned are essential. People also want to know that another shoe is not about to drop. Bring closure to your investigation and facilitate emotional healing by communicating with all levels of the organization *after* the investigation. Be communicative. Let your people know you and the organization care about them. Wasn't one of your original objectives to create a better and safer workplace? If so, tell them.

CHAPTER 7

Case Closure and Shutdown

Every undercover investigation eventually evolves to where the production of useful information reaches the point of diminishing returns. In some instances, the investigative effort has met every objective and the undercover investigator has identified every perpetrator. More common, however, is something short of this idealistic outcome. Typically, the investigation simply reaches the point where it has yielded enough information to permit the removal of the operative and allow the rest of the investigative team to take over. Generally, the properly engineered investigation has anticipated this eventuality and has designated and allocated the sources necessary to properly close the investigation. As I have mentioned in prior chapters, most workplace undercover investigations culminate with one or more of the following outcomes:

- Employee discipline
- Employee prosecution
- Restitution

However, before the case is shutdown, some "back-end" preparation must be accomplished. For the sake of our examination of this process, let's assume that the investigation has in fact reached that point of diminishing returns where any further effort will likely yield little new information. We also will assume that the investigator(s) is still in place and there is no suspicion of him or his true role in the workplace. We will further assume that the investigation has netted the identity of several employees who have stolen company property (the value of which is not necessarily important) and several who are involved in the use and sale of illegal drugs at work.

Selecting the Appropriate Outcome

Paramount in the proper closure of the undercover investigation is determining the desired outcome. Although this important decision should have been decided before the investigation began, often it is necessary to change or alter the investigative objectives as the operation unfolds. A good example might be the investigation of a small employee theft problem in which the undercover investigator discovers a *very big employee theft problem* and the collusive involvement of key customers. Clearly, if this finding was not anticipated, the investigative team would surely have to reconsider some of its key objectives and very possibly reengineer its planned case shutdown. And it is because of situations like this that so much planning and preparation must go into the investigation's front-end. In any event, the client organization and the investigative team must agree on the desired outcome and then engineer a process to achieve it. A significant component of that process is interviewing the people involved and proceeding with termination and/or prosecution.

Administrative and Operational Preparations

Once the desired outcome has been determined, the client-organization must make a number of administrative and operational preparations. For example, if it has been decided that those who have violated the company's theft and substance abuse policies will be terminated, it must be determined who will do the terminations and where and when they will be done. Consideration should also be given as to whether unemployment benefits should be opposed and how to handle future inquiries by prospective employers of those terminated seeking employment verification.

In a unionized environment, these and other considerations need to be made as well. For example, how much evidence should be provided to the union following the terminations and prior to its filing of a formal grievance? Should witnesses be identified before arbitration or during the actual arbitration? How rigorous should the union be opposed, and should special consideration be given to those in jail and unable to attend their own arbitration?

Some significant operational considerations should be made as well. For example, what impact will the terminations have on productivity, deadlines, customer service, profitability, and safety? Can the organization, division, unit, or team afford to lose all of those who have substantially violated company policy? How difficult will it be to find and train replacements? What will be the impact on morale and labor relations? For maximum deterrent value, should employee arrests take place on company premises and what sort of employee communications should be put into effect after the arrests? These and myriad other administrative and operational questions need to be contemplated and answered before the investigation can be shut down. Effective prior planning will save time and money later.

Employee Communications and Public Relations

Employees in every workplace want to be informed. Following the shutdown of an undercover investigation in which even a few employees are disciplined or arrested, the workforce wants information about what's taken place and why. One of the biggest mistakes the organization can make following an exposed and highly visible undercover investigation is to say nothing about it. The news of employee discipline and arrest will race through the organization. Rumors and speculation will fly. In order to derive maximum benefit and deterrent value from its investigation, management must communicate with its workforce following the investigation. Those communications must be frank (yet not defamatory), honest, and sincere. Management must communicate why the investigation was conducted, what it hoped to achieve, its outcome, and most importantly that the process is finished. The questions most frequently asked by employees following a highly visible investigation are: How does this affect me? Is the investigation still going on? Inevitably, the disclosure of an internal investigation (of any kind) creates employee fear and concern. Management must answer these questions and do all that it can to restore employee confidence and trust. Wise managers anticipate the need for these sorts of communications and prepare statements or other disclosures in advance.

Management must also anticipate the disclosure of the investigation to those outside of the organization. In large organizations it is appropriate that such matters be left to those in public relations. In smaller organizations the responsibility of answering to the media, customers, vendors, and stockholders may well be left to local management. And in spite of the obvious downside of such exposure or inquiries, the skilled communicator can turn the event into an opportunity that builds public confidence and actually enhances the organization's image. Take a moment and look at the Media Response Kit in Appendix F. With a little preparation and the slightest amount of confidence, the average manager can confront the media and turn what might otherwise seem like a media crisis into a once-in-a-lifetime media opportunity.

Just imagine being able to truthfully tell an eager television news correspondent, "Our research shows that more than 21 percent of all those who work in our industry have used an illegal drug at least once while on the job. Furthermore, while our investigation did identify several employees having some involvement with drugs, the public was never at risk. Our efforts identified those in need of help before they injured themselves or had the opportunity to hurt others. The same cannot be said about our competitors, who remarkably still do not even embrace employee drug testing or treatment in spite of all of the evidence I have mentioned."

Final Coordination

Finally, before the finished plan can be cast into stone, things like holidays, vacations, crew schedules, and the availability of key management must be considered. If employee arrests are to take place, coordination with the authorities must be arranged. The dates, time, and place(s) of the arrests must all be discussed. Additionally, security and safety issues must be addressed. Every detail should be reviewed and managed to the fullest extent possible. Contingencies and what-if scenarios should be thoroughly gone through. Nothing should be left to chance, for as most readers know, "what can go wrong . . . usually does."

Restitution and Recovery

Property crimes orchestrated by employees tend to lend themselves to some form of recovery by the employer. A properly engineered investigation should not only produce the identity of the transgressors but what became of the assets they stole or diverted as well. The investigation should be sufficiently thorough to allow the organization to exercise its prerogative in seeking recovery of the stolen goods or restitution for them. The effort, however, should not overlook recovery for the organization's contribution of resources and time to the investigation. Often not sought are the cost of the undercover investigation, management's time, and the income lost while the organization was deprived of its assets. These costs can translate into a considerable amount and should not be overlooked when contemplating restitution by the offending employees or their accomplices.

Prior to shutting down the investigation, the investigative team should thoroughly contemplate how much of the financial burden of the investigation can be shifted to the perpetrators and how might that best be done. Remarkably, this might be easier than one thinks. When prosecution is sought, the employer (the victim) can simply ask the court to consider restitution as part of the sentencing. By explaining the economic impact of the defendant's actions on the organization, a lighter sentence might be combined with the order to make restitution. Conversely, if prosecution is not an option or the court refuses to consider repayment, the employer can simply ask the offender to make some form of restitution in good faith. However, care should be taken in approaching a defendant prior to sentencing. It is unlawful to demand restitution or any other consideration in exchange for favorable criminal prosecutorial treatment. In some jurisdictions, the offense is classified as extortion and its consequences are quite serious.

Another option in seeking recovery is to pursue it through civil litigation. Combining all the offenders (employee and nonemployee) as codefendants in a single action makes both tactical as well as economic sense. Generally, under such circumstances, the more reputable defendants and those with the greatest amount to lose (other businesses, for example) will be the first to seek settlement. If they come forward, part of the settlement might be their continued cooperation in the action. Thus the employer-plaintiff's case not only becomes self-funded, but the employer has gained the cooperation of a very valuable witness(s).

Employee Interviews

As I have mentioned in this chapter and elsewhere in the book, employee interviews are a key component of any successful workplace investigation. In fact, the undercover portion of the investigation could be considered only a vehicle by which the investigative team reaches the point where employee interviews are possible. In other words, the information developed by the operative serves as the seed information that enables the proper selection of candidates for interview. However, unlike most general investigations where the interview process over time closes in on the perpetrators, these interviews begin with those most involved and work toward those less involved. The reason for this is simple yet deserves some explanation. However, before I leave this point, let me reiterate that the interview process is the most critical component of the entire undercover investigation. To not conduct employee interviews following the efforts of the undercover is tantamount to professional negligence. Those who use this powerful tool will tell you that, on average, 75 percent of the total information gleaned during the investigative process comes from their interviews. When all is said and done, only about 25 percent (and often less) of the useable information is actually developed by the undercover. And it is that simple fact that makes it so hard to understand why some undercover vendors don't offer their clients employee interviews. Not interviewing those involved following the undercover is the mark of incompetence and unsophistication. Investigative agencies that don't effectively use this powerful tool are not properly serving their clients.

Administrative Interviews

Administrative interviews, which are used for interviewing witnesses, friends, supervisors, and anyone else other than the offender, are simple and usually unstructured. They are usually only collateral to the subject or event. In most cases, these people are innocent and have not committed any known policy violations or other infraction. Most often, the only reason we interview them is to learn more about our subject or his activities. And although these interviews are less structured than their counterpart, investigatory interviews, I still like to obtain a written and even a tape-recorded statement when I conduct one of them, if possible. Like all statements, those obtained from administrative interviewees should be voluntary, factual, concise, and authenticated by a witness whenever possible. The truthfulness of the statement should be clear, as should be the fact that the interviewer made no threats or promises. I also like to ask the interviewee to share with me who else they think should be interviewed and why. And I make it a policy never to offer immunity in exchange for the subject's cooperation. Statements provided by administrative interviewees should always be signed by the interviewee and may be taken as a sworn declaration if desired.

Investigatory Interviews

Investigatory interviews are complex and can be fraught with liability even when properly conducted. They include those in which the subject is known to have committed the offense in question and those in which the interviewer has very good reason to believe that he has. For tactical reasons, the most serious offenders should be interviewed first. These individuals are usually the easiest to obtain admissions from and very often the most cooperative. If interviewed later in the process, they may either make themselves unavailable (quit or skip town) or have had ample time to collect their thoughts and create alibis. Thus the skilled interviewer (or team in some cases) will start at the top and work down the list of interviewees, such that each subsequent interviewee is less involved than the one prior. This procedure also allows the interviews to be concluded at any time without the concern that someone not interviewed might claim discrimination, bias, or disparate treatment. Theoretically, everyone that was interviewed either committed or was suspected to have committed more serious offenses than those not interviewed. It's tough to take offense with that, wouldn't you agree?

Unlike administrative interviews, investigatory interviews are very structured. Ideally, they unfold in some predetermined fashion as if they were scripted, moving the interviewee to the point she eventually volunteers an admission or a confession. The process usually has five components:

1. Introduction
2. Some sort of theme development and discussion
3. Provision of a written statement (or confession as the case may be)
4. Provision of a tape-recorded statement
5. Conclusion

The introduction is nothing more than a process by which the interviewer and interviewee are brought together and introduced. It should be done in such a fashion that the interviewer is properly identified and the interviewee put on sufficient notice that his or her participation is required and that their cooperation is appreciated. The interview should be conducted in a place that provides adequate privacy, yet is not so remote or secluded as to be inappropriate or seemingly threatening. Following the actual introduction of the two to each other (usually performed by a management representative known to the interviewee), it is best for the interviewer to reintroduce himself and attempt to put the interviewee at ease. When the interviewer is a person not known to the interviewee (as should be the case in most instances), the selection of the interviewer should be contemplated well in advance. As a general practice men should not interview women alone, and vice versa. The interviewer should have the skill and experience to conduct the interview. He should know employment and civil law sufficiently well so as to not make careless mistakes or expose himself, his organization, or the client to any foreseeable liability. The interviewer should present a professional image and know his material well. At all times the interviewer should treat the interviewee with respect and dignity.

Next the interviewer should introduce a theme and discuss the issue at hand. The introduction and use of an interview theme is called *theme development,* and it is the mechanism by which the interviewer transitions from his introduction to his direct questioning of the subject. To move directly from "Hi, my name is Gene." to "Why did you steal the money?" is not only rude, but it is ineffective as well. More appropriate is to build rapport and some meaningful foundation for the eventual line of questioning. For example, it may be appropriate to explain to the interviewee why management is concerned about employee theft and why even petty theft has a profound effect on the organization and its employees. By demonstrating to the interviewee that there are myriad reasons why management might be concerned about a particular behavior and wishes it to stop, the interviewee is afforded the opportunity to see their own behavior from another perspective within the context of the entire organization. By appealing to the interviewee's sense of loyalty to the organization and the need for honesty, an admission can usually be obtained. Once obtained, the admission needs to be fully developed and qualified as voluntary.

Written and Tape-Recorded Statements

Once the interviewee has admitted his transgressions and has told all he knows about the transgressions of others, a written statement should be obtained. Again, the statement should be voluntary, factual, concise, and authenticated by a witness, if possible. It is my practice as well to insist that the interviewee indicate that she knows she violated company policy (if in fact it is the case) and that she may be disciplined because of it.

It is also a good practice to ask the interviewee to state that her cooperation was voluntary and that she was not denied representation, if requested. In nonunion environments, the decision to allow representation is one that only management should make. Unless the organization has a policy or practice of allowing representation during such proceedings, there is no obligation to provide it. However, if the interviewee is party to a collective bargaining agreement, she has some very specific rights that were established in *NLRB v. Weingarten,Inc.*, 420 U.S. 241 (1975) as we saw in Chapter 6. Under *Weingarten*, once an employee makes a valid request for union representation, the employer must either grant the request or dispense with or discontinue the interview.[1] The employer, however, may continue the interview without union representation if the employee "voluntarily" agrees to remain unrepresented after having been apprised by the employer of the rights just described or otherwise made aware of those choices.

An employer does not have to guarantee an employee that a union representative will be present at an investigatory meeting in order to get the employee to leave the plant floor. Once a union representative is legitimately present at an interview, the employer cannot force him to remain silent; however, the employer can insist on hearing only the employee's account of the incident under investigation or insist that the representative hold his comments until the end of the interview. If a union representative is present at a meeting solely by virtue of a collective bargaining agreement, however, the employer may require the representative to remain quiet.

In a recent decision, the NLRB has held that an employer lawfully discharged an employee who refused to leave the plant floor and meet in the employer's office when no union representative was available. Although the employee had the right to refuse to speak with the employer during the actual interview, he did not have the right to refuse to adjourn to a more private location where he and the employer could determine whether the interview would be held without a union representative. Rather than conduct company business on the crowded plant floor, the employer was entitled to require the employee to come to his private office in the interest of maintaining plant order and discipline.

The NLRB has also held that an employer may lawfully discipline an employee for his refusal to attend a noninvestigatory meeting without union representation. The employer may also discipline a group of employees who walk out of a noninvestigatory meeting to protest the employer's denial of their demand for a union representative.

---

[1] Note that although *Weingarten* specifically addresses employer obligations, the interviewer as either a contractor or also an employee of the employer is the lawful agent of the employer for purposes of Weingarten and incurs the same obligations as the employer.

Finally, and I think most interestingly, the NLRB has ruled that reinstatement and back pay are inappropriate remedies for *Weingarten* violations if the employee was disciplined for just cause. Unless the discipline was the direct result of an employee's assertion of *Weingarten* rights, the Board cannot order "make-whole" remedies nor can it make punitive awards. Even blatant violations of *Weingarten* rights do not give rise to make-whole remedies when discipline is for just cause. Courts have held that a make-whole remedy is not appropriate if some other independent evidence, not obtained in the unlawful interview, demonstrates that the discharge was for good cause. I suggest, however, that for your own protection you get the advice of competent labor law counsel when you know you are going to interview in a union environment.

The tape recorder is a powerful tool, however; it should not be used until after the interviewee has provided a written statement. Years of experience has shown that introducing a tape recorder too early in the process will frighten or intimidate the interviewee. As a general rule, people don't like to be tape-recorded. Knowing this, the interviewer must carefully introduce that possibility to his subject. The best time for this is after the subject has provided a signed admission. This is also an excellent time to introduce a representative from the employer into the process. The management representative can then observe the completion of the interview and contribute as appropriate. This portion of the interview should be highly structured and to some degree rehearsed. For if it is being tape-recorded, both the interviewer and the management representative want to make the interviewee as comfortable as possible. This process provides the opportunity to capture, at least to some degree, the atmosphere in which the interview was conducted. For example, an appropriate question to ask the interviewee while on tape is how he has been treated during the interview process. One might also ask if the interviewee was held against his will or was he permitted to use the restroom and telephone or to take breaks. It is also very appropriate to ask why the interviewee told the truth and if any promises or threats were made by the interviewer or anyone else. It may be appropriate to ask the interviewee to read his written statement to the management representative and when finished ask that he acknowledge he wrote it and confirm its accuracy.

Once these and any other details are seen to, the management representative (not the interviewer) should tell the interviewee what will happen next. Under most circumstances, it is inappropriate to immediately discipline the employee following his interview. Instead, it is best to place the individual on some sort of administrative leave pending the completion of the investigation. Regardless of the gravity of the admission, it makes sense to finish all of the interviews before dispensing discipline. Doing so allows the employer the opportunity to examine all of the evidence and make fairer decisions. Postponing the disbursement of disciplinary action following the completion of the entire investigation also allows the employer time to prepare final checks, draft discharge notices, and make the appropriate internal disclosures.

From an employee relations standpoint, I also think it is best to allow those that have been tagged for termination to be given the chance to resign instead. Though the employer is still the moving party and the action does not offer any legal protections, allowing the offenders to resign looks kinder and is perceived as compassionate. It also helps minimize the pain. The employee who resigns (even under duress) is allowed to leave with some semblance of his dignity and self-respect. No one likes to be fired, and certainly no one particularly likes to be fired for gross misconduct. Employees who are fired, even for just cause, often leave angry. And anger can precipitate more misconduct and even violence. It is also true that those who are allowed to resign typically don't pursue unemployment benefits or file grievances. Interestingly, not everyone who is offered the opportunity to resign in lieu of termination will choose resignation. Because of principle, stubbornness, or anger some people select termination. However, if the number of disciplined individuals is large, even a small number of resignations dilutes the ranks of the would-be troublemakers.

Following the interviews, the investigative team should compile all of the information gleaned during the investigation and arrange it by each individual involved. The team can then guide the employer's decisionmakers through the information, examining each offender and the totality of information regarding them. Typically, the information on each individual can be separated into three groupings:

1. That which was developed by the operative
2. That which was provided by the employee during his or her interview
3. That which was provided by others during their interviews

Clearly, if the employee made an admission against their own self-interest, it would serve as the best evidence against them. In fact for employment purposes, if the admission was properly obtained, no other evidence is needed to effect the discipline. Unlike our criminal justice system, for employment purposes the admission is all that is needed to make the case. In some instances, it is wise for the employee to discard all of the other evidence in favor of an admission. In doing so, the disciplined employee can only challenge her admission. Because nothing else from the actual investigation (including the information developed by the undercover) has been used, she cannot challenge any of it. In other words, she cannot challenge the undercover, his reports, the process, or even those who were interviewed and spoke out or provided information about her. If the employer exclusively relies upon the subject's admission and nothing else, the subject will indeed have difficulty challenging the employer's decision.

Just a quick word about video-recording the interview. For years law enforcement agencies of all sizes have experimented with video-recording their interviews. Its usefulness is widely debated. In the private sector the demarcation is clear. The experienced interviewers in the industry today don't use video. It is expensive, intimidating (a reason it is often used during depositions), and has proven to be more trouble than it is worth. Although I know of several unsophisticated agencies that claim to video-record their interviews, none of the better or more experienced agencies do it. These same agencies like to show the subject the video of himself while breaking company policy or committing some infraction. This unsophisticated technique (though it sounds hi-tech) usually yields little more than an admission of what's on tape. It provides no incentive for the subject to admit to anything else or reveal the misconduct of his coworkers. What's more, it reveals to him, his union, and his attorney the quality and the limitations of the employer's evidence. The plaintiff's attorney that is contemplating taking the case on contingency might therefore be allowed the benefit of knowing the employer's only evidence is a poorly done, two-minute videotape in which his potential client "allegedly" is smoking marijuana. The attorney will not only take the case, he'll likely ask his new client to give his card to anyone else that was interviewed. But equally damaging, the practice also allows the attorney the enormous benefit of knowing that those who conducted the investigation were not very sophisticated or experienced (and probably did not read this book).

Don't videotape your interviews and don't show your evidence to the interviewee.

Physical Evidence Gathered During the Interview

Occasionally an interviewee will voluntarily surrender evidence during or immediately following his interview. This is most typical in drug investigations. In fact, it is so common in those cases that it is a good practice to make it a point to ask the subject if he is in *possession*. If evidence is then provided, it should be properly handled, packaged, and tagged. A chain of evidence should be established and when appropriate tested. Like all other evidence, it should be retained until the statute of limitations has run out on all possible claims and all actions that were brought have been adjudicated and appealed. If you have any doubts about handling evidence properly, ask your employment law attorney or the district attorney handling your case.

Role of Law Enforcement

The outcome of some investigations is prosecution. Regardless of the type of misconduct investigated, if one of the desired outcomes is the prosecution of the offenders, at some point the authorities must be involved. As I have mentioned elsewhere in this book, law enforcement's role, though often critical, should be limited. Both the undercover investigator and his supervisors must be careful of "agent status" so as not to become agents of the government. As agents, the investigator's powers become more limited and the subject's rights are expanded. For example, for the government (and its agents) to effect a search and seizure, probable cause is required and in most instances a warrant is necessary. Conversely, in the workplace, absent some expectation of privacy, the employer (and its agents) can search anything they want . . . any time. What's more, when dealing with the government agents, citizens have both due process and an assortment of other rights that protect them from personal and property abuse. Conversely, an employee when dealing solely with his employer does not have the right of due process or the other protections provided by the Constitution. Therefore, the more government-like the investigation, the more rights the subjects of that investigation will have. Consequently, the savvy investigator knows precisely how close his relationship with law enforcement should be.

For the best results, employee arrests should take place after the employer has dispensed its discipline. That way, the disciplined employee cannot claim that the discipline he received was the result of his being charged with a crime or being arrested. Additionally, postdiscipline arrests protect the employer against a defective or failed prosecution. If in fact the employer did base its decision to discipline on criminal charges brought against the employee and the charges are later dropped, what then are the grounds for the discipline? The complication can be completely avoided by following the plan outlined above.

But let's take a closer look.

Say the employee in question sold illegal drugs to the undercover investigator during the investigation and law enforcement intends to file criminal charges. Suppose the employee is successfully interviewed and provides both a written and tape-recorded admission. Then based on the admissions, the employer terminates the employee. A week later he is arrested and charged. Because he is a first-time offender, the court allows a plea to a lesser offense, say, simple possession of a controlled substance. The charge of trafficking is dropped, the defendant gets a suspended sentence, and he is given full credit for time served while awaiting trial. Because the employer based its discipline decision on the individual's pre-arrest admission of selling drugs, the fact that criminal charges for that crime were dropped is irrelevant. The terminated employee cannot use the fact that charges were dropped or that he was never found guilty of selling illegal drugs as grounds for re-instatement.

Conversely, had the employer waited to make its decision to terminate until after the arrest, it could create the appearance that the arrest influenced that decision. And it is for this very reason that I don't advocate the employer assisting with any arrests or even allowing them to take place on company premises. Although arguably the spectacle of employees being dragged out in handcuffs has some possible deterrent value, the downside is it creates the appearance that the employer was assisting law enforcement (possibly creating agent status) and that the decision to discipline was at least in part based on the arrests.

What's more, unless you are looking to create the impression that your workplace is some sort of police state and all policy offenders go to jail, don't allow arrests to take place on company premises. Who wants to work for a company like that?

Operative Removal

The timing of the removal of the operative is one of the most frequently debated subjects among undercover supervisors. However, to me the answer is a simple one: the operative should be kept in as long as possible. Where interviews follow the undercover effort, the operative should stay in place until such time he is named by enough interviewees as a co-offender that it seems illogical that he too would not have been called up and interviewed. To remove the operative sooner will only bring suspicion upon him. If he is removed before the interviews begin, it will appear clear to everyone that he was an informant. This very thing recently happened in one of my cases. Against his supervisor's instructions, the operative gave notice indicating his last day was the day before our interview team was to secretly arrive. Not only did this concern my client, a frequent user of undercover; it caused problems during our interviews. Several interviewees told us that they knew that "employee who had just quit" was our source of information. Consequently, it took excessive effort to obtain the admissions we would have otherwise easily obtained. The operative later told me he had violated his supervisor's instructions because he was concerned for his safety and did not want to be anywhere around when people were questioned. In fact, by his action, in just a matter of hours everyone's suspicion of him was raised and they wanted to know more about him. Luckily no one decided to go look for him. Had he stayed in place, we would have put him through what would have appeared to be an interview and then sent him home on administrative leave, just like everyone else. No one would have been the wiser.

When the operative is not exposed by interviewees, I will sometimes leave her in place for several weeks or a month following the shutdown and disciplinary phase of the investigation. If the undercover investigator is not compromised or otherwise exposed, she can be very valuable if left in place. Often after the disciplinary and corrective action is taken by the employer following a highly visible undercover, offenders who have been caught will sometimes become complacent. Some offenders will even brag of their cunningness and of having slipped through management's dragnet. These individuals are easy targets for the operative. More than once, such an individual has told one of my investigators that he was too sharp to be caught, as he handed over a bag of marijuana on the shop floor.

Another technique is to place a new undercover investigator into the new staff replacing those who have just been terminated. Although for some time most new hires will be suspect, the skilled operative placed this way can often get information otherwise not possible. Increasingly, my organization has requests for this type of undercover. We call them *workplace evaluations* and I will discuss them in more detail in Chapter 10.

Don't be in a rush to pull the operative. Remember that the purpose of the undercover is to develop information. As long as the operative is gathering information, keep her in place. The results may surprise you.

Employee Communication

I have mentioned several times already the importance of workplace communication following an undercover investigation. Enough cannot be said about this critical aspect of the investigation. I call these communications sessions *settle-down meetings* and to assist you in putting one together, I've included a sample in Appendix G. These simple meetings should be direct and straightforward. The presenter should be a high-level decisionmaker in the organization, preferably someone who was on the investigative team. They should be prepared to answer questions and defend the organization's actions. It is important, however, that such communications, whether written or spoken, not be undertaken until after all the discipline and corrective action has taken place.

In a healthy workplace, such communications are met with interest and appreciation. In environments where problems remain or where others continue to sympathize with some of those disciplined, the response will not be as warm. For this reason, the settle-down meeting serves as a litmus test. If management's best efforts are met with anger, outrage, and protests, the chances are very good that the employees expressing those emotions are themselves policy violators who are at odds with the organization's mission and purpose. The undercover investigators we leave in place following a routine shutdown prove this to be the case time and again. Maybe I'm asking the wrong audience, but would you *really* be offended if your employer had conducted an undercover investigation to stop a theft problem, to prevent sexual harassment, or to stop employee drug-dealing . . . and later honestly told you why it did it?

If revealing your investigation is met with harsh protestations, consider the need for another investigation.

CHAPTER 8

Litigation Avoidance

Employers confronted with complaints and/or evidence of serious employee misconduct face many difficult decisions. Most employers are generally aware that the failure to investigate allegations or evidence of serious misconduct on the part of employees is reckless and often negligent. Lawsuits can easily arise from an employer's failure to remedy alleged intolerable or unlawful behavior (i.e., discrimination and sexual harassment) or by their mismanagement of the foreseeable (i.e., inadequate security and workplace violence). However, few employers realize that a failure to investigate may in fact be unlawful.

While the courts have long held that, generally, employers have the right to run an orderly and efficient business and make a profit, the Federal Occupational Safety and Health Act (Fed-OSHA) and its state counterparts, as well as a large body of case law, require employers to provide employees with a workplace that is "free from recognized hazards that are causing or are likely to cause death or serious physical harm to . . . employees."[1] In 1995, California's Cal/OSHA went even further and addressed violence in the workplace by producing a comprehensive report and a Model Injury and Illness Prevention Program for Workplace Security. Two years before, the agency had issued Guidelines for Security and Safety of Health Care and Community Service Workers. Similarly, state and federal laws require that the workplace be kept free from the sales and use of illegal substances.[2] At the same time, there is no question that the investigation of one's employees can be troublesome and complex. And while the typical workplace investigation may consume time, energy, and financial resources, it can also create myriad potential legal liabilities.

It would therefore seem appropriate that within the process of investigation there be safeguards and mechanisms to reduce these risks. There are, and collectively that effort is known as a *litigation avoidance strategy*.

---

[1] 29 U.S.C. 654(a)(1).
[2] Title V of the Omnibus Drug Initiative of 1988.

This chapter will address federal and state mandates as well as case law at the federal and state levels relative to the implementation of this strategy. However, because our body of law is never static but always in process, if you are contemplating undercover I suggest legal counsel be sought and invited to join your investigative team. As I have repeatedly mentioned, undercover investigations in the workplace are complex and fraught with liability. Furthermore, because it is beyond the scope or intent of this book to address the specific laws of all 50 states, I have selected references mostly from the state of California. Because California has traditionally taken an aggressive approach toward protection of employee and individual rights, and has been the innovator behind much of today's tort law development, it serves as a suitable context for many of the important points I'm interested in making. By no means should this deter you from reading on. Although the pertinent statutes may differ somewhat in your jurisdiction, they are sufficiently uniform that what is covered in this chapter will be valuable to you.

Potential Liability for Failing to Investigate Reported Workplace Drug Abuse, Threats, and/or Assaults

In 1992, the National Crime Victimization Survey found that assaults while on duty at work represented approximately 11 percent of all violent crimes in the United States, while a sampling of 480 members of the Society of Human Resource Management revealed that one-third of their workplaces had experienced at least one known violent crime during the previous five years.[3] Homicide is the leading cause of death in the workplace in a number of states, including California, and in the District of Columbia. While the numbers represent a very small percentage of all workers, the liability associated with workplace homicide can be devastating to an organization both financially and, of course, in terms of its reputation.

Security professionals know that any threat of violence must be taken seriously. A threat or a seemingly minor assault that goes unchecked may well be a precursor to something far more serious. Experience tells us that most employees who kill a coworker or supervisor did not "just snap." In nearly every known case, the aggressor provided significant clues regarding his instability prior to the incident. His ultimate course of action and the resultant tragedy could have probably been averted had those around him considered the possibility that the threats were serious and taken appropriate and timely action. The cost of these errors can be staggering. The average cost of defending an inadequate security lawsuit exceeds $38,000

---

[3] Cal/OSHA Guidelines for Workplace Security (rev. 30 March 1995).

when the defendant business prevails. The cost is significantly greater if the case goes to trial. The average (nationwide) reported verdict for plaintiffs in wrongful death cases is $2.2 million. The average verdict in aggravated assault cases is approximately $1.2 million. Absent a verdict, settlements average $750,000.[4]

Victims (and survivors) of workplace violence often allege that the root of the problem is negligent hiring. For the claim to prevail, the plaintiff must prove (1) the existence of an employment relationship; (2) the employee's incompetence; (3) that the employer had actual or constructive knowledge of this incompetence; (4) that the employee's act or omission caused the injuries; and (5) that the employer's negligence in hiring or retaining the employee was the proximate cause of the injuries.[5] An action for negligent hiring may also be based upon the extent of the background investigation conducted by the employer, the employee's position and responsibilities, and the risk of harm to third parties posed by the employee.[6] At the same time, in California and elsewhere, significant obstacles stand in the way of conducting thorough employment background investigations. Employers in these jurisdictions, other than those hiring for a specific position that *statutorily requires* criminal background checks, are generally allowed access only to public records.[7]

What's more, there is no central repository for such records. Typically, each county or parish maintains its own records. The diligent employer therefore is faced with scouring the records of each county in which the prospect recently lived or passed through. A daunting task to say the least. Also in California, questions concerning convictions for marijuana-related offenses more than two years old are not allowed. Nor may an employer ask questions about arrests that did not result in convictions unless the applicant or employee is currently out on bail. California even prohibits (under Penal Code §11125) requiring any prospective employee to furnish a copy of their "rap sheet" (criminal record) or to even answer truthfully whether a rap sheet on the applicant exists.

Merely failing to conduct a thorough background investigation is not, however, sufficient grounds to hold an employer liable. The plaintiff must be able to produce evidence that there was negative information readily available that would have shown that the applicant posed a risk to the safety of others. If no such evidence exists, there can be no liability imposed on the employer.[8] Victims can sue for *negligent supervision* or *retention* once

---

[4] J. Chaney, S. Kaufer, and J. Mattman, eds., *Premises Security and Liability* (Laguna Beach CA: Workplace Violence Research Institute, 1997).

[5] Green and Reibstein, "It's 10 p.m., Do You Have to Know Where Your Employees Are?" 32 *Personnel Ad.* 70, 73 (April 1987).

[6] *Henley v. Prince George's County*, 305 Md. 320 (1986).

[7] See *Pittman v. City of Oakland*, 197 Cal. App. 3d 1037 (1988).

[8] See *Wasson v. Stracener*, 786 S.W.2d (Tex. Ct. App. 1990).

it was known or should have been known that the perpetrator was dangerous or otherwise unfit. For an employer to be found liable for negligent hiring, supervision, or retention, the offense need not be within the scope of employment but merely related somehow to the employment. In *Yunker v. Honeywell*, 496 N.W.2d 419 (Minn. Ct. App. 1993), the defendant rehired a former employee after he returned from a five-year prison term for strangling a female coworker to death. Not long after he was rehired, the employee was transferred twice due to his inability to get along with coworkers. After the second transfer, he threatened a female coworker with death for rejecting his romantic advances. Subsequently he voluntarily resigned after the woman reported the incident to her supervisor and requested a transfer. The day after his resignation, he went to the woman's home and shot her to death. Although the man was no longer an employee at the time of the murder, and the incident did not occur on the defendant's property, Honeywell was still found liable for negligent retention on the theory that Honeywell supervisors were well aware of the man's violent propensities yet exposed the victim to danger by failing to terminate the man after the two recent confrontations with coworkers.

Closely related to the tort of negligent retention is the tort of *negligent failure to warn.* Case law suggests that courts tend to impose liability for negligent failure to warn when the employer had specific knowledge about the violent propensities of an offender who had threatened a third party yet the defendant failed to warn them.[9]

More common is the claim of *intentional* or *negligent infliction of emotional distress.* This claim could arise from an employer's alleged reckless failure to immediately suspend an employee pending the results of an investigation when the subject of the investigation had in fact threatened others. Likewise, because employers have a duty to maintain a safe workplace, a claim of negligent infliction of emotional distress could be brought by both the victim(s) and those who witnessed a particularly violent workplace incident.

Another exposure has its source in the common employee handbook or manual. If the manual states that it is the company's policy to maintain a safe and drug-free workplace for employees, and if a known drug abuser-employee assaults a coworker, the injured worker may prosecute a claim for *breach of implied contract.* The plaintiff need only point out that the provision in the handbook constitutes a contract between the employer and the employee, and that the employee relied on that contract. The same set of circumstances might prompt another attorney to draft a complaint for damages based on employer *fraud and misrepresentation.*

Another legal theory that has been widely used by victims as the basis of lawsuits against employers, and that is recognized in virtually all states,

---

[9] See *Tarasoff v. Regents of University of California*, 17 Cal.3d 425, 436 (1976).

is the *doctrine of respondeat superior*. Under this theory, the employer can be held vicariously liable for the acts of employees when the offense was committed within the scope of employment. Broadly this theory asserts that the offender used his position in committing the misdeed or that the employer in any way benefited from not addressing the misdeed. A good example is the recent highly publicized case involving the chief executive officer (CEO) of a California corporation. Allegedly, the company's board of directors looked the other way as claims of sexual harassment mounted against the CEO. The claim asserted that while the CEO was not questioned regarding his misconduct, the organization posted huge profits *benefiting both the board and stockholders.*[10] Another example is the hypothetical nightclub manager who directs a bouncer to eject a patron who ends up getting injured in the process. While the bouncer clearly may have used excessive force, his actions were the result of instructions from the manager. Another example of the application of respondeat superior is the employee-substance abuser who, in the course of his employment, deals illegal drugs that ultimately cause the injury of another person. Again, the employer may be liable.

Legal Responsibilities of Employers Who Hire Private Investigative Firms

Based on the general principles of agency, the employer who hires a private investigative firm to conduct employee investigations can potentially be held liable for violations of the law that the employer authorized, either implicitly or expressly. The employer can also be held liable if found to have been negligent in its selection of an investigative firm.

A number of California appellate cases, most notably *Noble v. Sears, Roebuck & Co.*, 33 Cal. App. 3d 654 (1973), held that "the hirer of a detective agency for either a single investigation or for the protection of property, may be liable for the intentional torts of employees of the private detective agency committed in the course of employment." Id. at 663. This particular case involved a retail department store that hired private detectives to obtain information about someone who had allegedly been injured on the store's property. The detectives gained admittance to the plaintiff's hospital room and obtained information from the plaintiff through deception. *Solis v. Southern Cal. Rapid Transit Dist.*, 105 Cal. App. 3d 382 (1980), confirmed that persons or entities that retain private investigators may potentially be held liable for tortious invasion of privacy when the investigators conduct what the court referred to as an "unreasonably intrusive investigation" and obtain information by deception.

---

[10] Horn, Miriam, "Sex & the CEO", *U.S. News & World Report*, 6 July 1998, pp. 32–40.

Although not involving undercover per se, an insurance company was sued by a workers' compensation claimant after it came to light that the insurance company hired a private detective agency to investigate the activities of the claimant and to obtain photographs of her. Ultimately, one of the detectives deceived and enticed the claimant into a romantic relationship for the purpose of filming her. The claimant's lawsuit against the insurance company eventually reached the California Supreme Court. See *Unruh v. Truck Ins. Exch.*, 7 Cal. 3d 616 (1972). The court found that the insurer had embarked on a "deceitful course of conduct, involving intentional and willful assault, battery, and intentional infliction of emotional distress" on the plaintiff. Because of cases like this, corporate and insurance defense attorneys increasingly suggest their clients require indemnification agreements from vendors providing investigative services.

Avoiding Discrimination Lawsuits

Americans with Disabilities Act

In July 1994, every American business of 15 or more employees became subject to the Americans with Disabilities Act (ADA), 42 U.S.C. §12101 (see Appendix H). The ADA allows disabled workers to bring legal actions for discrimination against employers and seek damages up to $300,000. What's surprising is that the Equal Employment Opportunity Commission (EEOC), charged with enforcing the ADA, reports that 87 percent of the ADA-based complaints it receives are from people who are already employed as opposed to applicants claiming hiring discrimination.[11] The provisions of the ADA protect individuals (1) with a physical or mental impairment that substantially limits one or more of the major life activities of the individual; (2) who have a record of such impairment; and (3) who are perceived as having such an impairment. The ADA prohibits employers from discriminating against a "qualified individual with a disability" in job applications; hiring; advancement and discharge; compensation; job training; and other terms, conditions, and privileges of employment. 42 U.S.C. §12112. A "qualified individual with a disability" is one who, with or without *reasonable accommodation*, can perform the essential functions of an assigned position. Employers are allowed under the ADA to test for drug use, but they may not discriminate against a person who has successfully completed a drug rehabilitation program and who no longer uses illegal drugs. Current drug users are not protected.

The ADA is less specific about alcohol use and alcoholism.

There have also been cases in which an employee was alleged to have made serious threats and/or actually assaulted a coworker only to later have

---

[11] Joseph P. Shapiro, "The Americans with Minor Disabilities Act", *U.S. News & World Report*, July 6, 1998, pp. 41, 42.

sought protection claiming a mental disability. In *Adams v. Alderson*, 723 F. Supp. 1531 (D.D.C. 1989), *aff'd*, 1190 WL 45737 (D.C. Cir. 1990), the court determined that under the Federal Rehabilitation Act of 1973, an employee who physically assaulted his supervisor because of an adjustment disorder was not "otherwise qualified" and entitled to an accommodation from his government employer. It therefore seems that the danger posed by one's inability to control violent urges outweighs the need for job protection because of a perceived mental disability.

Title VII of the Civil Rights Act of 1964

The Civil Rights Act of 1964 attempted to eliminate gender and race discrimination in the workplace. Title VII of the Act criminalizes discrimination in hiring, firing, promoting, or giving raises or other benefits because of an employee's race, gender, color, religion, or national origin. While this federal law is limited to employers with fifteen or more employees, most states have similar laws affecting all employers.

To qualify as a discrimination case, one of two factors must be present. The first is known as *disparate* or *different treatment* of a member of a protected class based solely upon that difference. The second factor is *disparate impact*, which most often occurs when a company has a policy or administers a test that, usually unintentionally, results in a negative impact on an entire protected class of applicants or employees. A simple example that has been battled in courts around the nation is height requirements for firefighters, which have been held to be discriminatory against women and Asians of both sexes, who are on average shorter than white and black males. Similarly, a freight delivery company, which requires all drivers to be able to lift and carry 200-pound packages, could conceivably be sued under Title VII for discrimination against women.

Disparate sentencing for convictions for the possession of crack cocaine and powdered cocaine has brought charges of racial discrimination across the nation. The suits are based on the claim that powdered cocaine is a drug of choice among the economically advantaged whites, while crack cocaine, its cheaper counterpart, is used primarily by minorities. Thus in both engineering its investigations and meting out discipline, employers must ensure that company policies and practices are applied equally to all individuals and classes.

Civil Rights Act of 1991

Under the Civil Rights Act of 1991, employers have the burden of proof when their employment practices are challenged and must show that such practices are "job related and consistent with business necessity." For example, the presumption that most of the young Hispanic or black male warehouse workers tend to stick to themselves, speak in dialect, and wear a popular style of clothing sometimes associated with gangs would not constitute a sufficient basis on which to launch an investigation. In contrast, the presence of gang graffiti on company property, the factioning of workers into apparent rival groups, evidence of theft or illegal drug use, or credible reports of gang activity may be legitimate reasons to begin such an investigation. The rationale, of course, is that an investigative effort under these circumstances is reasonable for the safety of other workers and in view of the welfare of the company as a whole. Clearly the investigation would then rely on evidence of illegal activity rather than be based on suspicions about race and cultural differences. Again, this is why establishing and recording the investigation's objectives at the onset are so important. The following checklist provides a guide for assessing whether your organization has taken solid steps toward safeguarding against discrimination claims:

1. Does the company investigate suspicious activity without regard to race, color, sex, or national origin?
2. Has the company informed all employees of its drug and alcohol policies and made it clear that the policies will be strictly enforced?
3. Are substance abuse problems in management ignored while enforced elsewhere?
4. Is discipline consistently applied at all levels of the organization?
5. Are opportunities for rehabilitation consistent among all levels of employees?

Sexual Harassment

According to a 1988 survey, over 90 percent of Fortune 500 companies have received sexual harassment complaints; over 33 percent of them have been sued; and almost 25 percent have been sued more than once for sexual harassment.[12] The survey noted that an immediate supervisor or upper-level manager was the alleged harasser in two-thirds of the reported incidents, and that the human resource managers of these companies believed that about two-thirds of the claims were valid.

The EEOC has defined two categories of sexual harassment. The first is called *quid pro quo harassment.*" This claim arises, for example, when a supervisor conditions employment benefits or opportunities on the return of sexual favors to him. The other type of sexual harassment, *hostile environment harassment,* occurs when an employer creates, or allows to be created, a pattern of conduct pertaining to sex that contributes to an unpleasant, intolerable, or hostile work environment.

---

[12] "Enforcement Guidance," EEOC, May 1994.

Where harassment is pervasive and the employer fails to discover it, it will be held to have *constructive knowledge* of the harassment See *Hall v. Gus Constr. Co., Inc.*, 842 F2d 1010 (8th Cir. 1988). If the employer is determined to have actual or constructive knowledge of the harassment and fails to take immediate and appropriate corrective action, it will be held liable.[13]

The investigation of sexual harassment claims presents a unique set of problems. The EEOC requires that a thorough investigation of complaints be conducted, yet the nature of a sexual harassment claim is such that it is particularly difficult to investigate adequately without infringing upon the privacy rights of both the accused and the accuser. Courts have made it clear, however, that a prompt and thorough investigation on the part of the employer and the taking of remedial action can limit the damages if conducted properly. Employers should investigate sexual harassment complaints whether the complaint is made formally or not.

Because of the sensitive nature of sexual harassment investigations, and the potential for defamation lawsuits, each witness should be admonished to not discuss the matter with anyone other than the investigator. The investigator should emphasize that the purpose of the investigation is to get to the truth and that the best way of doing that is for everyone to feel assured that whatever they say to the investigator will remain as confidential as possible.

In the event that the investigation leads to disciplinary action, well-written and complete records of the investigation will support the employer's decision should any disciplined employee seek legal action.[14] These records will also be necessary if the investigation is inconclusive and the claimant subsequently files a Title VII sex discrimination lawsuit.

Since many claims of sexual harassment involve incidents that allegedly occur between two people without the presence of witnesses, such charges sometimes boil down to one person's word against another's, and no conclusion can be reached as to the truth of the allegations. Sometimes it is just an honest difference of interpretation of events. It is up to the employer, in any event, to reiterate the company's sexual harassment policy and to decide what disciplinary action, if any, is appropriate. Even in cases where no definitive conclusion can be reached, it is sometimes appropriate for the employer to offer to laterally transfer one of the parties, if possible, to alleviate the chance of future problems. At the very least, in most cases it can be concluded (and possibly verified by the undercover) that there has

---

[13] R. Sanaroff, "Sexual Harassment in the Fortune 500," *Working Woman*, 18 December 1988, p. 69.
[14] EEOC Manual, at 3279.

been some kind of conflict between the claimant and the alleged harasser that needs to be addressed.

Avoiding Unfair Labor Practice Claims

Under the National Labor Relations Act (NLRA) employees have the right to form, join, and assist unions. Any interference with, restraining, or coercing employees in regard to a protected activity is a violation of the Act and can subject the offending employer to heavy fines and sanctions. As an acting agent of the employer, the investigation team must be particularly careful to avoid even the appearance of attempting to interfere with union activity. Under no circumstances may any employer conduct surveillance on or otherwise monitor employees' union activities. Violations of these basic rights may subject both the employer and the investigative agency to claims of unfair labor practices.

The undercover investigator working in a union environment must know what constitutes an unfair labor practice as well as any provisions of the specific union contract under which he is working. Great care should be taken by the operative to exclude inappropriate information or make mention of union activities in notes or reports. As mentioned previously, I make it a practice to disallow even the word *union* in my operative's reports.

Union employees on strike have the right to picket their employer's premises but not to trespass on the premises during the strike. Nonstriking employees have the right to protect their safety by refusing to cross a picket line. Employees who strike over safety issues or unfair labor practices must be rehired when the strike is over, except for those who are convicted of crimes, including trespassing, during a strike or lockout. Rehiring of those convicted of crimes and those who strike for reasons other than safety issues or unfair labor practices is at the discretion of the employer.

Weingarten

In *NLRB v. Weingarten, Inc.*, 420 U.S. 241 (1975), the Supreme Court ruled than an employee is entitled to ask for and receive union representation at an employer's investigatory interview if the employee reasonably believes that the interview might result in disciplinary action against him or termination. Thus, the right to representation must not be offered by the employer but rather is triggered upon the worker's request. An employer who disciplines or terminates an employee for refusing to participate in an investigatory interview without a union representative present is in violation of §8(a)(1) of the Act.

Once the employee has requested union representation at the interview, the employer must either grant the request or dispense with or discontinue the interview unless the employee voluntarily agrees to participate after being informed by the employer or another party that he has the right to not participate without union representation. The employee does *not* have the right to union representation at a meeting held solely for the purpose of informing the employee about, and acting upon, a disciplinary decision that was made prior to that meeting. The best and safest practice for the employer, then, is to do nothing until the request for representation is made. If and when such a request is made, document it and either provide the representative or allow the employee to make the decision whether to continue without it. Regardless of the choice, document it. Also document the time and response to the request. If witnesses are used, have them do the same thing.

Weingarten also provides that the employer can insist on hearing only the employee's account of the incident or insist that the union representative hold his comments until the end of the interview. The employer *cannot require* that the representative remain silent unless the representative is present only because of a collective bargaining agreement that allows him to be there. The Supreme Court also ruled that the employer need not reinstate the employee with back pay in response to the employer's violation of *Weingarten* rights if some independent evidence, obtained *other* than through the unlawful interview, shows that the discipline was for good cause.

The NLRB has also held that employees do not have the right to demand union representation at a meeting that is not an investigatory interview, and that the employer may discipline employees who refuse to participate under those circumstances. Additionally, the NLRB has ruled that an employer may discharge an employee who refuses to meet with the employer in a private office to discuss whether the interview will be held without union representation.

As an interesting note on the seriousness in which existing collective bargaining agreements must be regarded, five Courts of Appeal are in agreement with the Third Circuit's recent ruling that if a request for accommodation under the ADA is made by a disabled employee, and the accommodation requested is in conflict with an existing collective bargaining agreement, the employer does not have to provide the accommodation.[15] Collective bargaining agreements take precedence even over the requirements of the ADA.[16]

---

[15] See *Whitaker v. Carney*, 778 F.2d 216, 222 (5th Cir. 1985), *cert. denied*, 479 U.S. 813 (1986).
[16] NIBM, "ADA: No Accommodation Needed in Conflict with Union Pact," *You and the Law*, vol. 28, no. 3 (March 1998).

Workplace Privacy

An understanding of the privacy rights of individuals in our country is fundamental to the proper engineering of any workplace investigation. The concept of invasion of privacy was first contemplated in the Fourth Amendment of the U.S. Constitution as a protection against unreasonable searches and seizures. Two hundred years later, the implications of the Fourth Amendment are still being interpreted by our courts at both the federal and state levels.

In 1989, Fourth Amendment issues entered into the debate over government-mandated drug-testing programs. *National Treasury Employees v. Von Raab*, 489 U.S. 656 (1989), involved applicants and employees seeking sensitive positions with the U.S. Customs Service who were required to produce urine specimens for drug screening purposes. The Court upheld the testing as "reasonable" under the Fourth Amendment because the government had a compelling interest in preventing drug users from holding positions involved in the interception of illegal drugs. Additionally, many of these employees were required to carry firearms. Under these circumstances, the Court held that the need for drug testing by the government outweighed the need for privacy on the part of applicants and employees in these sensitive positions. The principle was laid forth that employees in sensitive positions have a diminished expectation of privacy.

The Supreme Court again upheld mandatory testing, this time of blood, urine, and/or breath, when railway workers are involved in an accident or when a supervisor has a reasonable suspicion that the acts or omissions of the employee contributed to the accident. In *Skinner v. Railway Labor Executives Assn.*, 489 U.S. 602 (1989), the Court found that ensuring the safety of the public outweighs the employees' expectation of privacy. Both cases were decided on the basis of the 1987 case *O'Connor v. Ortega*, 480 U.S. 709 (1987), where the Court propounded a balancing test that mandates that the "invasion of the employee's legitimate expectations of privacy" be balanced against "the government's need for supervision, control and the efficient operation of the workplace." While these Supreme Court decisions apply only to government workplaces, the balancing test of *O'Connor* has been applied to a number of state privacy cases where the actions of a private employer were at issue.

The state constitutions of Alaska, Arizona, California, Florida, Hawaii, Illinois, Louisiana, Montana, South Carolina, and Washington address the right to privacy or recognize a right to freedom from intrusion into one's private affairs. The California Constitution, art. I, §1, states: "All people . . . have inalienable rights. Among these are enjoying and defending life and liberty, . . . and pursuing and obtaining safety, happiness, and privacy."

However, in *Nader v. General Motors* (1970), the court noted that "the mere observation of the plaintiff in a public place does not amount to an invasion of privacy. But, under certain circumstances, surveillance may be so overzealous as to render it actionable." The U.S. District Court of New York in 1972 reinforced the concept that legal action is appropriate when surveillance tactics cross the line and become an invasion of privacy. The case involved Jacqueline Kennedy Onassis and celebrity photographer Ron Galella, who had allegedly monitored Mrs. Onassis's activities by corrupting doormen, romancing Mrs. Onassis's personal maid, intruding into her children's schools through deception, and visiting shops and restaurants in order to find out what she purchased. The court held that Mr. Galella's activities were all exclusively for the "purpose of gathering information of a private and confidential nature" and were thus actionable on the grounds that the photographer "[had] no right to invade [the] defendant's right of privacy."

Most of the laws regarding privacy that apply to the private sector are derived from case law on the state level. The majority of states recognize a common law right to privacy, with invasion of that privacy as a legitimate basis for a lawsuit. Twenty states have adopted the definition of the right to privacy as formulated in the Restatement (Second) of Torts §652(a):

(1) One who invades the right to privacy of another is subject to liability for the resulting harm to the interests of the other;
(2) the right to privacy is invaded by:
    (a) unreasonable intrusion upon the seclusion of another; or
    (b) appropriation of the other's name or likeness; or
    (c) unreasonable publicity of facts of another's private life; or
    (d) false light publicity.

Under *Hill v. NCAA*, 7 Cal. 4th 1 (1994), the California Supreme Court set a new standard for invasion of privacy claims, a standard that is more favorable to employers than earlier California case law which was based on the 1987 *Ortega* standard of "compelling interest." *Hill* established that a private employer may be held liable for invasion of privacy only if the plaintiff can establish (1) a legally protected privacy interest; (2) a reasonable expectation of privacy; and (3) conduct by the defendant constituting a serious invasion of a privacy interest. The decision in *Hill* noted that "[p]rivate entities pursue private ends and interests" and would virtually never be able to show a "compelling public interest" for intrusions on individual privacy. The court concluded that a rigid and absolute definition of privacy rights, to the exclusion of practical and legitimate business concerns, has no foundation in the law. Five out of the seven justices in *Hill* viewed the "compelling interest" federal standard as unduly inflexible and placed the burden of proof on the plaintiff.

Some courts have ruled that particular acts of invasion of privacy constitute a violation of public policy, or are against the public good. Here are several examples in which a public policy violation claim prevailed:

- An employee was terminated for refusing to take a polygraph test that was prohibited by state law (*Perks v. Firestone Tire & Rubber Co.*, 611 F.2d 1363 (3d Cir. 1979))
- A nurse was terminated for refusing to expose her buttocks in front of an audience while on a rafting trip with coworkers (*Wagenseller v. Scottsdale Memorial Hosp.*, 147 Ariz. 370 (1985))
- A clerical worker, in a nonsafety-related position, was terminated for refusing to submit to a random drug test (*Luck v. Southern Pac. Transp. Co.*, 218 Cal. App. 3d 1 (1990), *cert. denied*, 498 U.S. 939 (1990))

The question of course is how does the right of privacy affect workplace undercover. The short answer is that it does not. However, the investigative process must be reasonable and the information collected must fill legitimate business needs. Clearly, using undercover for the purpose of gathering information regarding a suspected drug problem would be acceptable. Using undercover to learn of an employee's political leanings and union sympathies would not be acceptable. The objectives of the investigation must fall within permissible purposes and the process must be reasonable. The employer, however, can hedge its position and reduce its liability by closely monitoring the investigation process and not permitting the collection of information that suggests in even the slightest way a violation of one's reasonable expectation of privacy.

My investigators practice this precaution regularly. We strictly monitor the amount of time the operative spends with the subject *away from work*. We rarely allow them to visit a subject in his home. We minimize the off-duty time the operative spends on the case with his subjects even in a public place like a bar. Because our investigations typically focus on some form of "workplace misconduct," it is inconsistent for our operatives to spend any significant amount of time with the subjects outside the workplace—even if that off-duty time would be spent further developing the operative's cover. This runs contrary to the practice of many of our competitors. Many colleagues maintain that "bar time" and many other off-duty activities are essential to the success of the case and "getting offenders" that are too smart to commit their crimes in the workplace. If that is in fact the case, then what is the real purpose of their investigation? Are they attempting to solve a workplace problem for a private employer or enforce public law for the government?

All Americans should expect and enjoy the right of privacy. Don't trample the rights of others in the name of investigation or by twisting logic to think you're right simply because you're fighting crime. Be sensible and respect the rights of all people, including those you investigate.

Fingerprints and Photographs

There are no specific federal restrictions on employers' obtaining employee fingerprints and photographs, but some states have actually addressed how employers can use fingerprints and photographs. California Labor Code §1051 prohibits employers from requiring applicants or employees to furnish photographs or fingerprints as a condition of employment if they are going to be given to a third party who could use them with adverse effects for the employee. Simply stated, employers can collect employee fingerprints and photographs for their own use, but should avoid supplying them to anyone outside of the organization unless otherwise directed to do so (as in the case of a court order).

If fingerprints or photographs are required by the employer, the employee should be requested to furnish them only after an offer of employment has been made. To request them prior to an offer of employment could expose the employer to a discrimination claim.

Drug and Alcohol Testing

The law as it applies to drug testing is continually evolving. Since drug testing involves what many claim to be a highly invasive procedure through the scientific examination of bodily fluids, an employer contemplating such testing would be well advised to seek the advice of a labor and employment law attorney before proceeding. As is true with many of the investigative topics discussed in this book, state laws vary, often from one year to the next. In regard to drug testing, some cities, such as Berkeley, California and Boulder, Colorado, have instituted tighter restrictions on pre-employment drug testing than are required by their states. Regardless, drug testing by most private employers will not give rise to Fourth Amendment rights prohibiting unreasonable searches and seizures and the requirement of reasonable suspicion. Only *public* employers (federal, state, county, or city) are subject to Fourth Amendment restrictions. However, private employers are subject to other restrictions as mentioned and should nevertheless proceed cautiously.

Drug testing may also be required. Under the Omnibus Transportation Employee Testing Act (OTETA), five operating administrations under the federal Department of Transportation have instituted rules requiring alcohol and drug testing for employees under their auspices. These administrations are as follows:

- Federal Aviation Administration (FAA)
- Federal Highway Administration (FHWA)
- Federal Railroad Administration (FRA)
- Federal Transit Administration (FTA)
- Research and Special Programs Administration (RSPA)

New regulations imposed by the FHA apply to about 7 million *interstate* and *intrastate* drivers. Testing for drugs and alcohol are no longer required as part of a physical exam, but testing is required before returning to duty after the employee has been disciplined in relation to on-the-job drug or alcohol use. Let's look a little closer.

Pre-employment drug testing is imposed by many employers as a condition of employment. This requirement has been challenged on both federal and state levels, including the two bellwether states, New York and California. The New York state court, however, disapproved of pre-employment drug testing policies that do not advise the applicant of his or her right to obtain the original specimen and have it independently tested nor advise of the date when a specimen that tested positive would be destroyed. A California Court of Appeal in *Wilkinson v. Times Mirror Corp.*, 215 Cal. App. 3d 1034 (1989), held that a private employer's pre-employment drug and alcohol testing procedure did not violate the constitutional privacy rights of job applicants. The court also balanced the interests of the employer with the privacy issues of the applicant and noted that the policy in question was minimally intrusive because

1. The employer gave advance notice
2. There was guaranteed confidentiality
3. A follow-up report was given to the applicant
4. There was an opportunity to question and challenge test results
5. The specimens were collected by a third party in a medical setting
6. Rejected applicants could reapply after six months

In 1997, the California Supreme court analyzed the constitutionality of the city of Glendale's policy of mandatory urinalysis drug and alcohol testing for individuals who have conditionally been offered new positions with the city, encompassing both applicants and existing employees approved for promotion to new positions. The court held that drug testing was constitutional (in accordance with both the federal and state Constitutions) with respect to applicants, but *invalid* as applied to current employees seeking approval for promotion.

The ADA prohibits medical testing prior to an offer of employment; however, a test for *illegal* drugs is not considered a medical test under the Act. In order to avoid a conflict with the requirements of the ADA, any required pre-employment drug test must be designed to accurately identify only illegal drugs and cannot be given in conjunction with a physical exam. The ADA also disallows alcohol testing prior to an offer of employment.

Routine Drug and/or Alcohol Testing during Periodic Physical Exams

The ADA requires that employee physical exams must be voluntary or job-related and consistent with business necessity. Employees should be notified that drug and/or alcohol tests will be administered during physical exams if it is a requirement of continued employment. However, California's Confidentiality of Medical Information Act (California Civil Code §56.20–56.245) requires that an employer must obtain authorization from the employee before disclosing medical information relating to that employee. This little-known law also provides that "no employee shall be discriminated against in terms or conditions of employment due to that employee's refusal to sign an authorization" (California Civil Code §56.20(b)). A California employer cannot terminate an employee solely for refusal to authorize a drug or alcohol test or any other medical test, but the employer is allowed to inquire of the physician as to whether the employee is able to perform his job duties satisfactorily.

In contrast, Texas law requires an employee to consent to a drug test ordered by his employer as a condition of continued employment, and an at-will employee may be terminated for refusing to consent to a drug test so long as the drug test policy is reasonable. See *Farrington v. Sysco Food Servs., Inc.*, 865 S.W.2d 247 (Tex. Ct. App. 1993, *writ denied*); *Jennings v. Minco Technology Labs, Inc.*, 756 S.W.2d 497 (Tex. Ct. App. 1989, *writ denied*). Further, the state of Texas can deny unemployment compensation to any worker fired for refusing to submit to a required drug test.[17] Employers in any state where refusal to submit to drug testing carries serious consequences for the employee should make certain to protect themselves from potential legal action by obtaining *written consent* prior to testing.

Federal courts have found that periodic drug testing is not a violation of the Fourth Amendment prohibition against unreasonable searches and seizures and thus have approved of drug testing as a part of annual or periodic physical exams.[18]

Reasonable Suspicion Drug and/or Alcohol Testing

Under the ADA, all alcohol testing of current employees must be limited to reasonable suspicion testing or some other legitimate business reason. With either drug or alcohol testing, limiting testing to situations where reasonable suspicion exists should minimize legal challenges. The courts have identified what constitutes "reasonable suspicion" several times.

The FHA, in regulating drug testing of truck drivers, puts forth in 40 C.F.R. §382.307(a) that reasonable suspicion must be based on "specific, contemporaneous, articulable observations concerning appearance, behavior, speech or body odors of the driver." The Code further states that observations "may include indications of the chronic and withdrawal

---

[17] See *Kralik v. Durbin*, CA 3, No. 97-3106 (1997).
[18] See *Kaminiski v. Texas Employment Commn.*, 848 S.W.2d 811 (Tex. Ct. App. 1993).

effects of controlled substances." 49 C.F.R. §382.307(b). The Ninth Circuit, in two separate cases, held that in some safety-sensitive or security-sensitive circumstances, reasonable suspicion may be based on suspicion of *off-duty* drug use.[19] Refusal to submit to reasonable suspicion testing, when the testing policy is deemed to be appropriate, has been held to be appropriate grounds for termination of the employee.[20]

Postaccident Drug and/or Alcohol Testing

The OTETA, applying to airline pilots, air traffic controllers, railway workers, truck drivers, and so forth, requires postaccident drug and/or alcohol testing following certain types of accidents. The FHA defines an accident that will trigger testing as involving the loss of human life or for which the driver receives a citation under state or local law for a moving traffic violation. 40 C.F.R. §382.303(a). Generally, testing required of employees suspected of being under the influence when an accident occurred has not been successfully challenged in federal or state courts and is considered by many authorities as one of the safest circumstances under which employers can test employees.

Random Drug and/or Alcohol Testing

Although unannounced random drug testing appears to be the most effective means of detecting and deterring drug and alcohol use among employees, it is the most controversial. Currently, the only states that statutorily affirm the use of random testing of employees in nonsafety-sensitive positions are Arizona, Louisiana, and Oklahoma. As noted above, Texas allows drug testing, including random testing, with employee consent, and refusal to consent can be grounds for termination and denial of unemployment benefits. The California Supreme Court held in it's review of *Hill v. NCAA*, 7 Cal. 4th 1 (1994), that the NCAA's random drug testing program, which required student athletes to provide a urine sample in the presence of a same-sex witness, did not constitute an invasion of privacy according to the state Constitution. Although the court stated that private entities are covered by the constitutional privacy guarantee passed by California voters in 1972, private businesses need not always meet the strict standards imposed on government when infringing on privacy. The government must show *compelling* reasons, but private entities in many cases need only show that the invasion of privacy is justified by *legitimate business* interests and needs.

---

[19] See *International Bhd. of Teamsters v. DOT*, 932 F.2d 1292 (9th Cir. 1991); *Amalgamated Transit Union Div. 1279 v. Cambria County Transit Auth.*, 691 F. Supp. 898 (W.D. Pa. 1988).
[20] *American Fedn. of Govt. Employees v. Roberts*, 9 F.3d 1464 (9th Cir. 1993); *American Fedn. of Govt. Employees v. Martin*, 969 F.2d 788 (9th Cir. 1992).

While the *Hill* standards on random drug testing in California have, at the time of this writing, yet to be challenged in the private employment setting, the trend of California courts seems to be to recognize a legitimate need for employee drug testing as long as policies and procedures are reasonable according to the following standards:

- Testing of applicants to whom a conditional offer of employment has been made
- Testing of current employees on reasonable suspicion
- Random or periodic testing of employees in safety-sensitive positions[21]

However, the following conditions apply:

- Individuals to be tested are given advance notice of the test
- Proper chain-of-custody procedures are utilized
- Samples are tested at competent laboratories
- Means of analysis and/or confirmation is by gas chromatography/mass spectrometry or the most accurate method available as of the date of the testing
- Results are strictly confidential with the sole exception of informing only those with a need to know

Case law has reinforced employers' right to perform random drug testing for certain types of positions beyond those that fall under the authority of the Department of Transportation. In *Taylor v. O'Grady*, 888 F.2d 1189 (7th Cir. 1989), the court upheld mandatory, annual urine testing of correctional officers and supervisors because they had a reasonable opportunity to smuggle drugs into the inmate population and had access to firearms. In 1991 a federal district court held that mandatory drug and alcohol testing of hospital employees was constitutional when the affected employees were involved in "direct, hands-on patient care."[22]

Negligence in Administering Drug Tests

Another exposure an employer faces arises from the principle of agency in the event of its negligent selection of a testing laboratory. The employer can be liable under a negligence theory if (1) the drug tests were not conducted in accordance with appropriate protocol and standards; (2) the tests were susceptible to serious inaccuracies because of improper handling, reporting, or documentation; or (3) the test results were maintained negligently, resulting in the dissemination of inaccurate or incomplete

---

[21] *Rawlings v. Police Dept., Jersey City, New Jersey*, 133 N.J. 182 (1993).
[22] N. Abell, L. Edwards, E. Gordon, and S. Sonnenberg, *Issues in Workplace Privacy and Investigations*, Paul, Hastings, Janofsky, and Walker (Santa Monica 1995).

information.[23] A laboratory has a duty of reasonable care in conducting employer-mandated drug tests.[24]

Testing as a Condition of Returning to Work after Rehabilitation

Some state statutes require that the employer attempt to rehabilitate employees who abuse drugs or alcohol, prior to or in lieu of termination on the grounds of substance abuse.[25] Employers commonly require drug testing as a condition of returning to work during and/or after an employer-referred rehabilitation program. Particularly in safety-sensitive positions, substance abuse professionals typically recommend that the employee who has recently been in a rehabilitation program be subject to unannounced alcohol and/or drug testing as one incentive for keeping clean and sober. It is likely that the employee who has been in such a program recognizes the need for testing and will consent to future testing.

Visual or Video Surveillance

In spite of recent court rulings that tend to favor the employer over absolute privacy rights, the safest course of action during both drug testing and investigations is to conduct them as unobtrusively and with as little invasiveness as possible and to generally not allow surveillance in areas where employees have a *reasonable expectation of privacy*, such as private offices, restrooms, and locker rooms.

The use of undercover investigation to discover information about such illegal activities as theft and drug use must be handled with the utmost of care since both the investigative agency and the employer can be exposed to invasion of privacy and intentional infliction of emotional distress claims. Operatives must be clearly instructed to stay strictly within the bounds of what is permissible according to both state statutes and applicable case law. In drug investigations, operatives must steer clear of initiating or participating in any criminal activities unless permitted to do so by law enforcement. Under such circumstances, as detailed in prior chapters, the investigator must work under the direct supervision and direction of the controlling law enforcement agency. Theft investigations are nowhere as complicated; however, unreasonably intruding into the private lives and activities of the subject beyond that which is necessary to further the investigation may give rise to privacy claims. The undercover investigation must be engineered to minimize such intrusions and effectively justify them when they occur.

---

[23] *Kemp v. Claiborne County Hosp.*, 763 F. Supp. 1362 (S.D. Miss. 1991).

[24] M. S. McDonald and J. K. Staples, *Responding to Drugs and Alcohol in the Workplace*, Littler, Mendelson, Fastiff, Tichy & Mathiason (1995).

[25] See *Willis v. Roche Biomedical Labs., Inc.*, 21 F.3d 1368 (5th Cir. 1994).

In *Robinson v. Hewlett-Packard Co.*, 183 Cal. App. 3d 1108 (1986), the plaintiff sued for invasion of privacy based on his claim that his employer had him followed during an investigation. Although the claim was rejected because the plaintiff could not prove that he had been followed, the court implied that had he been able to establish this claim, then his allegation could have been a cause of action—the employer could have been liable for an invasion of privacy not necessary to effectively further the factfinding process or achieve the objectives of the investigation.

However, employers do have legitimate business reasons for monitoring and watching employees. Privacy issues rarely arise when employers monitor actual work activities. It is the monitoring of personal and private behavior and communication that normally causes the employee to feel violated and to seek legal action.

The least objectionable use of monitoring and surveillance by employers is monitoring work activities for the purpose of giving the employer an objective record of performance and productivity that can be used for employee evaluations. As long as all employees are monitored and held to the same standards, using these procedures for evaluation purposes can actually help eliminate charges of discrimination or favoritism by employers in disciplining or promoting workers.

Providing a safe and crime-free workplace is perhaps the most compelling justification for monitoring employees and conducting surveillance when appropriate. It is widely held that monitoring and surveillance of employees while at work can detect and/or deter illegal activity on the premises, including the staging of "accidents" in order to file fraudulent workers' compensation claims, assaultive behavior, use of drugs and alcohol in the workplace, and theft. Even the surveillance of government employees (a group that typically enjoys expanded rights relative to search and seizure) in work areas, conducted with their knowledge, does not invoke Fourth Amendment privacy issues because there is no expectation of privacy in such circumstances. In 1992 a postal employee unsuccessfully sued when the employer focused a camera in a work area specifically on him after becoming suspicious of his behavior. *United States v. O'Reilly*, 7 IER Cases 665 (E.D. Pa. 1992).

Another case involving the U.S. Postal Service turned out quite differently because the surveillance camera was hidden in an employee break room. The court held that because the break room was not a public area, the employees had a reasonable expectation of privacy. The court also noted that video surveillance was more intrusive than other types of surveillance and, as a result, the government's showing of necessity must be very high to justify this *extraordinarily intrusive* method. *State v. Bonnell*, 856 P.2d 1265 (1993).

Interestingly, video surveillance is not regulated by most states, but states that have a constitutional or statutory right to privacy, including California, have a basis on which employees in the private sector can make privacy claims. For example, in California a video recorder is a "recording device" according to the Invasion of Privacy Act, Cal. Penal Code §632. The Act sets forth criminal penalties for anyone (except those gathering evidence of a crime) who records confidential communication without the consent of all parties. However, California has no explicit limitations on visual or video surveillance in the workplace. Other states may. Limitations on surveillance by employers, or their agent, are primarily derived from case law. The following two California cases are typical of those in any of the states that have a constitutional or statutory right to privacy:

- A California appellate court held that surveillance of a dressing room that could easily be observed from an adjoining corridor did not constitute an invasion of privacy (*In re Deborah C.*, 30 Cal.3d 125 (1981))
- A department store clerk sued her employer when she learned that the employer had placed a hidden camera in a storeroom that contained a safe, a sink, and a phone. Some of the employees used the room for a variety of personal activities including confidential conversations, changing clothes and for personal hygiene. The jury rejected the claim that the employees had a legitimate expectation of privacy in the room since, as a storeroom, it was not an area that was in any way designated for private activities of employees

Employers and agents should be aware that in 1997 the NLRB ruled that an employer must bargain with its employees' union in advance about the installation and use of hidden surveillance cameras in the workplace.[26] The case came about when an employee reported his discovery of a hidden camera in the air vent of a restroom to a union steward who, in turn, reported the hidden camera to the union's officers. The human resource manager reported to one of the union's officers that the camera was placed in the restroom to aid in a theft investigation. An additional hidden camera was found in the employees' exercise room.

After filing a grievance over the use of the hidden camera, and the failure of the company to respond, the union filed a charge with the NLRB over the company's refusal to bargain about the use of hidden cameras. The case was heard before an administrative law judge who sided with the union. The company appealed, and the NLRB affirmed the decision of the judge, reasoning: "The use of surveillance cameras is not entrepreneurial in character, is not fundamental to the basic direction of the enterprise, and impinges directly upon employment security. It is a change in the [company's] methods used to reduce workplace theft or detect other sus-

---

[26] See Cal. Labor Code §1025–1028 and Federal Vocational Rehabilitation Act of 1973.

pected employee misconduct with serious implications for its employees' job security, which in no way touches on the discretionary core of entrepreneurial control."

The NLRB's final comment on the matter was that the "union has the statutory right to engage in collective bargaining over the installation and continued use of surveillance cameras, including the circumstances under which the cameras would be activated, the general areas in which they may be placed, and how affected employees will be disciplined if improper conduct is observed."

A Labor Board arbitrator held in 1987 that a company that was experiencing a high incidence of theft was required to bargain over the installation of a closed-circuit television system because it had a pervasive impact on the conditions of employment, was susceptible to abuse, and went beyond the broad scope of the employer's discretion under the management rights clause of the contract. *Super Marketing Serv. Corp.*, 89 Labor Arb. Rep. (BNA) 538 (1987).

Monitoring Phone Calls

The Omnibus Crime Control and Safe Streets Act of 1968 (Title III) prohibits private individuals, organizations, and employers from intercepting wire or oral communications. Amended as the Electronic Communications Privacy Act of 1986, 18 U.S.C. §§2510–2520, the statute does not specifically address the question of simple eavesdropping without an electronic or mechanical device; however, video cameras with sound tracks fall under the restrictions of this Act: "[A]ny person who willfully uses, endeavors to use, or procures another person to use any electronic, mechanical, or other device to intercept an oral communication when . . . such use or endeavor to use . . . takes place on the premises of any business or other commercial establishment the operations of which affect the interstate or foreign commerce . . . shall be punished."

Under Title III, wiretappings are currently limited to use in investigating crimes such as drug trafficking, currency reporting, and bribery and must be based on probable cause and the establishment that normal investigation techniques have not been nor will be successful. The wiretaps can be authorized for only 30 days or less and a warrant must be obtained from a court, with approval by the attorney general or assistant attorney general.

Violations of the Electronics Communications Act can result in the payment of actual damages suffered by the plaintiff plus any profits made by the violator, or $10,000 or $100 per day for each day of violation (whichever is greater), reasonable attorneys' fees and costs, and sometimes recovery for emotional distress.

A nonemployee whose telephone conversation with the employee was surreptitiously recorded by an employer also may maintain a civil action against the employer. *Awbrey v. Great Atl. & Pac. Tea Co.*, 505 F. Supp. 604, 609 (N.D. Ga. 1980).

The principal exceptions to the Act are the following:

1. Where there is consent of one party to the communication
2. Where an employer uses a telephone extension to monitor employees in the ordinary course of business, which can include
   (a) providing training on interaction with the public
   (b) determining whether an employee is discussing business matters with a competitor
   (c) determining whether an employee is making personal calls
   (d) a phone company monitoring calls for mechanical or service checks

Section 2515 of the Act prohibits intercepted wire or oral communications as evidence. The section reads: "Whenever any wire or oral communication has been intercepted, no part of the contents of such communication and no evidence derived therefrom may be received in evidence in any trial, hearing, or other proceeding in or before any court, grand jury, department, officer, agency, regulatory body, legislative committee, or other authority of the United States, a State, or a political subdivision thereof if the disclosure of that information would be in violation of this chapter."

At least 40 states have adopted electronic interception statutes similar to the Omnibus Crime Control and Safe Streets Act, making it illegal to intercept employees' conversations when participants in the conversation are not aware that they are being monitored. Employers as outside parties to a conversation are not allowed to tape conversations *between employees* unless the participants in the conversation have been forewarned that their conversations might be monitored.

Some states allow interception as long as one participant is aware of the interception; other states, including California, require that all parties give consent. Courts consistently have upheld state statutes that impose more restrictive provisions than federal laws. In states with one-party consent, employers may, without an employee's consent, tape a conversation they are having with that employee. This, of course, is a double-edged sword since employees are also allowed to tape any conversation that they have with their employer and the tape could be allowed as evidence in a court of law. However, this does not mean that employees have a *right* to tape conversations between supervisors and themselves if the company has a policy against taping such a conversation or if a supervisor instructs an employee not to tape.

A McDonald's Corporation employee insisted upon taping one such conversation despite her supervisor's warning that she could not do so and, if she proceeded to tape, that she would be discharged for insubordination. The employee continued the taping and she was subsequently discharged.

In the employee's lawsuit for discrimination based on race, gender, and national origin, and for retaliation for complaining about discrimination, the court held that McDonald's terminated her for a legitimate, nondiscriminatory reason. She had been insubordinate in failing to follow her supervisor's clear directive at the beginning of the meeting that she was not to tape the meeting. *Hernandez v. McDonald's Corp.*, 975 F. Supp. 1418 (Kan. Dist. Ct. 1997).

Generally, a ban on taping meetings is the safest policy. In lieu of taping, supervisors should be taught to prepare written documentation of meetings with employees, including a summary of their content, and to keep the documentation on file.[27]

California Penal Code §632 prohibits intentional eavesdropping or recording of a confidential communication without consent of *all* parties to the conversation. Criminal penalties apply to violations. In *Ribas v. Clark*, 38 Cal.3d 355, 359 (1985), the California Supreme Court defined *eavesdropping* as the "secret monitoring of conversations by third parties." Penal Code §632(c) defines *confidential communication* as any communication carried on in circumstances that indicate that any party wishes the communication to be confined to the parties involved.

Exceptions to the California law against interception of wire communications occur under the following circumstances:

1. When the conversation is related to the commission of a crime against a person (i.e., bribery or extortion, as opposed to property crimes)
2. When the caller uses obscene language with the intent to annoy

Under the rules of the California Public Utilities Commission, an employer must provide a beep-tone warning audible to all parties when monitoring or recording phone calls. Alternatively, the employer may announce to the parties that the call is being monitored, but only if no party other than the employee can be heard.

All monitored parties in California must give informed consent before an employer may eavesdrop upon or record a confidential conversation. An employer *may not* listen to or record private conversations. Violation of California Penal Code §632 is punishable by a fine of up to $2,500 and/or imprisonment for up to one year.

The Texas Code of Criminal Procedure and the Texas Civil Practice and Remedies Code both govern the illegal interception of oral communications in that state. The Code of Criminal Procedure allows an exception when the equipment is being used in the ordinary course of the telephone customer's business, but specifies actual damages of $100 per day or $1,000,

---

[27] "Labor Board Favors Thieves—Says Union Must Be Given Advance Notice of Hidden Cameras," *Ohio Employment Law Letter*, vol. 8, no. 6 (June 1997).

whichever is higher, and civil liability for violations. Chapter 123 of the Texas Civil Practice and Remedies Code gives a party to a communication the right to sue a person whose communication is intercepted without that party's consent. Employers are specifically discouraged from the use of wiretaps or similar devices based on the common law right of privacy.

Monitoring of Email

State and federal law is still evolving where rights of privacy in regard to employees' email is concerned. Generally, as an electronic communication, email has been held by some courts to fall under the provisions of the Electronic Communications Privacy Act (ECPA). Section 2701 of the ECPA provides an exception for "the person or entity providing the wire or electronic communications service." The exception states that that person or entity (employer) is not liable for offenses regarding *stored* communications, which is sometimes interpreted to include voice mail and email stored on equipment owned by the employer. However, the crucial issue on which there is no consensus as yet is whether the employer can be said to "own" the email system when it is merely a subscriber to a commercial provider's system.

If the owner of the computer equipment (i.e., the employer) is legally considered to be the "provider of the service," then according to §2702(b)(5) of the ECPA, an employee authorized to use email for business purposes has no right of protection from intrusions by the employers, particularly on a strictly "in-house" email system. Questions like these illustrate why it is imperative to consult with legal counsel prior to attempting to monitor communications involving relatively new technologies. Particularly with such issues as yet unresolved, it is important for the employer to diminish the expectation of privacy in email by creating a monitoring policy including notice to employees of intent to monitor and, if possible, obtaining written consent from employees.

Two California employees filed an invasion of privacy lawsuit stemming from a situation where they were fired after their employer monitored email containing sexual and other personal messages. A state appellate court held that they had no reasonable expectation of privacy in their email because they had signed a waiver that the equipment was restricted to business use and because they had been told that their email would be periodically reviewed. *Bourke v. Nissan Motor Corp.* (Cal. Ct. App. 1993) (unreported).

Whether the employee accesses his computer files through a password also affects the level of privacy that can be expected. *United States v. Maxwell*, 1995 CCA LEXIS 129 (1995), dealt with the appeal of a federal employee who was convicted of using email at work to send indecent messages to another service member. The court held that the "appellant clearly had an objective expectation of privacy in those messages stored in computers which he alone could retrieve through use of his own assigned password."

Employers have also been held liable in sex discrimination and race discrimination cases, based in part on offensive email messages to coworkers, which went *unmonitored* to the point where they were found by the court to be ongoing harassment sufficient to create a hostile work environment. For protection, employers should give adequate notice to all employees by having them sign a statement acknowledging that they understand their communications may occasionally be accessed by the employer.

Investigative Interviews

As mentioned in the previous chapter, investigative interviews are one of the most effective investigative tools available. And because they are so effective, the sophisticated investigative team will engineer their undercover investigation invariably to include interviewing at least the most serious offenders. To do otherwise is simple professional negligence. However, for the untrained and unsophisticated investigator, no investigative action poses more legal risk and exposure than interviewing. No litigation strategy would be complete without addressing this legal minefield.

Intentional Infliction of Emotional Distress

As all security professionals know, employers or their agents may interview employees as a part of an investigation as long as that investigation has a legitimate business purpose and the interviews are conducted properly. Aggressive, coercive, or intimidating behavior on the part of the interviewer may give rise to the claim of *intentional infliction of emotional distress*. Under Texas case law, in order to establish a claim for intentional infliction of emotional distress, the plaintiff must establish that

1. The defendant acted intentionally or recklessly
2. The conduct was extreme and outrageous
3. The defendant's action caused plaintiff emotional distress
4. The emotional distress suffered by plaintiff was severe[28]

In *Dean v. Ford Motor Credit Co.*, 885 F.2d 300, 306 (5th Cir. 1989), the court held that "extreme and outrageous" conduct must "go beyond all possible bounds of decency, and . . . be regarded as atrocious, and utterly intolerable in a civilized community." Such determination is usually left

---

[28] NIBM, "Workplace Taping Ban is the Best, Safest Policy," *You and the Law*, (March 1998), p. 7.

up to the jury, so community standards will affect the outcome of a trial resulting from a claim for this particular tort. As such, the interviewer had best know the legal landscape before charging forward. Other successful claims for intentional infliction of emotional distress include the following rather blatant examples:

- An employee suspected of theft was required to strip to her underwear in a public restroom in front of a female supervisor and a customer (*Bodewig v. K-Mart, Inc.*, 54 Or. Ct. App. 480 (1981), *rev. denied*, 292 Or. 450 (1982))
- A supervisor intentionally drugged a female subordinate and sexually assaulted her (*Gilardi v. Schroeder*, 672 F. Supp. 1043 (N.D. Ill. 1986), *aff'd*, 833 F.2d 1226 (7th Cir. 1987))
- A male employee was discharged after refusing to pull down his pants and expose himself in full view of coworkers (*Madani v. Kendall Ford Inc.*, 312 Or. 198 (1991))

The following rejected claims were far less convincing to the courts:

- An employee was threatened with job loss unless his performance improved (*Sossenko v. Michelin Tire Corp.*, 172 Ga. App. 771 (1984))
- An employee was dismissed after testing positive for marijuana (*Satterfield v. Lockheed Missiles & Space Co.*, 617 F. Supp. 1359 (Dist. S.C. 1985))
- An employee was discharged for refusing to break off an affair with a coworker (*Patton v. J.C. Penney Co.*, 301 Or. 117 (1986))
- A West Virginia employee sued her employer after telling her to "cut the crap" and calling her a liar during a theft investigation involving a $17,000 shortage; the court ruled that though the statements of the interviewer were not appropriate they did *not* constitute outrageous behavior

Intrusion into Seclusion

It should be no surprise that the courts allow interviewees other claims as well. The tort of *intrusion into seclusion* once applied only to physical intrusions into employee workspaces but now can include psychological violation in some jurisdictions. In *Phillips v. Smalley Maintenance Servs., Inc.*, 711 F.2d 1524 (11th Cir. 1983), an employee was repeatedly interrogated behind "locked doors" about sexual activities between her and her husband. The court ruled that these repeated and intrusive inquiries supported the employee's invasion of privacy claim in regard to intrusion into the employee's psychological seclusion.

Other cases where judges have ruled that the acts of employers intruded upon the seclusion of employees, thereby invading their privacy, include the following:

- The principal officer of a company opened and read the private mail of another company officer (*Vernars v. Young*, 539 F.2d 966 (3rd Cir. 1976))
- A manager broke open an employee's personal lock on a company locker and went through her purse and other personal belongings (*K-Mart Corp. v. Trotti*, 677 S.W.2d 632 (Tex. Ct. App. 1984))
- An employer pressured his employee into taking a polygraph examination based on rumors of off-the-job drug use (*O'Brien v. Papa Gino's of Am., Inc.* 780 F.2d 1067 (1st Cir. 1986))

Conversely, invasion of privacy claims based on intrusions into the plaintiffs' seclusion were rejected by the courts in the following cases:

- An employer interviewed employees and examined company records while investigating coworker reports of a supervisor's inappropriate relationship with a subordinate (*Rogers v. IBM Corp.*, 500 F. Supp. 867 (W.D. Pa. 1980))
- A nurse was asked by coworkers why she left the job after a forced resignation (*Avallone v. Wilmington Med. Ctr., Inc.*, 553 F. Supp. 931 (D. Del. 1982))
- An employee claimed that he was asked to fill out a questionnaire with offensive and intrusive questions, but did not cooperate in answering those questions (*Cort v. Bristol-Meyers Co.*, 385 Mass. 300 (1982))
- A man committed suicide upon concluding that his wife was having an affair after his wife's employer showed him her attendance record (*Kobeck v. Nabisco, Inc.*, 166 Ga. Ct. App. 652 (1983))
- Off-the-job drug use was detected by a workplace drug test (*DiTomaso v. EDS*, 3 IER Cases (BNA) 1700 (E.D. Mich. 1988))
- An employer requested disclosure of medications taken by an employee before a routine drug test was administered (*Mares v. Conagra Poultry Co.*, 773 F. Supp. 248 (D. Colo. 1991), *aff'd*, 971 F.2d 492 (10th Cir. 1992))
- When an employer discovered a relationship between a manager and subordinate, the court held that there was no bad faith or "other reckless prying" (*Watkins v. United Parcel Serv., Inc.* 797 F. Supp. 1349 (S.D. Miss. 1992))

False Imprisonment; Assault and Battery

False imprisonment is both a crime and a tort. False imprisonment claims can arise if the employer restrains the employee by force or by fear for purposes of search or interrogation. Under California Penal Code §236, the crime of false imprisonment is defined as "[t]he unlawful violation of the personal liberty of another." Where the tort of false imprisonment is concerned, the employee must be conscious of the confinement or be harmed by it. See *Restatement (Second) of Torts* §35 (1965). "The Tort requires direct restraint of the person for some appreciable length of time, however short, compelling him to stay or go somewhere against his will."[5] Witkin, Summary of California Law 378 (9th ed. 1988).

In 1930, in *Vandiveer v. Charters*, 110 Cal. App. 347, a California appellate court explained the nature of the basis for a claim of false imprisonment: "The restraint constituting false imprisonment may arise out of acts, words, gestures or the like, which induce a reasonable apprehension that force will be used if the plaintiff does not submit, and it is sufficient if they operate upon the will of the person threatened, and result in the reasonable fear of personal difficulties or personal injuries. . . . A voluntary display of force, intended to deprive plaintiff of his liberty, even without actual laying hands on plaintiff, has been held sufficient, but there is no legal wrong unless the detention was involuntary in the sense of being contrary to the will of the plaintiff."

In short, false imprisonment is established by proof of actual force or an express or implied threat of force. See *Ware v. Dunn*, 80 Cal. App. 2d 936 (1947).

Most claims of false imprisonment arise when a police officer or a private citizen makes a false or improper arrest. Private investigators (and employers for that matter) rarely have to make arrests, but an acting party can be held liable for false arrest if he furnishes false or inaccurate information to police officers who subsequently make an arrest based on that information. Confrontational interviews with accused persons can lead to claims of false imprisonment if the investigator threatens or creates the reasonable fear that he will detain the subject through force or have the person arrested if she tries to exit the interview. To minimize this potential claim, the interviewer should attempt to convince the subject to sign the written statement, ideally in the presence of a witness who also signs, wherein the interviewee states that she was not held against her will or in any way felt threatened or coerced. Experience suggests that for the best protection, the following language should be included in the interviewee's statement: "This statement is given freely and voluntarily on my part. No threats or promises were made to me to induce me to make this statement and I hereby acknowledge it was made of my own free will."

In the event that the subject agrees with this statement but refuses to affirm it in writing, the interviewer should read it back to her in front of a witness, asking the subject to confirm that the statement reflects that which she stated orally. The interviewer should then ask the subject to explain why she refuses to sign the statement. The reason given should be noted on the statement and signed by the interviewer and the witness. It has been my experience that a properly witnessed statement that is unsigned by the subject is sometimes even more believable in a court of law than a signed, but unwitnessed, statement.

If the subject fails to sign a statement or orally agree in the presence of a witness that the interview process was free of threats or coercion, the interviewer should consider tape-recording that portion of the interview. Again it should be well established that the subject was free to leave at any time and never held against her will.

Under no circumstances should the interviewer ever initiate physical force to restrain, coerce, or otherwise control the subject of an investigation. In the event that a subject becomes violent, the police should be called immediately. Like false imprisonment, assault and battery can be either a *willful tort* or a criminal act. California Penal Code §240 defines assault as "an unlawful attempt, coupled with a present ability, to commit a violent injury on the person of another." Section 241 of the Code provides that an assault is punishable by a fine not exceeding $1,000, by imprisonment not exceeding six months, or by both. California Penal Code §242 defines battery as "any willful and unlawful use of force or violence upon the person of another." A battery is punishable by a fine not exceeding $2,000, by imprisonment not exceeding six months, or both (§243). A subject who is in any way "roughed up" or who falls while being restrained could later file criminal charges of assault and battery then file a civil suit for damages. Witnesses, including a security officer or law enforcement officer, should be present when confronting any subject strongly suspected of having a propensity for violence.

Use of Consumer Reports and Investigative Consumer Reports

In the course of most undercover investigations, it is likely that background investigations of the subjects will be necessary. If for no other purpose than operative safety, a simple search of public criminal records is often appropriate. However, under the Fair Credit Reporting Act (FCRA) as amended in 1997 (see Appendix I), an employer's decision that is based in whole or in part on information contained in a consumer report and that adversely affects an employee's or job candidate's current or prospective employment must provide that person with

1. Written notice of the adverse action and a copy of the report and summary of rights, including the right to dispute the report, prior to taking the adverse action
2. The name, address, and telephone number of the consumer reporting agency that furnished the report

3. A statement that the decision to take adverse action was based in whole or in part upon information contained in a consumer report[29]

When ordering a consumer report, employers must state a legitimate purpose for the inquiry and obtain written authorization from the employee (or prospective employee).

The FCRA also affects the employers use of *investigative consumer reports*, which are a compilation of information gathered through personal interviews. These types of reports generally focus on the subject's character and general reputation. Prior to obtaining an investigative consumer report on an employee, the employer must disclose to the employee, in writing, that such a report may be sought. A statement informing the employee of her rights to obtain a copy must be included. As in the case of a consumer report, employees (or prospective employees) are entitled to receive a copy of the investigative consumer report and a summary of rights prior to any adverse action being taken on the basis of the report.

Clearly the FCRA poses some interesting challenges for those conducting background investigations relative to an undercover. An investigation would be quickly compromised every time the employer sought a subject's permission before conducting a background investigation. There are several simple solutions. The first is to simply not do background investigations during the undercover. This, however, may put the operative at risk and in fact be negligent. The second solution is better but may not always be practical. *Simply obtain authorization from every employee prior to the investigation.* Because it would be inappropriate to take action against an employee solely based on his background investigation under such circumstances, neither the findings of the background or the employer's intentions relative to the undercover need to be revealed. However, there is another option and it is the strategy I use most often. Because the FCRA defines the investigative agency conducting the background investigation as a consumer reporting agency (CRA) and the reports they generate as consumer reports only when they are requested by the employer, and because certain consumer rights begin only when the employer uses the reports, we simply don't provide the results to our client. In doing so we avoid triggering the FCRA and any obligations under it for the client-employer. The downside, of course, is that only we are able to view and use the results. Our clients rarely object because the reason for conducting the backgrounds is most often operative safety. What's more, based on our response and the precautions we take during the case shutdown, the client can generally figure out who we think the bad actors might be.

---

[29] *Wilson v. Monarch Paper Co.*, 939 F.2d 1138, 1142 (5th Cir. 1991); *Twyman v. Twyman*, 855 S.W.2d 619, 621 (Tex. 1993); *Tidelands Auto Club v. Walters*, 699 S.W.2d 939, 942 (Tex. Ct. App. 1985).

Honesty Testing

The federal Employee Polygraph Protection Act (EPPA) of 1988, 29 U.S.C. §§2001–2009, severely restricts the use of lie detector tests, effectively eliminating the use of polygraph testing by most private sector employers in applicant screenings and under most circumstances involving current employees. The Act additionally prohibits employers from disciplining, discharging, or discriminating against any employee for refusing to submit to a polygraph or other "lie detector" test or for taking action to preserve his rights under the Act. Employers are further prohibited from discriminating against an employee based on the results of any such test.

The term *lie detector* is defined by the Act to include polygraph, deceptograph, voice stress analyzer, or other mechanical or electrical device used to render diagnostic opinions about the honesty or dishonesty of an individual. 29 U.S.C. §2001(3). The Act does not regulate paper-and-pencil "honesty tests" or any other nonmechanical means of testing honesty.

Interestingly, the Act does *not* apply to federal, state, or local government employers and employees. Other exceptions are the following:

- Employers manufacturing, distributing, or dispensing controlled substances may administer polygraphs to applicants who would have direct access to manufacture, storage, distribution, or sale of a controlled substance and current employees as a part of an ongoing investigation misconduct involving same
- Private security firms charged with protecting certain types of facilities that affect public health, safety, and security, such as nuclear power plants, public water supply facilities, shipments or storage of radioactive or other toxic waste materials, and public transportation, or with providing protection of currency, negotiable instruments, and precious commodities
- Employee in an ongoing investigation of thefts or other incidents causing economic loss to the employer, such as embezzlement, misappropriation, or an act of unlawful industrial espionage or sabotage; where there is a reasonable suspicion that the employee was involved in an incident under investigation and had access to the property in question (29 U.S.C. §2006(d))

The law requires that any employee suspected of theft and subject to polygraph testing must be given written notice that:

1. Specifies the particular incident being investigated and the basis for testing that employee
2. Identifies a specific economic loss or injury suffered by the employer
3. States that the employee had access to the property
4. Describes the basis for the employer's reasonable suspicion

The requirement is met if the decision is reasonable and suspicion is grounded in *observable, articulable* facts; if the authorization is signed by a person legally empowered to bind the employer; and it is retained by the employer for a minimum of three years.

Procedural requirements for administering polygraph under the exceptions include the following:

1. Written notice to employee of date, time, location, nature of test, and right to consult an attorney or employee representative before each phase of the test
2. Written statement from the employee acknowledging his or her rights under EPPA
3. Employee opportunity to review all questions to be asked during the test
4. Refraining from conducting the test where a medical condition may cause abnormal reactions during the examination.

During the actual testing phase

- An examiner licensed by the state in which the test is to be conducted must conduct the test
- The examiner may not ask questions not presented in writing to employee or applicant before the test, or ask questions that pertain to religion, racial matters, political beliefs, sexual behavior, or unions
- The examiner may not administer more than five polygraph tests per day; and the employee or applicant may terminate the test at any time

After the test, and before taking action based on the results, the employer must

1. Interview the employee on the basis of test results
2. Give the employee a copy of test questions and responses
3. Give the employee a written copy of any conclusions reached from the test

And it doesn't end there. Limitations on the use of test results by employers include the following:

1. Results of a polygraph test may not be the sole basis for the employer's decision regarding the employee
2. Refusal to submit to a test may not provide the sole basis for an employer's decision regarding an employee; however, a negative inference may be drawn from that refusal

Only the employer has the right to see the results of a polygraph test. A present employer may not ask about any polygraph tests that the employee may have taken for previous employers.

Employees who feel their rights were violated by a polygraph test have up to three years to file legal claims. Employers may be liable for civil penalties of up to $10,000. Employees whose rights are found to have been violated may be entitled to reinstatement and back wages.

The EPPA is the controlling law in any business involving interstate commerce *unless* state polygraph law is even more restrictive. According to California Labor Code §432.2, employers may *not* require an applicant or employee to submit to a polygraph test as a condition of employment, but employers *may* request that an employee submit to a polygraph test so long as he is advised in writing of the provisions of the federal EPPA. The federal law, in this case, is more restrictive than state law.

Workplace Searches

Private sector employers, including investigators, are not subject to Fourth Amendment protections against unreasonable searches and seizures unless the investigation is being conducted at the behest of the police or a government agency. In that event, a valid warrant must accompany every search. Failure to obtain a valid warrant results in the exclusion of any evidence obtained from the warrantless search, commonly known as "the fruit of the poison tree."

O'Connor v. Ortega, 480 U.S. 709 (1987), as noted earlier in this chapter, is currently the leading Fourth Amendment case addressing workplace searches. While its holding is not binding on private sector employees, it is useful in understanding the basis of many state statutes and case law. *Ortega* derives from a search of the desk and filing cabinets of a doctor at a state hospital amidst allegations of improper conduct. During the search the employer seized personal letters and cards, a photograph, and a book of poetry. The doctor sued on the grounds of invasion of privacy. The court ruled that a public employee has a reasonable expectation of privacy in his office, desk, and file cabinets that contain only personal files. However, the employer may search such areas if it has "reasonable grounds for suspecting that the employee is guilty of work-related misconduct" or if the search is necessary for a business-related purpose such as retrieving a file. No warrant is required under those circumstances.

Private employers are generally allowed to conduct searches of their premises for business-related purposes so long as they do not search areas where employees legitimately have reasonable expectations of privacy. The employer should diminish expectations of privacy by providing written notice to employees that lockers, desks, filing cabinets, company vehicles, and all other company property are subject to search without employee consent.

In order to remind employees that the company property that they may use daily is not the employee's private property, employers should switch employee desks, lockers, and vehicles periodically, as well as supply all necessary locks and retain a copy of the key to each lock. Employees should also be notified that failure to cooperate with the company search policy might result in discipline up to and including termination. See *Simpson v. Commonwealth Unemployment Comp. Bd. of Review*, 450 A.2d 305 (Pa. Commw. Ct. 1982), *cert. denied*, 464 U.S. 822 (1983).

Each employee should be required to sign a copy of the search policy, acknowledging consent to searches of company property for any reason. However, some courts have found that searches conducted randomly, for no *specific* reason are, by definition not *reasonable* searches and constitute an invasion of privacy. See *McGann v. Northeast Ill. Regional Commuter R.R. Corp.*, 8 F.3d 1174 (7th Cir. 1993).

In *K-Mart Corp. v. Trott*, 677 S.W.2d 632 (Tex. Ct. App. 1984), *aff'd per curiam*, 686 S.W.2d 593 (Tex. 1985), K-Mart was found liable for searching an employee's locker for stolen merchandise because they had to cut her personal lock off of a locker in order to conduct the search. Had the employer provided the lock, and had the employer been determined to have had *reasonable suspicion*, the case likely would have been dismissed.

Conducting Workplace Searches

The procedures that pertain to a workplace search include the following:

1. In workplaces with a unionized work force, consider having a union steward present during the search both as a means of honoring agreements, if applicable, and as a means of avoiding the appearance of impropriety
2. In a nonunion workplace, consider allowing the employee to choose his own witness
3. Ensure that the search is reasonable or in compliance with established policy of random searches
4. Get authorization from human resources department or appropriate official before the search is conducted
5. Tell the subject the purpose of the search, and limit the search to what is appropriate in the context of that purpose
6. Have at least two management officials present during the search
7. Try to obtain consent from the employee; if the employee refuses to give consent or cooperate, inform the employee of possible disciplinary consequences per company policy
8. Do not be confrontational or physically force any part of the search

9. Use professional search equipment such as metal detectors or trained dogs in appropriate settings
10. Seize the contraband in plain view of the subject(s)
11. Allow the employee to explain during the interview
12. Mark and retain any contraband in secure location and preserve the chain of custody; in the case of illicit drugs or paraphernalia, seal contraband in an envelope for delivery to lab or law enforcement personnel
13. All participants in the search should prepare a memo to be filed
14. Take photographs of contraband before it is moved, if possible
15. If the employer is committed to prosecuting, call the police
16. Consider turning the search over to the police if there is a reasonable basis for believing that illegal activity has occurred
17. Avoid using force[30]

Clear notice of the company's search policy is mandatory if the employer or investigative agency plans to conduct searches of employees' clothing, purses, lunch boxes, and other personal effects. This type of search is highly invasive and thus carries with it the highest level of potential liability other than the collecting of blood and urine samples; frankly, it plays little or no role in most undercover investigations. Regardless, it is imperative that the search policy be clearly stated both in the employee handbook and in separate notices given to each employee along with a requirement that they sign the notice or face disciplinary action. These types of searches should rarely, if ever, be conducted without probable cause unless, for instance, the company has a policy of routinely searching *every* employee's lunch box upon exit from the premises.

Singling out individual employees for searches of clothing or other personal effects without the high level of reasonable suspicion likely to be acceptable to a judge and/or jury could open up a Pandora's box of liability. If the search of a singled-out employee fails to turn up the anticipated evidence, the employee may feel humiliated and, if the suspicions of the employer were in fact groundless, perhaps feel that she is the victim of discrimination.

The employer should explain the basis for the suspicion and request that the employee consent to the search, even if the employee has previously signed a more generalized consent to search form. If the employee refuses, she should be reminded of the company's policy of disciplining employees who refuse to comply with searches. The over-zealous employer who grabs the employee or the employee's purse or lunch box makes himself vulnerable to charges of assault and battery along with invasion of privacy. Generally, the employee who is subject to this invasive type of

---

[30] 15 U.S.C. §1681m(a) and Cal. Civil Code §1785.20.

search should be given a reasonable opportunity to submit to the search, and the search should be conducted out of the view of coworkers other than designated witnesses or representatives. The object is not to humiliate the subject in front of her coworkers, but rather to determine whether illicit activity has occurred and to take the *appropriate* steps in a professional manner to curb such activity in the future.

Investigating Threats of Violence

During some undercover investigations, threats of violence do sometimes occur. More frequent are those circumstances in which the operative overhears or learns of a threat made by one employee toward another employee. This poses an interesting dilemma for both the client-employer and investigative agency. On one hand, employers must take reports of threats of violence seriously and have a lawful duty to protect employees. California's Cal/OSHA has gone so far as to classify workplace violence into three categories:

Type I. An employee or small business owner shot during the commission of a robbery.

Type II. An assault by someone who is either the recipient or the object of a service provided by the affected workplace or the victim. Examples: medical facilities, social welfare service providers, and alcohol and drug treatment centers.

Type III. An assault by an individual who has some employment-related involvement with the workplace. Usually involves a threat of violence, or a physical act of violence resulting in a fatal or nonfatal injury to an employee, supervisor, or manager of the affected workplace by the following types of individuals:

(1) A current or former employee, supervisor or manager; or

(2) Some other person who has a dispute with an employee of the affected workplace, e.g., current/former spouse or lover, relative, friend, or acquaintance.[31]

"Most commonly, the primary target of a Type III event is a co-employee, a supervisor or manager of the assailant. In committing a Type III assault, an individual may be seeking revenge for what he or she perceives as unfair treatment by a co-employee, a supervisor or a manager. Increasingly, Type III events involve domestic or romantic disputes in which

---

[31] N. Abell, L. Edwards, E. Gordon, and S. Sonnenberg, *Issues in Workplace Privacy and Investigations*, Paul, Hastings, Janofsky, and Walker (Santa Monica 1995).

[32] Cal/OSHA Guidelines for Workplace Security (rev. 30 March 1995).

an employee is threatened in their workplace by an individual with whom they have a personal relationship outside work," says Cal/OSHA.

While Cal/OSHA mandates that incidents of workplace violence be investigated *after* they occur, the employer conducting an undercover investigation must make some difficult decisions. It can either immediately conduct the investigation and jeopardize the undercover effort or postpone its investigation until after the undercover is complete. I usually opt for the second option. Most often compromising the undercover investigation is just too great a risk. Postponing the investigation until some later time, if possible, makes not only economic sense but is arguably not postponement at all. For isn't the undercover investigation an *investigation* and cannot the undercover investigator be used to further management's effort regarding a credible threat?

If possible, the operative should obtain information regarding the threat and report the following:

1. The name of the person who made the threat
2. The name of the person(s) against whom the threat was made
3. The specific language of the threat
4. Description of any physical conduct by the threatening party that would tend to substantiate that the individual intends to follow through on the threat
5. The names of any other witnesses to the threat or violent conduct
6. The time and place where the threat or violent conduct occurred
7. Description of any threats or violent behavior by the alleged perpetrator prior to the current incident
8. Any other information that will assist in the investigation and help ensure that the threat will not be carried out

After the initial information is collected, a decision must be made as to whether further action is necessary. If there is a need to interview additional witnesses, this must be done as soon as possible. The employer may decide to take the cautious approach and suspend the alleged perpetrator, with or without pay, pending conclusion of the investigation. That person should have an opportunity to tell his version of events, but under no circumstances should the person against whom the threats were directed conduct the investigation or interview the alleged perpetrator.

The employer should consider whether it is advisable, based on what is known at that point, to have security personnel or a police officer present during the interview of the threatening employee. If it appears that this is a situation where a temporary restraining order may be warranted, having a police officer or security officer as a witness to any further threats can help expedite obtaining such an order.

Of course, if a violent incident has already occurred, police should handle the situation initially and the interview should be postponed until after the facts are gathered.

California's Code of Civil Procedures §527.8 allows California employers to pursue, on behalf of their employees, temporary restraining orders and injunctions that prohibit an individual from engaging in unlawful violence or *threats of violence* against employees. If the person allegedly making the threats is an employee of the employer requesting the injunction, the judge must hear evidence concerning the employer's decision to retain, terminate, or otherwise discipline the person. If, after considering all available evidence, the judge finds clear and convincing evidence that the defendant engaged in unlawful violence or made a credible threat of violence, the judge shall issue a permanent injunction prohibiting further unlawful violence or threats of violence. Violation of this statute is a misdemeanor. If the individual violates the injunction on two or more occasions in a seven-year period, he may be sent to state prison for up to three years.

Assuming that the incident was relatively minor, during the initial interview with the alleged perpetrator, the investigator should concentrate on defusing the situation by listening to his version of events rather than being confrontational or recounting witnesses' statements and seeming to have already arrived at a conclusion. If the employee is a union member and requests the presence of a union representative, the request must be accommodated or the interview terminated per *Weingarten* as discussed earlier in this chapter.

Particular care should be taken to conduct the interview in a manner that will minimize the chances of a lawsuit should the employee be terminated. For instance, coercing the employee to come to the office under threat of criminal prosecution could give rise to a claim of false imprisonment. In conducting the interviews, and in writing the report, the investigator should approach the situation with the understanding that there is a possibility that the subject may file a civil suit if discharged, or that he may follow through with the threat. The investigation process must be thorough, professional, and well documented. All conclusions and resulting decisions should be carefully thought out as to potential consequences, both pro and con.

If the employee is terminated, in order to safeguard against a discrimination lawsuit based on the violent or potentially violent employee's possible disability under the ADA, the employer must be prepared to show that there is (1) a *significant* risk of substantial harm; (2) a *specific* identifiable risk; (3) a current and not speculative or remote risk based on *factual evidence* regarding that particular individual; and (4) a risk that cannot be reasonably accommodated without undue hardship to the employer. Witness statements regarding direct threats, particularly if there is more than one witness, may provide the documentation necessary to circumvent liability for discrimination claims under the ADA.

Wrongful Discharge

As mentioned earlier in this chapter and elsewhere in this book, the employer and the investigative agency may both be named as defendants if an employee decides to file a lawsuit as a result of being terminated or otherwise disciplined based on the findings of the investigation. It is at this point that the accuracy and completeness of the investigative files are of utmost importance since they will serve as evidence. There must be solid documentation to support the position that the action taken was the most reasonable under the particular set of circumstances.

Although there is no way to guarantee that the employer and investigative agency will never be sued as a result of conducting an investigation that results in disciplining employees, the best course of action is to plan and conduct the investigation in a manner that will minimize the chances of being sued. Even if you, as the defendant, were legally and ethically without fault, a lawsuit is time-consuming and expensive to defend. Even a frivolous case can be dragged out for years. The cost and inconvenience to the organization and those involved can be unimaginable. As a result, my strategy has always been to plan ahead, minimize the risk, and fight aggressively when challenged. Often when the case is believed to be groundless or frivolous, the best defense is a strong offense. In any event, I recommend the following strategy:

1. Properly engineer your investigation. Use only qualified and experienced resources and clearly define your objectives before you begin.
2. Know the law. Obtain competent, experienced employment law counsel before you begin. Obey the law and follow the rules.
3. Respect the rights of others. As demonstrated throughout this chapter, aggressive and abusive conduct creates liability. Respect the subjects' rights and treat them respectfully. Be kind and be fair.
4. Document, document, document. If it's worth doing *or thinking*, it's worth documenting. Don't succumb to the temptation of documenting your efforts or results later. It never happens and as a defendant you look foolish and unprofessional.
5. Take action against only those cases you know you can prove. Manage your risks and minimize your exposures.
6. Remember this is business, not war. Winning is not everything and those of us who don't get what we want can generally try again later. The same cannot be said for those on the battlefield.

CHAPTER 9

Measuring Results

Measuring our investigative results is often difficult, if not impossible. Few investigators like to do it, most dread it. Typically, at the completion of an investigation, the last thing one wants to do is spend more time critiquing one's effort and measuring its return. Often the return cannot be immediately measured anyway. In some cases, the result is more subjective than objective. In other instances, *there is no perceivable return that can be measured.* In any event, our investigative efforts nevertheless *must always be measured.* Without measurement, analysis, or critical review of the investigative process and results, neither process improvement nor identifying and nurturing best practices are possible. It seems strange to me that we apply these fundamental business practices to every other aspect of our operation and business, but rarely are they applied to the process of investigation.

Furthermore, if the individual responsible for the investigation doesn't measure results, someone else ultimately will. It may be one's immediate supervisor when conducting personnel performance reviews, the budget review committee when deciding the proper allocation of corporate resources, or the criminal justice system when deciding guilt or innocence. Ultimately, someone always measures the results of our investigative efforts. Isn't it strange, then, that the very people who conduct these investigations sometimes don't measure their own results. In the long term, does it make sense that the professional investigator always allows others to determine the value of their effort? Does it make sense for someone else to justify our value to our organization instead of taking responsibility ourselves for providing that justification? It seems almost professionally negligent to ignore this important responsibility. To do so is a disservice to our customer and our career.

Benchmarking

For years I've done some form of *benchmarking* before initiating my investigations. This often-overlooked component of the investigative process is fundamental to measuring results. Because benchmarking allows us (sometimes literally) to "take a snapshot" of the condition, state of affairs, or damage that has been done to our customer before our effort begins, we're able to conduct some form of comparative analysis when our effort is complete. The challenge is finding the time to make this preinvestigation assessment and deciding what to measure.

In cases involving property crimes, some of the benchmarking work has already been done for the investigator. A loss has been reported and values are easily attached if not already calculated by someone else. For example, take the situation in which an inventory variance of $100,000 is reported during a routine cycle count. Most likely the report will detail what inventory is missing (by line item), when it was last accounted for, who accessed it last, and its value. Upon further audit and analysis it is determined that the inventory is in fact missing (and was not simply misplaced, miscounted, or misidentified) and the actual variance (now called a *loss*) is $124,000. The estimated restock date is 30 days out and the economic impact to the organization's revenue stream will exceed $200,000 (after calculating profit, additional transportation costs, and processing). So what was initially considered a $100,000 problem is now a $200,000 problem. Additionally, without any investigation, it is reasonable to conclude that that portion of the organization responsible for this inventory has process and system failures of some degree and that if they are not identified, the losses could possibly continue or even escalate. Furthermore, if process and system vulnerabilities contributed to this loss (in fact there is no way that they did not), it is possible that other vulnerabilities exist but have not yet been exploited. In fact, as is typically the case, those employees legitimately using our processes and systems, know of these vulnerabilities long before they are exploited (or reported, if ever).

Thus it should be clear that the situation is not just a large inventory loss but a confusing myriad of complex problems and opportunities. The investigator must therefore accumulate information and analyze the problem in its totality in order to effectively benchmark.

Let's briefly look at another situation. Suppose the suspected problem is employee substance abuse. Undoubtedly, those bringing the situation to the attention of the investigator would have some reason to suspect a substance abuse problem. But the investigator should dig further and ask more questions before accepting his assignment. One of his first actions should be benchmarking.

Though substance abuse problems intuitively seem more difficult to benchmark, they are actually quite easy. As discussed earlier in this book, substance abuse problems affect an organization in a variety of ways, some of which are very significant. Among these are the following:

· Higher than normal employee turnover
· Higher than normal employee absenteeism rates

- Excessive disciplinary problems
- Unusual thefts or the frequent unexplained disappearance of property
- Suspicious acts of vandalism and sabotage
- Excessive waste or scrap
- Unexplained increased consumption of employer-provided benefits
- Alcohol containers or drug paraphernalia found on company premises or in company vehicles
- Employee apathy and low morale
- Unexplained loss of employees or customers
- Gradual decline in profitability

Although some of these effects can only be measured subjectively, clearly the investigator is left with a multitude of things to analyze and measure before initiating his investigation. In fact, by looking beyond the allegation of an employee substance abuse problem by an anonymous informant or concerned employee, the investigator has a huge opportunity to collect information across the organization. The effort is not only likely to confirm or refute the allegation, but if confirmed, will also encourage the proper allocation of resources to properly investigate it.

Information and Data Collection

Often the information and data we pursue for benchmarking purposes will also be used in our investigation. For example, if it has been decided to use undercover to root out a suspected employee theft and substance abuse problem, then some of the information gathered during our preinvestigation analysis will be very valuable in selecting the work area into which the investigator should be placed. Thus, if our analysis reveals that notebook computers have been the principle target of the thieves and most of the turnover, absenteeism, and discipline has been among the mailroom clerks, then maybe the best place to put the undercover investigator is in the mailroom.

One of the best and most practical tools for the collection of the desired information is a simple security audit checklist. Most security professionals either have or have access to these valuable tools. Those that don't can find them readily available either through the libraries of the trade organizations to which they belong or on the Internet. An excellent site is that of the American Society of Industrial Security. The address is *www.securitymanagment.com*. Any qualified security consultant will also possess these checklists and will routinely conduct these smaller, narrower audits for a nominal fee.

The focused audit should be conducted as discreetly as possible. A covert audit if possible is best. However, often the information desired cannot be gathered covertly, in which case one should consider a plausible and reasonable cover for the audit. A good cover might be to claim that the organization is the subject of a routine insurance audit, a government compliance audit, or a simple and cursory ISO audit. In several of our cases, we audited the entire organization in order to create the appearance of not targeting any particular area or workgroup. The process, if done properly, will not only permit the collection of information for benchmarking purposes but will likely produce some other unexpected eye-popping results.

In one such case, the results changed the entire course of our investigation. The client-employer had suspected for some time that employees were systematically stealing some of the cheese it manufactured. In fact, its estimated losses were huge. These losses, initially identified as "shrink," reached such proportions that management concluded that organized theft was the only possible explanation. Production costs were running 10 percent over historical norms and upper management was scrambling for answers. Upon the request for assistance, we immediately suggested an audit, not only for the reasons I outlined above but because I was concerned that something more was going on. From what the client told me, I suspected that there were both production and inventory problems. I also suspected that the client had a huge, undocumented waste problem.

Tip: In a manufacturing environment, when one sees production costs increasing, inventories remaining constant or declining, and profits falling through the floor, the experienced investigator should first look at the waste stream. All things equal, if the amount of waste or scrap has not increased, the unfortunate diagnosis is usually theft.

As it turned out, the amount of wasted product was enormous. On some days the amount of waste equaled that which was approved for customer shipment! The carelessness, complacency, and lack of supervision were appalling. Several of the people that were interviewed during the audit cautiously suggested that some of the problems could be related to employee drug abuse. Upon closer examination, it was quickly determined that at least some of the problems *were* drug related. Completing our audit and analysis, we came to the collective conclusion that our hapless client had an enormous employee substance abuse problem.

After several months of undercover investigation, our operatives identified the dealers and a very large number of on-the-job users, but no theft. Just 30 days after our interviews that followed the undercover portion of the investigation, my client told me that only one-third of the terminated employees had to be replaced and the amount of waste had been reduced by an astonishing $400,000. A year later the client told me that our investigation had resulted in long-term production increases and a huge reduction in waste. In one year, the client realized nearly a $5 million increase in profits (largely by eliminating waste) and employed fewer people to do it.

Just imagine the investigative result that produces increased profits with fewer employees. An employer would have to be out of its mind not to embrace such an outcome. In fact, such remarkable outcomes are common when the investigation is properly scoped and engineered. Let's look closer at the potential return on a case like this.

Analysis

Suppose the undercover investigation resulted in the termination of five employees. Let's also suppose that the workforce before the investigation employed 100 individuals. If the investigation produced results that identified system, process, and procedure improvement opportunities that if implemented could increase the productivity of each employee by just 5 percent, the net productivity gain would easily outweigh that which was lost by terminating the five employees. In other words, by sufficiently increasing the productivity of the remaining employees, the lucky employer may not have to replace all of those workers that the investigation caused it to lose. As mentioned several times in this book, I have worked with clients that terminated up to one-third of their workforce following an undercover investigation and did not replace anyone. By improving the productivity of the "survivors," the employer may find that it is not necessary to replace some if not all of those terminated.

But here's another scenario. Suppose no one is terminated as a result of the findings of the undercover investigation but management learns enough from it to improve productivity and maybe even quality. Again using the sample 100 employee workforce, if the investigation netted productivity improvement opportunities that if implemented improved the productivity of ten employees by 10 percent, the net effect would be the equivalent to a productivity gain of one additional employee. If the average production employee cost the employer $25,000 annually, the investigation effectively produced a recurring revenue stream of $25,000 per year. If the effective life of those productivity improvements were just two years, the gross yield would be $50,000. If the same investigation uncovered safety risks, inventory shrink vulnerabilities, and improved morale by exposing supervisory weaknesses, the yield would be considerably greater.

Let's look at a more realistic example. Suppose the workforce in question numbered 1,000 employees and the undercover investigation resulted in the following:

- Thirty-five terminations for policy violations, 20 of them from the target department
- The productivity of the target department (a total of 100 employees) improved sufficiently such that only ten of those terminated needed to be replaced
- One questionable workers' compensation claim that had lingered for years was irrefutably determined to be a fraud; the claimant had been on full disability for five years and had not returned to work

- The behaviors of one alleged sexual harasser was confirmed
- A serious employee theft problem was stopped and $50,000 worth of stolen power tools and equipment was returned to the employer
- Employee morale soared to an all time high

Sounds too good to be true? Run this list by someone who's familiar with undercover and has done several of them. See what they say. I suspect they will tell you that such results are not uncommon and in fact may be conservative. The problem is that most investigators never measure their results. Let's try to do so in this case:

Result	Benefit
Thirty-five terminations for policy violations.	Empirically, not much benefit. Some of these terminated will need to be replaced and trained. The cost could be significant.
The productivity of the target department (a total of 100 employees) improved sufficiently such that only ten of those terminated needed to be replaced.	Good deal. Of the 20 terminated in the target department, only ten were replaced. If each of those that were not replaced had earned $30,000 per year, the organization will realize an annualized gain of $300,000 (easily offsetting the cost of hiring and training the employees who had to be replaced.
One questionable workers' compensation claim that had lingered for years was irrefutably determined to be a fraud. The claimant had been on full disability for five years and not returned to work.	If self-insured, the savings could be enormous. Excluding the recovery of benefits already paid, conservatively the organization could save $30,000 in future payments.
The behavior of one alleged sexual harasser was confirmed.	Sexual harassment claims are serious business. The defense of a single claim could exceed $100,000. In this case, the undercover produced enough evidence to terminate the offender, effect other corrective action, and prevent a lawsuit, saving the organization at least $10,000 in legal fees (very conservative) by not having to respond to a suit filed by the victim.

| A serious employee theft problem was stopped. | The company's losses due to theft were huge. However, during the investigative interview process, several employees voluntarily returned $50,000 in stolen power tools. |
| Employee morale soared to an all time high. | Good news. However, very difficult to value. Improved morale may translate into better attendance, less turnover, higher productivity, less waste, and better customer service. |

What was the total benefit? By including wage savings, in just one year this employer enjoyed a measurable $390,000 gain. Subtracting out the cost of the investigation and the cost of replacing and training those who were terminated, the net gain is still in excess of $225,000! *Conservatively*, the employer will throw a quarter of a million dollars to the bottom line as a result of just one undercover investigation. Amazing!

Leveraging Your Successes

But there is more. If, as suggested above, an employee theft problem was identified and stopped, there are additional downstream benefits. By stopping an ongoing theft problem, the bottom line will be increased immediately and the benefits will be enjoyed indefinitely. I will not even attempt to calculate the return on such an outcome. But suppose the investigation was engineered such that a recovery was possible. Suppose the total loss due to employee theft combined with the cost of the investigation was $500,000. Two recovery options are possible.

The first option is to go after the thieves. By pursuing the perpetrators civilly the employer could recover both the loss and the cost of dealing with it. As mentioned elsewhere in this book, recoveries of millions of dollars are possible. As I write this very chapter, my firm is involved in such an effort. And although the employer's loss exceeds $20 million, $2 million or more has already been recovered. Our hope is that at least one-half of the total loss will ultimately be recovered from the perpetrator. Most security professionals do not need to make too many recoveries like this in their career to justify their value. But amazingly, all too many never even consider it. Unfortunately, the old mantra "prosecution" is just too deeply ingrained.

The second option is to make an insurance claim. Most organizations carry some form of fidelity insurance and don't even know it. If you are unsure, ask your risk manager. A fidelity claim is a relatively easy pursuit.

However, some strings are attached. The loss must be reported quickly and the claim must be made in timely fashion. The insured also must surrender subrogation rights and agree to cooperate fully with the carrier. The cooperation the carrier will be looking for will include the production of documents, records, and witnesses. This may sound easier than in fact it may be. In complex fraud cases like the one mentioned above, not only are employees involved but also vendors and customers are involved as well. In some cases, the carrier will go after these parties and in doing so may severely damage business relationships. A large-scale investigation could reach huge proportions and precipitate media interest and unwanted exposure in the industry or community. For the publicly held company, this may simply not be acceptable.

Conversely, exposing a dishonest competitor may not be a bad idea. By cooperating with the insurance company and/or the authorities in these high-profile cases, spin can be used to produce valuable and otherwise very expensive PR of the good sort.

The employer can also leverage the investigative result internally. In most organizations in which the problems we have discussed take place, most of the workforce knows about them. I have said many times at the start of an undercover investigation that the only people that don't know whose behind the problem are the people that hire our firm and the operatives we select to conduct the investigation. In reality this is often the case. Most of the workforce knows exactly what is going on and who is behind it. The problem of course is that no one is willing to reveal it to management, and thus the need for an investigation. But the employer nevertheless can and should communicate with the workforce after the investigation. By revealing why the investigation was undertaken and disclosing the results, the employer can garner employee confidence and loyalty. It can show that, while it cares for its workers, ethics and policy compliance are mandatory. The employer can leverage this message into one of goodwill and confidence. It is a mistake to do otherwise.

In the end, the investigative result will assuredly be measured, subjectively or objectively, and some value attached to it. Everyone the investigation touches or who learns of it will judge it. Anticipating this criticality from the beginning of the process, the security professional must engineer his investigative effort accordingly. In the final analysis, the security professional should be prepared to demonstrate that his expenditure of time and corporate resources produced measurable results and provided a reasonable return on investment.

CHAPTER 10

The Future

At those occasional casual settings where my colleagues and I have a chance to congregate and relax together, the future of workplace undercover is often debated. I find it interesting that those who don't use or have never conducted undercover investigations hold some of the strongest opinions. Those who claim to be experts and proudly admit they run three or four cases a year also entertain me the most. To make such claims is the equivalent of claiming to have a college degree because you live near a university. If an agency does not run undercover every day, and conduct several dozen undercover investigations a year, they are *not* in the undercover business. In any event, the debate remains: What is the future of workplace undercover?

My opinion is that undercover is here to stay. It is a viable and effective tool. It enables the gathering of information not possible by any other means. Most importantly, it is one of the few forms of investigation that is interactive. It not only permits one to learn what is going on, *but also why it is going on*. Other than interviewing, no other form of investigation is as revealing.

Admittedly undercover investigation has its downside. It is complicated and expensive. If improperly conducted, an undercover can be terribly disappointing and even counterproductive. The untrained and unsuspecting undercover investigator has the opportunity to violate all manner of civil and criminal law. The complexities and liabilities are enormous and can be literally terrifying. However, when properly managed, the undercover investigation is no more difficult or dangerous than another form of workplace investigation. But it is a breed unto its own. And because it is such a powerful form of investigation, it will likely be around for a very long time.

New Roles and New Challenges

In my career I have had the fortune of placing undercover investigators in every conceivable job and environment except the cockpit of a commercial airliner and in the uniform of a sworn law enforcement officer. I have placed operatives into government positions, onto military bases, in hospitals, factories, warehouses and even into foreign countries. However, the investigative needs of industry are changing and I foresee a dynamic shift in interest in this powerful tool.

As America's population grows older, our economy will change. Like some of the European countries of today, it is foreseeable that the demands of an aging population will significantly alter our tax base and ultimately our economy. Clearly, the elderly will increasingly need affordable housing and healthcare. Entrepreneurial businesses will seize the opportunity to fill these needs. Two such firms are clients of mine today. However, as new industries are born so are new problems and criminal opportunities, and employers will need cost-effective strategies to deal with them. One of the tools these employers will use will be undercover.

Already we have heard of cases involving elderly abuse and mistreatment. Unable to defend themselves and often unable to effectively communicate, the elderly are easy victims. Properly placed undercover investigators in environments where the elderly live may be the only answer.

A similar burgeoning industry is childcare. Here again the exposure to abuse and criminal conduct is not only enormous but is terrifying as well. Undercover investigators posing as staffers can effectively infiltrate such facilities and monitor the operation and its employees in a way no other monitoring can. Not even covert cameras can learn what's said around the staff lunch table or what small children are told to do or think. Only properly conducted undercover can root out and identify abuse and negligence.

A growing challenge is also evident in the healthcare industry. No longer can hospitals allow visitors and staff members to roam freely about the hospital and its campus. Baby thefts, equipment sabotage, and even random murder have heightened the concerns of every hospital administrator and security professional. Because of the open environment, hospitals are prime targets for thieves, vandals, and other criminals. More locks, cameras, or guards are not the answer. And although these important tools play a critical role in keeping hospitals safe while protecting their assets, different strategies are needed. Once again undercover may be an effective answer. Operatives placed into the staff and posing as patients or visitors can easily serve as cost-effective tools in augmenting existing security architectures. I have conducted dozens of such investigations and know from those experiences that the hospital environment uniquely lends itself to the use of undercover. Because of the high mobility most staffers and visitors enjoy and its open environment, hospitals make perfect environments for highly effective and successful undercover investigations.

Another role for undercover is in the contract security industry. As the demand for contract security officers grows, so will the problems. With record low unemployment and pressures to hold down wages, it is increasingly difficult to find the personnel qualified to fill the growing need for security officers. The challenges for those in the industry are enormous. The result is often the fielding of a less-trained, less-qualified officer.

Contract security supervision and management is affected as well. Having to reach deeper into the available labor pool, the contract security vendor must compete aggressively for qualified personnel. The labor shortage creates the temptation to staff with individuals that heretofore would have never been considered for these critical positions. The result is often disappointing. High turnover, vacant posts (absenteeism while on duty), shoddy reporting and recordkeeping, and even criminal activity are just a few of the outcomes.

But what if customers demanded that periodically operatives be covertly placed into their contract security force? And what if the officers were told about it? I know the answer, because I've tried it. The result is better customer service. The vendor knowing full well that it is being covertly monitored will likely go out of its way to ensure the job is done properly and the customer is satisfied. Although this is a fairly expensive undertaking, I am surprised it is not done more often, particularly on the larger contracts. If the effort uncovers problems or process improvement opportunities, the return on investment pencils out quite easily.

Another growing industry is that of temporary and contract labor. As of this writing, Manpower, Inc., is the largest private employer in the United States. Headquartered in Milwaukee, Wisconsin, Manpower employs roughly 600,000 people and operates 3,200 offices in 50 different countries. Its revenues in 1998 were roughly $10.5 billion. Organizations like Manpower and its customers need to monitor employee productivity and safety. Both the vendor and the customer must be assured that the people placed into the environments they create are treated properly and do the jobs they are expected. What better way to monitor such an environment than with undercover? Like the contract guard force, the temporary labor pool makes an easy vehicle for operative placement and movement. The transience (some temporary workforces are more stable than others), the mobility, and the social nature of these workforces makes them exceptionally well suited for undercover. Both the vendor and customer would be well served by periodically using undercover in these environments. I am confident that undercover will increasingly be used in these situations in the future.

Another yet underused opportunity for undercover is in the hi-tech industry, not in the traditional manufacturing, distributing, and servicing end (that's already being done) but in product research and development (R&D). Big players in the industry have suffered enormous setbacks and losses due to the theft of trade secrets and other intellectual property. The typical creative side of the industry is highly educated, loosely supervised, and very casual—a perfect environment for undercover. Its seems logical that these environments be covertly monitored with undercover. However, the reality is quite different. Although these environments suffer their share of employee substance abuse problems, lost notebook computers, petty thefts, and attacks by competitors looking for unprotected intellectual property, management is hesitant to act. As many experienced readers know, senior management in such organizations are loathe to over-extend its influence in these "creative strongholds." The mere thought of placing an undercover investigator into such an environment is almost unthinkable. Remember, it is from these bastions of civil liberty that we hear the greatest protestations regarding drug testing, telephone monitoring, and access control.

Well, the tide will change. It must change. The technology companies of today will be tomorrow's has-beens if they cannot maintain their competitive and technological edge. The very technological advances they create will be used against them to steal their secrets, their ideas, and their people. Already the bolder enterprises are taking action. Discreetly, some of America's hi-tech powerhouses are using undercover to monitor and protect their most important secrets. The effort is cost effective and entirely appropriate.

Tomorrow's successful corporations will use undercover to not only protect their intellectual property but their other assets as well. This is a huge opportunity, don't miss it. If your organization is not currently occasionally using undercover, it should be. If you doubt it, ask a competitor.

Workplace Undercover Investigation for the Government

I have only done a small amount of undercover for the government and it has always puzzled me why we haven't been asked to do more. Some types of government investigations would clearly be inappropriate if conducted by a contractor. But there are many situations in which contract undercover would not only be appropriate but would be preferred. Consider the following possible applications:

- Investigation of equal employment opportunity complaints by the Department of Labor
- Covert monitoring of habitual offending employers by the Immigration and Naturalization Service (INS)
- Investigation of discrimination complaints by the Department of Fair Housing and Education
- Covert monitoring of food processing facilities
- Covert monitoring of waste disposal sites

- Covert monitoring of the entire transportation industry
- Covert monitoring of the food and drug industry

Please be clear that I am not suggesting that one industry or another deserves special monitoring or investigation. I am simply offering ideas to stimulate creativity and a little thinking outside of the box. Upon reflection, I think you will agree that there are literally thousands of opportunities for the more aggressive use of contract undercover at all levels of our government. I think we will see more of it in the future.

Workplace Evaluations

Over the years I have been occasionally asked to place undercover investigators into environments that had no apparent problem. For one such client alone, I have placed over 40 undercover investigators into its workforce. These efforts are sometimes called *look-see investigations* and are done for a variety of reasons (most of them appropriate). I prefer to call these investigations *workplace evaluations*. Greatly simplified and more expedient, these useful investigations can be extremely effective in measuring employee morale, employee attitudes, the quality of supervision, and the effectiveness of critical processes.

Workplace evaluations still require a properly trained investigator and a skilled case manager; however, there is usually no need for the rest of the investigative team. For example, if the issue of concern is the quality of off-shift supervision, a quickly placed operative can gather the information desired in several weeks and a single report serve as his work product. The report, as well as a debriefing with key management, is all that is necessary in order to allow corrective action. No muss, no fuss . . . in and out.

For a client like ours mentioned above, our primary objective is to determine that all line employees are treated properly and that their grievances (as rare as they are) are heard and acted upon. That's it! This particular employer is committed to a work environment in which all employees are consistently treated with respect and dignity, so committed in fact that it is rare that we do *not* have an operative in their workforce. And for a return on that investment the employer enjoys extremely low turnover, almost no absenteeism, a large team of highly motivated supervisors, happy customers, and no union. What price would your organization be willing to pay for benefits like these? Why not ask them?

A Final Word

For many, the term *undercover investigation* conjures up feelings of fear and outrage. Admittedly the reputation of this valuable investigative tool is mixed. Few know that better than those who use undercover everyday. However, undercover is a powerful mechanism, and when used properly it is unmatched in its effectiveness and ability to provide a return on investment. I hope that I have convinced you of that. For if I have, I have met my objective and the effort behind this work has been worth every word.

Be safe out there.

APPENDIX A

Sample Undercover Proposal

Scope

For some time, management at the Aurora, Colorado facility has had concerns about employee theft and substance abuse. Available information and unconfirmed allegations suggest that a serious problem may exist and that it may be fairly widespread. Corporate management is also concerned that an employee substance abuse problem could lead to other problems and might easily affect productivity and safety.

As a result, local and corporate management seek the assistance of a qualified external resource to investigate the allegations of employee misconduct and determine who may be involved. It is XYZ Company's intent to maintain a drug-free work environment and ensure a safe and healthy workplace for all of its employees, and at the same time to protect its assets.

Objectives

- Investigate the allegations of employee theft and determine the true nature and scope of the problem. Additionally, investigate and report on other forms of employee misconduct or crimes against the business.
- Gather any and all information concerning the problem in such a fashion as to allow management the opportunity to enforce its policies and effect appropriate corrective and/or disciplinary action.
- Conduct the factfinding process so that it is least disruptive to the organization and its operations.
- Engineer the process so that it provides the customer the highest possible return on investment.

Recommendations

It is recommended that XYZ Company ("the Client") pursue the objectives above incrementally. To that end and with the guiding assistance of Business Controls, Inc., the following is recommended:

A. Preparation and Planning

Determine the Client's specific needs and confirm the project's objectives, and develop an appropriate investigative strategy. Make necessary logistical preparations and coordinate initial investigative effort.

B. Information Gathering and Problem Identification

Surreptitiously place at least two undercover investigators into the workforce. Allow the investigators adequate time to gain the confidence of their coworkers and gather the desired information. Augment the undercover portion of the investigation with other forms of information gathering as appropriate.

C. Verification and Analysis

Interview the employees believed to be most involved. Obtain both written and tape-recorded statements from those interviewed. Cross-reference the information obtained, verifying and corroborating results where possible.

D. Disbursement of Disciplinary and Corrective Action

Business Controls, Inc. will not make recommendations regarding discipline. However, a detailed written summary of the investigative process and interviews will be provided to the Client at the completion of the project.

E. Prevention and Education

Business Controls, Inc. will provide, upon request, recommendations relative to workplace substance abuse prevention and education, and other aids to better protect assets and reduce employee temptation. The exact scope and nature of this service cannot be determined without first conducting the investigation.

Logistics

A. Material Needs

Business Controls, Inc. will need copies of current policies and procedures relative to pre-employment screening, theft, substance abuse, employee discipline, and copies of all labor agreements.

B. Our Investigator's Availability

The undercover portion of the project will likely run one to four months, or longer. The Client's objectives and the scope of the problem will drive the length of the investigation. Our investigators' availability varies depending upon the skills and experience required for the cover position. Once cover positions have been determined, we will know better the availability of the required investigators. All of our investigators are full-time, regular employees, and are licensed (where required) and insured. We do not use contract investigators.

Investment

A. Preparation and Planning

No charge.

B. Information Gathering and Problem Identification

The undercover investigator will be provided at a cost of $X per week per investigator, based on a five (5) day, eight (8) hour a day workweek. Fees for work performed beyond a five (5) day week or more than eight (8) hours in any one day worked will be prorated. The above rates include the cost of case supervision/management, the submission of the investigator's daily report, and the preparation of the Undercover Summary Reports that will be provided to the Client for every ten (10) work days of the assignment. Any communication costs, transportation, relocation costs (out of town investigators only), accommodations, special equipment, and utility expenses incurred by Business Controls, Inc. during the investigation will be in addition to the above fees. All security deposits and other cash outlays, which may be charged to the Client and ultimately recovered by Business Controls, Inc., will be returned or credited to the Client at the conclusion of the assignment. Given the facts as they are now known, a budget allowing 16 to 24 weeks of undercover should be ample.

With the Client's approval, Business Controls, Inc. may elect to augment the undercover portion of the investigation with other forms of information gathering. Should this service be used, the following rates will apply for the respective staff utilized:

Field Investigator/researcher	$ per hour
Surveillance Investigator	$ per hour
Interviewer	$ per hour
Associate	$ per hour
Executive	$ per hour

C. Verification and Analysis

This portion of the investigation involves the interviewing of those employees believed to be most involved in the violations of Client policy, as described by the Client, with the purpose of expanding Business Controls, Inc.'s information base and obtaining statements.

Should this service be used, the following rates will apply for the respective staff utilized at the interviews:

Interview Coordinator	$ per hour
Interviewer	$ per hour
Associate	$ per hour
Executive	$ per hour

In preparation for the interview process, our Interview Coordinator will compile the necessary reports and materials. This preparation time will be billed at the Interview Coordinator rate.

Any typing, photocopies, reproduction of audio and/or videotapes, transcription, mileage, transportation, and accommodation expenses incurred by Business Controls, Inc. during this phase of the work will be in addition to the above hourly rates. Administrative expense charges are as follows:

Photocopies	$ per copy
Mileage	$ per mile
Word Processing	$ per page
Tape Copy	$ per copy
Video Copy	$ per copy
Transcription	$ per page
Communication	as incurred

The number of employees interviewed will drive the investment for this portion of the investigation. Without more information the total number of interviews cannot be determined at this time.

Business Controls, Inc. will arrange transportation and lodging unless otherwise agreed. Business Controls, Inc. will seek and obtain the most economical fares/rates whenever practicable.

Return on Investment

The return on investment for a proactive drug and alcohol program is well documented. According to reports by the American Society for Industrial Security, a quality employee substance abuse awareness program returns $7.00 for every $1.00 invested.[1] The Institute for a Drug Free America maintains that the return may be measured in lower absenteeism, lower turnover, improved quality, higher productivity, and fewer lost-time accidents. In the case of employee theft and other forms of misconduct, actual return on investment can only be determined after more is learned about the scope and nature of the problem.

Frequently Asked Questions

Q. What is the length of the typical investigation?

A. Although the lengths of our investigations vary, undercover investigations rarely run less than 16 weeks. In every case, it is the size of the problem, the number of employees involved, and the skill of the investigators that drive the length of the process.

Q. What will be the total cost for the project?

A. The total investment is impossible to determine. However, a budget of $ per month per investigator should be adequate. The number of interviews will drive the cost of the interviews following the undercover portion of the investigation.

Q. How are the investigators trained and how often are their reports generated?

A. Each is taught about the drugs of abuse, employment law, and the process of investigation. Those who have not received our formal training either have prior law enforcement experience or have other qualifications that meet our strict standards. During the course of the investigation, the undercover investigator will generate a report every day he or she works. The computer-generated reports are up-loaded to our network daily and immediately provided to the case manager for review.

Q. How are the police involved and is prosecution necessary?

A. Law enforcement is involved to some degree in all of our drug investigations. However prosecution is an option that should be decided upon by both the Client and law enforcement. We make no decision regarding the prosecution of anyone.

Q. Are drug investigations dangerous?

A. Drug investigations can be very dangerous. However, at the first evidence of danger or a potentially violent situation we will make recom-

---

[1] William C. Cunningham, "The Hallcrest Report II," Hallcrest Systems, Inc., 1990.

mendations regarding the appropriate precautions. No one has ever been hurt during one of our drug investigations. Our highly structured process and trained staff help ensure the safety of our employees and the clients who engage us.

Licensing and Insurance

All but five states require private investigators to be licensed. Colorado requires no licensing. The investigation as now scoped should not require any work outside Colorado. However, if that changes we will obtain a license in the appropriate state or associate with another licensee.

In accordance with state and federal law, Business Controls, Inc. carries the required workers' compensation insurance. We also carry general liability, and errors and comissions insurance. A certificate of insurance is available upon request.

Qualifications

Business Controls, Inc. is a professional corporate undercover investigations firm and is registered as a Colorado corporation. The firm currently offers services throughout the United States, Canada, Mexico, Asia, and Europe. The firm specializes in the investigation of theft, dishonesty, and substance abuse in the workplace. Additionally, we offer pre-employment screening services, management training, litigation support, and an assortment of products and books related to our industry. Our clients include some of the most successful corporations, insurance companies, and law firms in the country.

Our mission: "Use innovation and technology to consistently provide our client partners with corporate undercover and special investigation services that are superior in quality and value, while ensuring they receive the highest possible return on their investment."

Our vision: "To build a world-class organization committed to continuous growth and market dominance, in which each employee has the opportunity to enrich themself professionally and financially to the fullest extent he or she desires."

Our values: "We treat all people with respect and dignity; we conduct all business with uncompromising integrity; we are loyal to our organization and mission; we encourage flexibility, innovation, and teamwork."

Mr. Eugene F. Ferraro, CPP, CFE will be the project leader. He is the President of Business Controls, Inc. and specializes in the investigation of employee dishonesty, substance abuse, and criminal activity in the workplace. He has supervised or managed well over 1,000 workplace undercover investigations. Mr. Ferraro has been designated a Certified Protection Professional (CPP) by the American Society of Industrial Security and serves as the chairman of its Standing Committee on Workplace Substance Abuse and Illicit Drug Activity. He is also a member of the National Association of Certified Fraud Examiners and is a Certified Fraud Examiner. Mr. Ferraro is a former military pilot, intelligence officer, and a graduate of the Naval Justice School. He holds a Bachelor of Science degree from the Florida Institute of Technology.

Affiliations

- American Society of Industrial Security
- Associated of Certified Fraud Examiners
- Professional Private Investigators Association of Colorado
- National Council of Investigative and Security Services
- National Association of Professional Process Servers

References

Trade and professional references will be provided upon request.

APPENDIX B

How to Select a Corporate Investigation Firm

License	In most states, private investigators and their agencies must be licensed. Request a copy of their license and required permits.
Experience	Ensure the agency as well as the employees they assign to your project have the experience necessary to do the job properly. Interview them and ask difficult questions.
Reputation	Reputations vary widely in the industry. The best agencies are well known in the business community and are active in their trade associations. Ask for references and check them thoroughly. Ask about their litigation and claims experience.
Willingness to Testify	All investigators must be willing to testify. You should be aware of any unwillingness to do so before the assignment begins.
Reports	Detailed reports should follow all investigative efforts. The information provided in a report should be complete, concise, and correct. Ask for samples and examine them thoroughly.
Insurance	All quality agencies carry general liability and errors and omissions insurance. Require a Certificate of Insurance and ensure the coverage is *occurrence* not *claims-made*.
Police Involvement	Employee prosecution is not always necessary. It is complicated and often expensive. The decision to prosecute should be made for business reasons only.

Attorney Involvement	Experienced agencies insist on the involvement of their client's attorneys. Those that don't should not be hired.
Return on Investment	All professional agencies provide proposals before accepting an assignment. If one is not offered, request one. The proposed investigation should offer an acceptable return on investment. If it does not, consider other options.

APPENDIX C

Common Drugs of Abuse

Alcohol

Alcohol (actually ethyl alcohol or ethanol) is the most commonly used and abused drug in the United States. It is a fast-acting central nervous system depressant that functions as an analgesic with sedative/hypnotic effects. Alcohol is addictive, and prolonged abuse can cause brain, liver, and heart damage. Its misuse accounts for about 250,000 deaths a year, ranking behind only cancer and heart disease. Nearly half of all highway fatalities are alcohol related.

Employee abusers are more frequently absent (especially Mondays and Fridays) and late. They use more sick time and often have problems at home that affect their ability to perform on the job. Abusers are typically in denial and project the cause of their problems on others.

Narcotics

The term *narcotic*, in the medical sense, refers to opium, opium derivatives, or their synthetic substitutes. As a group, these drugs are called *opiates* and are indispensable in the practice of medicine for they are the most effective substances known for the relief of intense pain. They are also highly addictive and frequently abused. The opiates include such drugs as codeine, morphine, and heroin. Usually taken orally or intravenously, some opiates are often smoked.

Employee abusers appear sleepy and lethargic. They move slower than others and are less productive. They tend to keep to themselves and aggressively protect their privacy.

Stimulants

In many ways, stimulants make our employees appear more alert, eager, and productive. However, this effect is at best short term, at worst it is just an illusion. What often appears to be productivity and enterprise is actually idling, wasted effort, and mistakes in the making. Abusers believe that stimulants enhance their creativity and endurance. In reality, they rob employees of their energy and rationality. Abusers suffer frequent and severe mood swings, making them difficult to manage and unpredictable to coworkers. Abusers often try to control their mood swings by using another drug, most often that drug is alcohol.

Cocaine

Cocaine (cocaine hydrochloride), which stimulates the central nervous system, is a white crystalline substance extracted from the coca plant. Though it has some medicinal value as a topical anesthetic, it is commonly abused and is considered highly addictive. Its immediate effects include dilated pupils, elevated blood pressure, increased heart rate, and euphoria.

Employee abusers may appear hyperactive and moody. They frequently have financial problems and often borrow money from their coworkers or employer. They bristle at criticism and quickly blame others for their mistakes and shortcomings. Fortunately, the popularity of this drug is declining. In many workplaces, cocaine has been replaced by methamphetamine.

Methamphetamine

Also known as *crank*, *meth*, *crystal-meth*, or *speed*, methamphetamine is a synthetic drug easily manufactured using shelf reagents and simple laboratory equipment. Because it is cheaper than cocaine and has longer lasting effects, methamphetamine has in many workplaces replaced cocaine as the drug of choice among stimulant abusers. Today, it is one of the most common illegal drugs found in the workplace.

Employee abusers are less productive and more prone to accidents and mistakes. They tend to be cliquish and secretive. They take more restroom breaks and are frequently absent while on the job (not at their desk or assigned workstation during the workday). They frequently miss deadlines and are quick to blame others.

Hallucinogens

Hallucinogens are powerful mind-altering drugs that drastically affect the user's mood, ability to reason, and sensory perception. They are also very unpredictable. Users' experiences vary, and no two "trips" are alike. Users often experience vivid hallucinations, panic, and a condition known as *synaesthesia*, or sensory crossover. Users lose depth perception, time perception, and emotional control. Emotions may range uncontrollably from ecstasy to terror.

Marijuana

Marijuana is one of the most common drugs of abuse in the workplace, second only to alcohol. Though a hallucinogen, in small quantities its effects are similar to alcohol, so it is often used by the recovering alcoholic or abstaining drinker. In larger doses, marijuana can cause vivid hallucinations, memory loss, and lethargy.

The principal psychoactive component, THC (delta-9-tetrahydrocannabinol), is a complex fat-soluble molecule retainable in the fatty tissue of the body. Because THC is not easily eliminated, it accumulates in the body of a regular user. As a result, the frequent user becomes less tolerant of the drug and steadily requires less of it to achieve the desired effect. Abusers may smoke less, but they tend to smoke more frequently. In many cases, the heavy marijuana smoker remains impaired all of his waking hours. This sort of abuser will smoke frequently throughout the workday in order to keep the concentration of THC in the body above that which is necessary to remain impaired. Often the abuser will use other drugs as well, increasing the risk to himself and others.

Employee abusers are less productive, make more mistakes, and have difficulty concentrating and learning. Long-term users suffer memory loss and damage to their reproductive systems. When under the influence of marijuana, their attention span shrinks and they have difficulty operating machinery and motor vehicles. When impaired, they are more prone to accidents and costly mistakes.

LSD and PCP

Lysergic acid diethylamide, or LSD, is colorless, odorless, and tasteless. However, it is one of the most powerful hallucinogens known. Most typically ingested orally, LSD has effects that are fast acting and long lasting. Users may experience vivid hallucinations interrupted by intense changes in mood. Impaired senses affect judgment and spatial orientation. Sometimes the effects last for hours.

On the job use is rare; however, in very small doses LSD may be substituted for methamphetamine or another stimulant. Employee abusers of LSD are inattentive, irritable, and prone to mistakes.

Phencyclidine, or PCP, was originally compounded as an anesthetic and analgesic, but because of its unpredictability and sometimes frightening side effects, its medical use was discontinued in 1967. PCP is typically added to a tobacco or marijuana cigarette and smoked. Its effects often last for hours.

Employee abusers are irritable, irrational, and sometimes physically violent. They are unable to concentrate and thus are prone to mistakes and accidents. Overdose may cause convulsions, coma, and death.

Prescription Drugs

Prescription drugs—usually stimulants or sedatives—are also frequently abused in the workplace. Typically first used properly under the supervision of a physician, prescription drugs are sometimes overused or continued when no longer needed. Physical or psychological dependency may develop. If the user can no longer obtain the drug legally, he or she may resort to illegal sources or substitute another drug for it.

Librium, Xanax, and Valium are some of the more common prescription drugs abused in the workplace. Employees who sell these drugs at work usually do so thinking they are helping a friend or coworker. They very rarely sell them to make a profit.

Employee abusers frequently mix prescription drugs with alcohol, thus compounding the effect of the drug. Abusers tend to be more frequently absent or tardy. They are often moody and irritable. As job performance declines, the employee increasingly becomes a disciplinary problem. Personal health and family problems are also typical in cases of long-term abuse.

APPENDIX D

The Controlled Substance Act

The legal foundation for the federal strategy of reducing the consumption of illegal drugs is the Comprehensive Drug Abuse Prevention and Control Act of 1970, Title II, which is better known as the Controlled Substance Act (CSA). There are four fundamental parts to this comprehensive federal law: (1) the mechanisms for reducing the availability of controlled substances; (2) the procedure for bringing a substance under control; (3) the criteria for determining control requirements; and (4) the obligations incurred by international treaty arrangements. Specifically, the law regulates the manufacture, purchase, and distribution of drugs according to their potential for abuse. The federal Drug Enforcement Agency (DEA) is responsible for enforcement and oversees the classification of all drugs. These classifications, or schedules, are as follows:

Schedule I

The drug or substance has a high potential for abuse and currently has no accepted use for medical use for treatment in the United States. Examples of Schedule I drugs are marijuana, hashish, heroin, and LSD.

Schedule II

The drug or substance has a high potential for abuse but currently has an accepted medical use in the United States with severe restrictions. Abuse may lead to severe psychological or physical dependency. Examples of Schedule II drugs are cocaine, morphine, amphetamines, and PCP.

Schedule III

The drug or substance has a potential for abuse less than the drugs or substances of Schedules I and II and currently has an accepted medical use in the United States. Abuse may lead to moderate or low physical dependency or high psychological dependency. Examples of Schedule III drugs are Codeine, Tylenol with Codeine, and Vicodin.

Schedule IV

The drug or substance has a low potential for abuse relative to Schedule III substances and currently has an accepted medical use in the United States. Abuse may lead to limited physical or psychological dependency relative to Schedule III substances. Examples of Schedule IV drugs are Darvon, Darvocet, Phenobarbital, and Valium.

Schedule V

The drug or substance has a low potential for abuse relative to Schedule IV substances and currently has an accepted medical use in the United States. Abuse may lead to limited physical or psychological dependency relative to Schedule IV substances. Examples of Schedule V drugs are the low-strength prescription cold and pain medicines commonly found in most homes.

Penalties

Possessing, compounding, or trafficking in scheduled drugs without permit or license is against the law. Federal penalties are severe and carry punishments of up to 40 years in a federal prison and fines up to $500,000! Some state laws are even tougher. Repeat offenders can be sentenced for life.

APPENDIX E

Anti-Drug Abuse Act of 1988

Sec. 5151 Short Title.

This subtitle may be cited as the "Drug-Free Workplace Act of 1988."

Sec. 5152 Drug-Free Workplace Requirements for Federal Contractors.

(a) DRUG-FREE WORKPLACE REQUIREMENT.—
(1) REQUIREMENT FOR PERSONS OTHER THAN INDIVIDUALS.—No person, other than an individual, shall be considered a responsible source, under the meaning of such term as defined in section 4(8) of the Office of Federal Procurement Policy Act (41 U.S.C 403(8)), for the purposes of being awarded a contract for the procurement of any property or services of a value of $25,000 or more from any Federal agency unless such person has certified to the contracting agency that it will provide a drug-free workplace by—
(A) publishing a statement notifying employees that the unlawful manufacture, distribution, dispensation, possession, or use of a controlled substance is prohibited in the person's workplace and specifying the actions that will be taken against employees for violations of such prohibition;
(B) establishing a drug-free awareness program to inform employees about—
(i) the dangers of drug abuse in the workplace;
(ii) the person's policy of maintaining a drug-free workplace;
(iii) any available drug counseling, rehabilitation and employee assistance programs; and
(iv) the penalties that may be imposed upon employees for drug abuse violations;

(C) making it a requirement that each employee to be engaged in the performance of such contract be given a copy of the statement required by subparagraph (A);

(D) notifying the employee in the statement required by subparagraph (A), that as a condition of employment on such contract, the employee will—

(i) abide by the terms of the statement and

(ii) notify the employer of any criminal drug statute conviction for a violation occurring in the workplace no later than 5 days after such conviction;

(E) notifying the contracting agency within 10 days after receiving notice under subparagraph (D)(i) from an employee or otherwise receiving actual notice of such conviction;

(F) imposing a sanction on, or requiring the satisfactory participation in a drug abuse assistance or rehabilitation program by, any employee who is so convicted, as required by section 5154; and

(G) making a good faith effort to continue to maintain a drug-free workplace through implementation of subparagraphs (A), (B), (C), (D), (E), and (F).

(2) REQUIREMENTS FOR INDIVIDUALS.—No Federal agency shall enter into a contract with an individual unless such contract includes a certification by the individual that the individual will not engage in the unlawful manufacture, distribution, dispensation, possession, or use of a controlled substance in the performance of the contract.

(b) SUSPENSION, TERMINATION, OR DEBARMENT OF THE CONTRACTOR.—

(1) GROUNDS FOR SUSPENSION, TERMINATION, OR DEBARMENT. —Each contract awarded by a Federal agency shall be subject to suspension of payments under the contract of termination of the contract, or both, and the contractor thereunder or the individual who entered the contract with the Federal agency, as applicable, shall be subject to suspension or debarment in accordance with the requirements of this section if the head of the agency determines that—

(A) the contractor violates or individual has made a false certification under subsection (a);

(B) the contractor violates such certification by failing to carry out the requirements of subparagraph (A), (B), (C), (D), (E), or (F) or subsection (a)(1); or

(C) such a number of employees of such contractor have been convicted of violations of criminal drug statutes for violations occurring in the workplace as to indicate that the contractor has failed to make a good faith effort to provide a drug-free workplace as required by subsection (a).

(2) CONDUCT OF SUSPENSION, TERMINATION, AND DEBARMENT PROCEEDINGS.—

(A) If a contracting officer determines, in writing, that cause for suspension of payments, termination, or suspension or debarment exists, an appropriate action shall be initiated by a contracting officer of the agency, to be conducted by the agency concerned in accordance with the Federal Acquisition Regulation and applicable agency procedures.

(B) The Federal Acquisition Regulation shall be revised to include rules for conducting suspension and debarment proceedings under this subsection, including rules providing notice, opportunity to respond in writing or in person, and such other procedures as may be necessary to provide a full and fair proceeding to a contractor or individual in such proceeding.

(3) EFFECT OF DEBARMENT.—Upon issuance of any final decision under this subsection requiring debarment of a contractor or individual, such contractor or individual shall be ineligible for award of any contract by any Federal agency, and for participation in any future procurement by any Federal agency, for a period specified in the decision, not to exceed 5 years.

Sec. 5153 Drug-Free Workplace Requirements for Federal Grant Recipients.

(a) DRUG-FREE WORKPLACE REQUIREMENT.—

(1) PERSONS OTHER THAN INDIVIDUALS.—No person, other than an individual, shall receive a grant from any Federal agency unless such person has certified to the granting agency that it will provide a drug-free workplace by—

(A) publishing a statement notifying employees that the unlawful manufacture, distribution, dispensation, possession, or use of a controlled substance is prohibited in the grantee's workplace and specifying the actions that will be taken against employees for violations of such prohibition;

(B) establishing a drug-free awareness program to inform employees about—

(i) the dangers of drug abuse in the workplace;

(ii) the grantee's policy of maintaining a drug-free workplace;

(iii) any available drug counseling, rehabilitation, and employee assistance programs; and

(iv) the penalties that may be imposed upon employees for drug abuse violations;

(C) making it a requirement that each employee to be engaged in the performance of such grant be given a copy of the statement required by subparagraph (A);

(D) notifying the employee in the statement required by subparagraph (A), that as a condition of employment in such grant, the employee will—

(i) abide by the terms of the statement; and

(ii) notify the employer of any criminal drug statue conviction for a violation occurring in the workplace no later than 5 days after such conviction;

(E) notifying the granting agency within 10 days after receiving notice of a conviction under subparagraph (D)(ii) from an employee or otherwise receiving actual notice of such conviction;

(F) imposing a sanction on, or requiring the satisfactory participation in a drug-abuse assistance or rehabilitation program by, any employee who is so convicted, as required by section 5154; and

(G) making a good faith effort to continue to maintain a drug-free workplace through implementation of subparagraphs (A), (B), (C), (D), (E), and (F).

(2) INDIVIDUALS.—No Federal agency shall make a grant to any individual unless such individual certifies to the agency as a condition of such grant that the individual will not engage in the unlawful manufacture, distribution, dispensation, possession, or use of a controlled substance in conducting any activity with such grant.

(b) SUSPENSION, TERMINATION, OR DEBARMENT OF THE GRANTEE.—

(1) GROUNDS FOR SUSPENSION, TERMINATION, OR DEBARMENT. —Each grant awarded by a Federal agency shall be subject to suspension of payments under the grant or termination of the grant, or both, and the grantee thereunder shall be subject to suspension or debarment, in accordance with the requirements of this section if the head of the granting agency or his official designee determines, in writing, that—

(A) the grantee has made a false certification under subsection (a);

(B) the grantee violates such certification by failing to carry out the requirements of subparagraph (A), (B), (C), (D), (E), (F), or (G) of subsection (a)(1); or

(C) such a number of employees of such grantee have been convicted of violation of criminal drug statutes for violations occurring in the workplace as to indicate that the grantee has failed to make a good faith effort to provide a drug-free workplace as required by subsection (a)(1).

(2) CONDUCT OF SUSPENSION, TERMINATION, AND DEBARMENT PROCEEDINGS.—A suspension of payments, termination, or suspension or debarment proceeding subject to this subsection shall be conducted in accordance with applicable law, including Executive Order 12549 or any superseding Executive order and any regulations promulgated to implement such law or Executive order.

(3) EFFECT OF DEBARMENT.—Upon issuance of any final decision under this subsection requiring debarment of a grantee, such grantee shall be ineligible for award of any grant from any Federal agency and for participation in any future grant from any Federal agency for a period specified in the decision, not to exceed 5 years.

Sec. 5154 Employee Sanctions and Remedies.

A grantee or contractor shall, within 30 days after receiving notice from an employee of a conviction pursuant to section 5152(a)(1)(D)(ii) or 5153(a)(1)(D)(ii)—

(1) take appropriate personnel action against such employee up to and including termination; or

(2) require such employee to satisfactorily participate in a drug abuse assistance or rehabilitation program approved or such purposes by a Federal, State, or local health, law enforcement, or another appropriate agency.

Sec. 5155 Waiver.

(a) IN GENERAL.—A termination, suspension of payments, or suspension or debarment under this subtitle may be waived by the head of an agency with respect to a particular contract or grant if—
(1) in the case of a waiver with respect to a contract, the head of the agency determines under section 5152(b)(1), after the issuance of a final determination under such section, that suspension of payments, or termination of the contract, or suspension or debarment of the contractor, or refusal to permit a person to be treated as a responsible source for a contract, as the case may be, would severely disrupt the operation of such agency to the detriment of the Federal Government or the general public; or
(b) EXCLUSIVE AUTHORITY.—The authority of the head of an agency under this section to waive a termination, suspension, or debarment shall not be delegated.

Sec. 5156 Regulations.

Not later than 90 days after the date of enactment of this subtitle, the government wide regulations governing actions under this subtitle shall be issued pursuant to the Office of Federal Procurement Policy Act (41 U.S.C. 401 et seq.).

Sec. 5157 Definitions.

For purposes of this subtitle—
(1) the term "drug-free workplace" means a site for the performance of work done in connection with a specific grant or contract described in section 5152 or 5153 or an entity at which employees of such entity are prohibited from engaging in the unlawful manufacture, distribution, dispensation, possession, or use of a controlled substance in accordance with the requirements of this Act;
(2) the term "employee" means the employee of a grantee or contractor directly engaged in the performance of work pursuant to the provisions of the grant or contract described in section 5152 or 5153;
(3) the term "controlled substance" means a controlled substance in schedules I through V of section 202 of the Controlled Substances Act (21 U.S.C. 812);

(4) the term "conviction" means a finding of guilt (including a plea of nolo contendere) or imposition of sentence, or both, by any judicial body charges with the responsibility to determine violations of the Federal or State criminal drug statures;

(5) the term "criminal drug statute" means a criminal statute involving a manufacture, distribution, dispensation, use or possession or any controlled substance;

(6) the term "grantee" means the department, division, or other unit of a person responsible for the performance under the grant;

(7) the term "contractor" means the department, division, or other unit of a person responsible for the performance under the contract; and

(8) the term "Federal agency" means an agency as that term is defined in section 552(f) of title 5, United States Code.

Sec. 5158 Construction of subtitle.

Nothing in this subtitle shall be construed to require law enforcement agencies, if the head of the agency determines it would be inappropriate in connection with the agency's undercover operations, to comply with the provisions of this subtitle.

Sec. 5159 Repeal of Limitation on Use of Funds.

Section 628 of Public Law 100–400 (relating to restrictions on the use of certain appropriated amounts) is amended—

(1) by striking "(a)" after "Sec. 628."; and

(2) by striking subsection (b).

Sec. 5160 Effective Date.

Sections 5152 and 5153 shall be effective 120 days after the date of the enactment of this subtitle.

This transcription of the "ANTI-DRUG ABUSE ACT OF 1988" has been prepared in this format by Business Controls, Inc. only for the purpose of providing information. Its accuracy is based on government documents available at the time of publication. Should you have questions concerning the act or compliance, we suggest you seek the advice of counsel.

APPENDIX F

Media Response Kit

Media Statement #1

We currently are having a management-driven investigation taking place at our facility. The investigation is drug-related and involves violations of company policies.
We are in the fact-finding stage. We are using an outside consulting firm to aid us in this portion of the investigation.
At this time, we have asked some employees to stay home. They are receiving full pay. We have taken no disciplinary action. We expect the investigation to continue through the early part of next week.
Company policy prohibits the possession, use, sale, or distribution of illegal drugs or controlled substances on company property.
This is not part of a company-wide effort. We have nothing else to say at this time. The investigation is still under way. At this time we have no further comment.

Follow Nondisclosure Guidelines.

Media Statement #2

We will be concluding our investigation soon. We can confirm that there were a relatively small number of violations of company policies pertaining to illegal drugs. Where appropriate, corrective action will be taken. Currently some employees have been asked to stay home while we complete the information-gathering process. They will receive full pay during this time.
As in any situation involving an internal investigation, the surrounding circumstances will be treated with complete confidentiality to protect the privacy of the individuals involved. At this time we have no further comment.

Follow Nondisclosure Guidelines.

Media Statement #3

We have concluded our investigation, and disciplinary action is being dispensed. This was a management-driven investigation. It is drug-related and involved violations of company policy. Realizing that we needed professional assistance to guide us through the information-gathering phase, we hired the consulting firm of Business Controls, Inc. to assist us. Business Controls, Inc. specializes in the investigation of employee substance abuse and employee dishonesty and misconduct.

Company policy prohibits the possession, use, sale, or distribution of illegal drugs or controlled substances on company property and recommends immediate termination of any employee who violates that policy. This is not part of a company-wide effort. At this time we have no further comment.

Follow Nondisclosure Guidelines.

Sample Questions to Management and Responses

Q: What is the company's policy regarding drugs?

A: The employment of an individual who has engaged in harmful or illegal acts that involve or affect the company or that occur on property (including company vehicles) may be terminated immediately. Acts of misconduct include (1) use, possession, sale, dissemination, or other involvement in illegal drugs or controlled substances; (2) unauthorized use of alcohol; and (3) impairment due to alcohol, drugs, or controlled substances.

Q: Doesn't the company help employees with drug problems—not fire them?

A: The EAP and other programs have been made known and available to employees. Some have chosen to utilize these resources and that information has remained confidential and is not related to this situation.

Q: Is it fair to fire employees if they do not know the policy?

A: Any time one is dealing with illegal substances, it can be assumed that the company cannot condone it.

Q: How was the information gathered?

A: A variety of methods were used. The decisions made regarding the employees involved were made based on solid facts and evidence.

Q: Will it happen again?

A: We certainly hope it will not be necessary.

Q: What is the policy for off-site activities, such as these?

A: We are not here to dictate personal life styles; however, when it affects company business, we get involved.

Q: What substances and activities were involved?

A: We are concerned with violations of company policies that prohibit the possession, use, sale, or distribution of illegal drugs or controlled substances on company property.

Q: Are you going to press charges?

A: If violations of the law have taken place, it is law enforcement's responsibility to take action. We play no role in that area.

Q: Why not?

A: Our objective is and has always been to enforce company policies. The authorities will deal with the enforcement of public law.

Q: Where was the investigation centered?

A: It was a wide-ranging investigation, not isolated to any specific areas.

Q: How many people are (were) involved?

A: Fewer than—.

Q: What caused the company to begin the investigation?

A: Employees and managers expressed concerns about this type of activity and what they perceived to be violations of laws and policy. We have a responsibility as a corporate citizen.

Q: When did you first learn about specific problems here?

A: Like most employers, we have been concerned about the problem for some time and have been investigating the issue since it came to our attention.

Q: Which areas and which levels are involved?

A: We did not limit the investigation. Information was pursued without regard to area or level within the organization.

Q: How long has the outside firm been involved?

A: They have been aiding us during the information-gathering portion of the investigation.

Q: Is the outside firm a private investigation firm?

A: Yes. Realizing that we needed outside expert help, we hired Business Controls, Inc. They specialize in the investigation of employee substance abuse, dishonesty, and misconduct.

Q: Was there any illegal drug dealing?

A: Yes, but not large amounts. We were concerned about all violations of the company policy, which prohibit the possession, use, sale, or distribution of illegal drugs or controlled substances on company property.

Q: Have you increased your security as a result of this investigation?

A: No. [Or: In these types of cases, emotions run high. The consulting firm has advised adding additional security as a precautionary measure.]

Q: What actions have you taken?

A: A range of actions, from verbal reprimands to termination.

APPENDIX G

Settle-Down Meeting

Introduction

1. Introduce self and staff
2. Discuss problem and concerns of company
3. Decision to investigate
4. The investigation not a "witch hunt"

Purpose

1. To identify extent of problem and those who were involved
2. Salvage as many people as possible
3. Learn how to prevent problems from reoccurring

Result

1. Serious drug problem, use, and sale
2. Employee theft
3. Serious alcohol problem

Implications

1. Effects on the individual
2. Effects on the company

Close with a restatement of company policy and possibility of future re-investigation, if necessary.

Extension of thanks to the loyal and honest employees . . . "Now, let's get back to what we do best."

APPENDIX H

The Americans With Disabilities Act

The Americans With Disabilities Act (ADA) is a federal antidiscrimination statute designed to remove barriers that prevent qualified individuals with disabilities from enjoying the same employment opportunities that are available to persons without disabilities.

Like the Civil Rights Act of 1964 that prohibits discrimination on the bases of race, color, religion, national origin, and sex, the ADA seeks to ensure access to equal employment opportunities based on merit. It does not guarantee equal results, establish quotas, or require preferences favoring individuals with disabilities over those without disabilities.

However, while the Civil Rights Act of 1964 prohibits any consideration of personal characteristics such as race or national origin, the ADA necessarily takes a different approach. When an individual's disability creates a barrier to employment opportunities, the ADA requires employers to consider whether reasonable accommodation could remove the barrier. The ADA thus establishes a process in which the employer must assess a disabled individual's ability to perform the essential functions of the specific job held or desired. While the ADA focuses on eradicating barriers, the ADA does not relieve a disabled employee or applicant from the obligation to perform the essential functions of the job. To the contrary, the ADA is intended to enable disabled persons to compete in the workplace based on the same performance standards and requirements that employers expect of persons who are not disabled.

However, where that individual's functional limitation impedes such job performance, an employer must take steps to reasonably accommodate and thus help them overcome the particular impediment, unless to do so would impose an undue hardship. Such accommodations usually take the form of adjustments to the way a job customarily is performed or to the work environment itself.

This process of identifying whether, and to what extent, a reasonable accommodation is required should be flexible and involves both the employer and the individual with a disability. Of course, the determination of whether an individual is qualified for a particular position must necessarily be made on a case-by-case basis. No specific form of accommodation is guaranteed for all individuals with a particular disability. Rather, an accommodation must be tailored to match the needs of the disabled individual with the needs of the job's essential functions.

This case-by-case approach is essential if qualified individuals of varying abilities are to receive equal opportunities to compete for a diverse range of jobs. For this reason, the ADA cannot supply the "correct" answer in advance for each employment decision concerning an individual with a disability. Instead, the ADA simply establishes parameters to guide employers in how to consider, and take into account, the disabling condition involved.

The Equal Employment Opportunity Commission (the Commission or EEOC) is responsible for enforcement of Title I of the ADA, 42 U.S.C. 12101 et seq. (1990), which prohibits employment discrimination on the basis of disability. The Commission believes that it is essential to issue interpretive guidance in order ensure that qualified individuals with disabilities understand their rights and to facilitate and encourage compliance by covered entities. This Appendix represents the Commission's interpretation of the issues discussed, and the Commission will be guided by it when resolving charges of employment discrimination. The Appendix addresses the major provisions of the ADA and explains the major concepts of disability rights.

The terms "employer" or "employee or other covered entity" are used interchangeably throughout the Appendix to refer to all covered entities subject to the employment provision of the ADA.

The act was signed into law on July 26, 1990. It is wide-ranging legislation intended to make American society more accessible to people with disabilities. It is divided into five titles:

1. Employment (Title 1). Business must provide reasonable accommodations to protect the rights of individuals with disabilities in all aspects of employment. Possible changes may include restructuring jobs, altering the layout of workstations, or modifying equipment. Employment aspects may include the application process, hiring, wages, benefits, and all other aspects of employment. Medical examinations are highly regulated.
2. Public Services (Title II). Public services, which include state and local government instrumentalities, the National Railroad Passenger Corporation, and other commuter authorities, cannot easily deny to people with disabilities participation in programs or activities which are available to people without disabilities. In addition, public transportation systems, such as public transit buses, must be accessible to individuals with disabilities.

3. Public Accommodations (Title III). All new construction and modifications must be accessible to individuals with disabilities. For existing facilities, barriers to service must be removed if readily achievable. Public accommodations include facilities such as restaurants, hotels, grocery stores, retail stores, etc., as well as privately owned transportation systems.
4. Telecommunications (Title IV). Telecommunications companies offering telephone service to the general public must have telephone relay service to individuals who use telecommunications devices for the deaf (TTYs) or similar devices.
5. Miscellaneous (Title V). Includes a provision prohibiting either (a) coercing or threatening or (b) retaliating against the disabled or those attempting to aid people with disabilities in asserting their rights under the ADA.

The ADA's protection applies primarily, but not exclusively, to "disabled" if he or she meets at least any one of the following tests:

- He or she is substantially impaired with respect to a major life activity.
- He or she has a record of such impairment.
- He or she is regarded as having such an impairment.

Other individuals who are protected in certain circumstances include (1) those, such as parents, who have an association with an individual known to have a disability, and (2) those who are coerced or subjected to retaliation for assisting people with disabilities in asserting their rights under the ADA.

While the employment provisions of the ADA apply to employers of 15 employees or more, its public accommodations provisions apply to all sizes of business, regardless of number of employees. State and local governments are covered regardless of size.

The ADA uses the term *disabilities* rather than the term *handicaps* used in the rehabilitation Act of 1973. Substantively, these terms are equivalent. As noted by the House Committee on the Judiciary, "the use of the term 'disabilities' instead of the term 'handicaps' reflects the desire of the committee to use the most current terminology. It reflects the preference of persons with disabilities to use that term rather then 'handicapped' as used in previous laws, such as the rehabilitation act of 1973."

The use of the term *Americans* in the title of the ADA is not intended to imply that the Act only applies to U.S. citizens. Rather, the ADA protects all qualified individuals with disabilities, regardless of their citizenship, status, or nationality.

APPENDIX I

The New Fair Credit Reporting Act

Changes to the Fair Credit Reporting Act

The Fair Credit Reporting Act (FCRA), originally enacted in 1970, was extensively amended in 1996. The bulk of the amendments to the law went into effect on September 30, 1997, and affects most employers. The changes primarily deal with the obligation of the CRA (Consumer Reporting Agency) and the User (employer) to furnish notices and disclosures to the Consumer (applicant). Although there were many changes to the FCRA that affect the credit industry, the focus of this Appendix is to shed light on the new law and its impact on the applicant screening process.

Definitions

Consumer Reporting Agency: Anyone who engages, in whole or in part, in the practice of assembling consumer credit information or other information on consumers for the purpose of furnishing consumer reports to third parties.

Consumer Report: Any report from a CRA reflecting the credit worthiness, credit standing, credit capacity, character, general reputation, personal characteristics, or mode of living which is used solely or partially for the purpose of serving as a factor in establishing the consumer's eligibility for credit, insurance, or employment purposes.

Investigative Consumer Report: A consumer report (or portion thereof) in which information on a consumer's character, general reputation, personal characteristics, or mode of living is obtained through personal interviews.[1]

User: A recipient of a consumer report or investigative consumer report.

Consumer: The individual that was the subject of the consumer report or investigative consumer report. For employment purposes, this may either be an applicant or an employee.

Adverse Action: Relating to employment, a denial of employment or any other decision for employment purposes that adversely affects any current or prospective employee.

What's New

The amended Fair Credit Reporting Act (FCRA) now requires a Consumer Reporting Agency (CRA) and Users (employers) to provide several types of notices and make specific disclosures to the Consumer. The FCRA establishes new Consumer rights and new obligations for CRA and the User:

- Intent to obtain a consumer report must be disclosed in a stand-alone document
- Consumer must authorize, in writing, the procurement of a report
- When used for employment purposes, requires the User to provide a copy of the report to the Consumer in advance of any adverse action, along with a prescribed notice of consumer rights [§607(c)]
- Limits information that antedates the report by more than 7 years
- Requires the CRA to obtain certification of compliance of the law from Users
- Provides for penalties and legal fees for violations of the FCRA [§§616, 619]

Obligation of Users (Employers)

- Prior to obtaining a consumer report for employment purposes, the user must disclose to the consumer their intent in a clear and conspicuous disclosure (stand-alone document) [§604(b)(2)(A)]
- Obtain from the consumer written authorization prior to procurement of the report [§604(b)(2)(B)]
- If an investigative consumer report is obtained, the consumer must be notified of its preparation no later than three days after the date on

---

[1] An interview, in this context, is asking questions that go beyond the scope of verifying factual information, i.e., dates, degrees, etc., and call for opinion, i.e., performance or character. These include, but are not limited to, contacts made with past employers, educational institutions, neighbors, friends, references, or associates of the consumer.

which the report is first requested.[2] The consumer must be advised of their right to request additional disclosures as to the nature and scope of the report and be given a copy of the prescribed summary of consumer rights [§606(a)(1)]

- Certify to the CRA that all laws will be adhered to and that all notices and disclosures will be provided to the consumer [§§604(b)(1), 604(f)]
- Prior to taking any adverse action, based in whole or in part upon information provided in the consumer report (or investigative consumer report), the Consumer (applicant) must be given a copy of the consumer report (and/or investigative report) and a copy of the consumer summary of rights [§604(b)(3)]
- If adverse action is taken, the User must notify the consumer either in writing, orally, or by electronic means. The User must provide the Consumer with the name, address, and phone number of the CRA that provided the report. The Consumer must be advised that the CRA did not make the adverse decision and does not know why the decision was made; that the Consumer has a right to obtain a free copy of the report from the CRA if ordered within 60 days; and that the consumer has a right to directly dispute with the CRA the accuracy or completeness of a report [§§612, §615(a)]

Obligation of CRA (Vendor)

- Cannot report negative information that is more than seven years old, ten years for bankruptcies[3] [§605(b)]
- Has a duty to maintain accuracy of public record and other information [§§606(d)(3), 613, 623(a)(1)]
- The CRA is required to provide a notice to Users of their responsibilities under the FCRA (User notice) [§607(d)]
- When an adverse decision is made based upon information provided by a CRA, the CRA will respond to consumer inquires within the time frame prescribed [§§611, 612]

Consumer Rights (Applicant)

- The Consumer must be told if information in their file has been used against them. Anyone who uses information from a CRA to take action against a Consumer (i.e., denying an application for credit, insurance, or employment) must tell the Consumer prior to taking any

---

[2] It must be clearly and accurately disclosed that an investigative consumer report, including information as to character, general reputation, personal characteristics, and mode of living, whichever are applicable, may be made.

[3] Interestingly, employers may not use bankruptcy information when making an employment decision.

adverse action and give them the name, address, and phone number of the CRA that provided the consumer report

- At the request of the Consumer, a CRA must give the Consumer the information in their file, and a list of everyone who has requested it recently. There is no charge for the report if a User has taken action against a Consumer, because of information supplied by the CRA, if requested within 60 days of receiving notice of the action. A Consumer is entitled to one free report every 12 months, upon request, if the applicant certifies that (1) they are unemployed and plan to seek employment within 60 days, (2) they are on welfare, or (3) the report is inaccurate due to fraud. Otherwise, a CRA may charge up to $8.00
- If a Consumer tells a CRA that their file contains inaccurate information, the CRA must investigate the claim (usually, within 30 days)
- Inaccurate information must be corrected or deleted. A CRA must remove or correct inaccurate or unverified information from their files, usually within 30 days after a dispute. In addition, the CRA must give an applicant a written notice stating it has reinserted the item. The notice must include the name, address, and phone number of the information source
- A Consumer can dispute inaccurate items with the source of the information. If an applicant tells anyone, such as a creditor who reports to a CRA, that there is a disputed item, they may not then report the information to a CRA without including a notice of the dispute
- Access to a Consumer's file is limited. A CRA may provide information about a Consumer only to those with a legitimate permissible purpose as recognized by the FCRA, usually to consider an application with a creditor, insurer, employer, landlord, or other business
- A Consumer's consent is required for reports that are provided to employers, or reports that contain medical information
- A Consumer may choose to exclude their name from the CRA's lists for unsolicited credit and insurance offers. If a Consumer requests, completes, and returns the CRA form provided for this purpose, the Consumer must be taken off the lists indefinitely
- A Consumer may seek damages from violators in state or federal court if an FCRA violation has been made

Conclusion

The amendments to the FCRA mandate some change. However, the full impact of these changes is not yet known. It will likely take years before the legislature and courts answer many of the questions this law has created. In the meantime, employers should

- Separately disclose a report request potential and obtain written consent from the consumer
- Certify to the CRA that disclosures and consent have been made and obtained; provide preadverse action disclosures and investigative report disclosures
- Prior to adverse action, provide consumer report and summary of rights
- Provide postadverse action notice stating CRA contact information; that CRA is not the decisionmaker; their right to obtain a free copy of the report; and their right to dispute

Bibliography

American Society for Industrial Security. *Substance Abuse, A Guide to Workplace Issues.*1990. Alexandria, VA.

Barefoot, J. Kirk. *Undercover Investigation.* 3rd ed. Boston: Butterworth-Heinemann, 1995.

Balevic, H. J. *Drug Abuse in the Workplace.* Selfpublished S.1. Henry J. Balevic, 1985.

Baron, A. S. *Violence in the Workplace.* Vewtura, CA. Pathfinder Publishing of California, 1993.

Fay, J. *Drug Testing.* Boston: Butterworth-Heineman, 1991.

Ferraro, E. F. *Employer's Guide to Workplace Substance Abuse.* Denver Marathow Press, 1999.

Simmons, R. J. *Employer's Guide to Workplace Security and Violence Prevention.* Losangeles, CA. Castle Publications, Ltd., 1994.

U.S. Department of Justice. *Crime Data Brief: Crime and Substance Abuse.* Washington, D.C.: Government Printing Office, 1995.

U.S. Department of Justice. *State Drug Resources: 1992 National Directory.* Washington, D.C.: Government Printing Office, 1993.

U.S. Department of Labor. *Workplaces Without Drugs.* Washington, D.C.: Government Printing Office, 1993.

Index

accidents/injuries, 114–115
Adams v. Alderson, 197
addiction, 110–112. *See also* drugs;
 substance abuse
agencies, selecting, 57, 58–61,
 255–256
 avoiding bad choices of, 79
 licensing and, 58
agent status, 188
aggressors, profile of, 17–18
alcohol, 257. *See also* drug/alcohol
 testing
 crime and, 5–6
 impact of on business, 6–7
 prevalence of, 6
American Society of Industrial
 Security, 235
Americans with Disabilities Act
 (ADA), 196–197, 201, 274–277
 drug/alcohol testing and, 206–207
amnesty, 74
Anti-Drug Abuse Act of 1988,
 263–268
arbitration
 evidence in, 165–167
 testimony in, 167–170
 winning through criminal
 prosecution, 170–171
arrests, coordinating, 180, 188–189
assault and battery, 221
Association of Certified Fraud
 Examiners, 12–13, 139
attorneys
 agency selection and, 60

 in case management, 85–87
 role of in investigations, 74–76
attorney work product, 75–76, 85–86
audits
 information gathering via, 127
 security checklist for, 235–236
awareness programs, 3
 substance abuse, 109–110
Awbrey v. Great Atl. & Pac. Tea Co.,
 214

background investigations
 employee, 21
 negligent hiring and, 193–194
 pre-employment, 123–124
benchmarking, 233–235
"beyond a reasonable doubt"
 standard, 47
billing, 34–38
 invoice types, 60–61
Bourke v. Nissan Motor Corp., 216
Brasco, Donnie, 70
breach of implied contract, 194
business failures, 12
buy-busts, 153
buy reports, 97

cartels, 3
case files, 101–103
 organization of, 102
 sexual harassment, 199
 storage/security of, 102–103
case management, 81–87
 defined, 81

case management (*continued*)
　levels of, 81–82
　team members in, 82–87
case managers, 33, 82–84
case shutdown, 177–190
　administrative/operational
　　preparations for, 178–180
　coordinating with authorities, 171,
　　180
　employee communications/public
　　relations and, 179–180, 190
　employee interviews in, 181–187
　law enforcement role in, 187–189
　operative removal and, 189–190
　outcome selection and, 177–178
　restitution/recovery and, 180–181
case supervisors, 33
Certificate of Insurance, 60
chemical dependence, 111–112
childcare industry, 242
cigarettes, 153
Civil Rights Act of 1964, 197
Civil Rights Act of 1991, 197–198
Civil War, 2
Clapton, Eric, 3
client-employers
　in case management, 84–85
　commitment of to investigation,
　　28–38
　doctrine of respondeat superior and,
　　194–195
　enabling by, 117–118
　financial obligations of, 24–25
　legal obligations of, 23–24
　moral obligations of, 22–23
　obligation of to investigate, 24, 191
　in operative selection, 63
　responsibilities of in hiring private
　　investigators, 195–196
　role of in investigations, 78
　substance abuse awareness
　　programs and, 109–110
　time required from, 28–31, 33–34
　understanding of substance abuse
　　for, 119
clinicians, 19
cocaine, 2, 258
　epidemic, 4–5

rock, 4
code names, 90, 94
codependency, 118–119
cognitive consistency, 149–150
cold hires, 68
collective bargaining agreements, 201.
　See also organized labor
communication, 87–103
　avoiding excessive preinvestigation,
　　73
　case files, 101–103
　confidential, 215
　electronic, 99–100
　employee, 179–180, 190
　ineffective postinvestigative,
　　174–175
　monitoring, 213–217
　skills for, 62
　of substance abuse policies, 124
　in team meetings, 101
　telephone, 100–101
　written reports, 87–99
"compelling interest" standard, 203
competitors, exposing dishonest,
　240
Comprehensive Drug Abuse
　Prevention and Control Act of
　1970, 261–262
confidential communication, 215
　attorney work product as, 75–76,
　　85–86
Confidentiality of Medical
　Information Act, 207
constructive knowledge of
　harassment, 199
consultants, 72
consumer reports, 221–222, 279–283
contraband materials, 153
contract employees, 243
contracts
　breach of implied, 194
　service, 57–58
　verbal, 46
contract security, 7–8, 72
　responsibilities of in clients in
　　hiring, 195–196
　undercover in, 242–243
controlled hires, 68–69

Controlled Substance Act (CSA), 261–262
conversion, 143–144
costs, 33–38
    of fraud to employers, 12–13
    human, 106
    recovering (*See* restitution)
    savings through terminations, 237–239
cover position selection, 64–67. *See also* placement
cover stories, 69–70
credit reports, 221–222, 279–283
crime
    alcohol and, 5–6
    prevalence of employee, 10–13
criminal immunity, 77
criminal justice system, impact of drug crime on, 5
custodian of record, 102–103

D.A.R.E., 3
Dealers, see drug dealers
Dean v. Ford Motor Credit C., 217–218
denial, of substance abuse, 115–117
different treatment, 197
disability claims, 115
disciplinary actions
    basing on employee admissions, 128–129
    determining appropriate, 33–34
    in drug investigations, 121–124
discrimination
    email as evidence of, 217
    ensuring freedom from, 23–24
    failure to investigate, 40–41
    lawsuits, avoiding, 196–198
disparate impact, 197
disparate treatment, 197
doctrine of respondeat superior, 194–195
documentation, 120, 121. *See also* reports
dogs, narcotics, 137
doper logic, 8–9, 108–110
drug/alcohol testing, 7
    as condition of returning to work, 210

government-mandated, 202, 205–206
    of investigators, 62, 134
    negligence in administering, 209–210
    during physical exams, 206–207
    postaccident, 208
    pre-employment, 206
    privacy rights and, 202, 205–210
    random, 208–209
    reasonable suspicion and, 207–208
drug culture, 2, 108–109
drug dealers, 111
    employee, 8–9
    making purchases from, 132–135
Drug Enforcement Agency (DEA), 2, 4
Drug-Free Workplace Act of 1988, 263–268
drug-free workplaces, 9–10
    employers' role in, 106–107
drug investigations, 105–138
    amnesty offers before, 74
    disbursement of disciplinary/corrective action phase in, 128–129
    discipline/corrective action in, 121–124
    and employee prosecution, 137–138
    importance of purchases in, 134–135
    information development in, 131–132
    interventions and, 119–121
    planning/preparation phase of, 125
    prevention/education phase in, 129
    problem identification/information gathering in, 125–128
    process of, 124–129
    purchase guidelines for, 132–134
    relationships building in, 130–131
    role of law enforcement in, 77–78
    supporting investigation for, 135–137
    time required for, 30–31
    verification/analysis phase of, 128
drug paraphernalia, 48–49
drugs. *See also specific drugs*

drugs (*continued*)
  of abuse, 107, 257–260
  crime and, 3
  impact of on business, 5–8
  prescription, 260
  in U.S. culture, 1–2
  war on, 2–5
due process, 42
duty to investigate, 40

elderly abuse, 242
Electronic Communications Privacy
    Act of 1986 (ECPA), 213, 216
email, 99–100
  monitoring, 216–217
emotional distress, infliction of,
    194
  in interviews, 217–218
employee assistance programs (EAPs),
    122–123
employee counseling programs, 7
employee manuals, 194
Employee Polygraph Protection Act
    (EPPA), 223
employee relations, 173–175
employees
  admissions by, 128–129
  background investigations of, 21
  employer liability for acts of,
    194–195
  empowerment of, 30
  prevalence of criminality of, 10–13
  prosecution of in drug
    investigations, 137–138
  reasons for theft by, 139–141
  screening before hiring, 123–124
  sensitizing to investigation, 73–74
  understanding substance abuse by,
    107–110
  vs. independent contractors, 37–38
employers. *See* client-employers
enabling, 52, 117–118
entrapment, 43, 87
  multiple buys as defense against,
    155–156
Equal Employment Opportunity
    Commission (EEOC), 196
evaluations, workplace, 190, 245
evidence

  in arbitration/grievance procedures,
    165–167
  corroborating, 154–156
  markers, 154
  physical, gathered during
    interviews, 187
  in unemployment hearings, 172
expectations, in interventions,
    120–121
Exxon Valdez, 6–7

failure to investigate, 39–41, 192–
    195
failure to represent, 163–164
Fair Credit Reporting Act (FCRA),
    123, 221–222, 279–283
Fair Labor Standards Act of 1938, 38
false imprisonment, 219–221
Federal Bureau of Narcotics, 2
fences, 150
fingerprints, 205
forensic analysis, 127
Fourth Amendment rights, 202, 205
fraud, 149
  cost of to employers, 12–13
  employee handbooks and, 194
  prevalence of, 139
freedom from intrusion, 202–203
front, 113
front-end, 32
functional abusers, 111

Galella, Ron, 203
gangs, 13–16
good faith investigation standard, 47
government, investigations for,
    244–245
graffiti, gang, 16
greed, 9, 140–141
grievance procedures, 165–171
  evidence in, 165–167
  testimony in, 167–170
  winning through criminal
    prosecution, 170–171
guarantees, 57
Guidelines for Security and Safety of
    Health Care and Community
    Service Workers, 191
guns, 153

Hallcrest Report II, 58
hallucinogens, 258–259
Hall v. Gus Constr. Co., Inc., 199
Hazelwood, Joseph, 6–7
healthcare industry, 242
Hernandez v. McDonald's Corp.,
    214–215
Hill v. NCAA, 203, 208–209
hiring
    negligent, 193–194
    screening before, 123–124
    undercover investigators, 67–69
hi-tech industry, 243–244
hold-harmless agreements, 57–58
honesty testing, 223–225
Hoover, J. Edgar, 3
hostile environment harassment, 198
housing, investigator, 70–72

incident management teams, 19
incident reports, 97
indemnifications, 57–58
independent contractors, 37–38
informants, 62
information gathering
    methods for, 126–128
    for results measurements, 235–239
insurance
    agency selection and, 59–60
    Certificate of, 60
    claims, recovery through, 239–240
intentional infliction of emotional
    distress, 194, 217–218
Internal Revenue Service (IRS), 37
interventions, 119–121
    defined, 19, 119
    documentation in, 120, 121
    interviews in, 120–121
interviews
    administrative, 181–182
    in case shutdown, 181–187
    infliction of emotional distress in,
        217–218
    information gathering through, 128
    in interventions, 120–121
    intrusion into seclusion in, 218–219
    investigative, 182–187, 217–219
    physical evidence gathered during,
        187

pre-employment, 124
in theft investigations, 154–155
theme development in, 183
threat of violence investigations
    and, 230
union rights and, 184–185, 200–
    201
videotaping, 186–187
written/tape-recorded statements
    in, 183–187
intrusion into seclusion, 218–219
investigations. *See also* drug
    investigations; theft
    investigations
alternatives to, 54–56
common mistakes in, 78–80
defined, 27
determining desired outcome of,
    33–34, 41–47
effect of on employee relations,
    173–175
elements required in, 27
employer obligation to perform, 24,
    191
fear of abuse of, 159
future of, 241–246
for the government, 244–245
information gathering through, 127
justification of, 1–26
objective articulation in, 56
objectives for, 38–56
preparation for, 27–61
risks of, 25–26
role of in drug-free workplaces,
    9–10
of sexual harassment, 199–200
time required for, 52–53
who should be involved in, 74–78
as workplace evaluations, 245
investigative interviews, 217–219
Investigative Summary Reports,
    94–97
investigative teams, 82–87
investigators
    in case management, 82
    cover positions for, 64–67
    demand for, 62–63
    double standard of, 30
    drug use by, 134

investigators (*continued*)
  identification of dysfunctional
    persons by, 20–21
  networks of, 20
  placement of, 31–32, 67–69,
    147–148
  profile of professional, 61–62
  relocation of, 70–72
  removal of, 189–190
  selecting, 62–64
  selecting for theft investigations,
    144–147
  selecting the wrong, 79–80
  sponsors of, 30, 130–131
  supplemental, 150–152
  testimony preparation for, 167–170
  theft by, 152
  use of actual name by, 68–69
  using multiple, 64
  wages of, 34
invisible markers, 154

justice, pursuit of, 42

Kagel, Sam, 51–52
Kennedy Onassis, Jacqueline, 203
kleptomania, 142
K-Mart Corp. v. Trott, 226
Krout & Schneider, Inc., 7

labor relations, 163–165. *See also*
    organized labor
law enforcement
  in case management, 87
  case shutdown and, 187–189
  crime reporting laws and, 162–163
  differing mission of, 32–33
  involvement in union workshop
    investigations, 171
  meetings with, 101
  reasons to involve, 162–163
  role of in investigations, 76–78
  willingness to involve, 60
legal issues
  attorney confidentiality and, 75–76,
    85–86
  employer obligations, 23–24, 191
liability

client, 84–85
  for failure to investigate, 192–195
  from independent contractors,
    37–38
  interviews and, 182
  releases of, 57–58
  weighed against possible outcome,
    52
licensing, 58
lie detector tests, 223–225
litigation, hostile, 174
litigation avoidance, 191–231
  of assault and battery claims, 221
  of discrimination lawsuits, 196–198
  drug/alcohol testing and, 205–210
  email monitoring and, 216–217
  failure to investigate and, 192–195
  of false imprisonment claims,
    219–220
  and honesty testing, 223–225
  interviews and, 217–219
  phone call monitoring and, 213–216
  private investigative firms and,
    195–196
  of sexual harassment lawsuits,
    198–200
  surveillance and, 210–213
  and threats of violence, 228–230
  of unfair labor practice claims,
    200–201
  and use of consumer reports,
    221–222
  workplace privacy rights and,
    202–217
  and workplace searches, 225–228
  of wrongful discharge claims, 231
Los Angeles, gangs in, 13–14
LSD, 259–260

make-whole remedies, 184–185
management. *See* client-employers
management referrals, 122–123
mandatory sentencing, 7
Manpower, Inc., 243
marijuana, 40, 95, 109, 111, 168, 259
McGann v. Northeast Ill. Regional
    Commuter R.R. Corp., 226
media, statements to, 165, 269–271

media response kit, 179, 269–271
medical information, disclosing,
    206–207
meetings
  settle-down, 190, 273
  taping, 214–215
  team, 101
methamphetamine, 258
Miranda v. Arizona, 42
misconduct
  defining, 41
  determining if evidence of exists,
    39
Model Injury and Illness Prevention
    Program for Workplace Security,
    191
morale, 114
motivation
  for theft, 139–141
  for violence, 18–19

Nader v. General Motors, 202–203
narcotics, 257
National Council on Alcoholism, 5–6
National Crime Victimization Survey,
    192
National Labor Relations Act (NLRA),
    53, 160, 200
National Labor Relations Board
    (NLRB), 212–213
  Weingarten and, 161–162, 184, 185,
    200–201
*National Treasury Employees v. Von
    Raab*, 202
negligence
  in administering drug/alcohol tests,
    209–210
  failure to warn and, 194
  in hiring, 193–194
  in supervision/retention, 193–194
NLRB v. Weingarten, Inc., 161–162,
    184, 185, 200–201
Noble v. Sears, Roebuck & Co., 195
nondisclosure guidelines, 173
notes, investigator, 88–89

objectives, 38–56. *See also* results
  articulating, 56

importance of clear, 79
Occupational Safety and Health Act
    (OSHA), 162
  "general duty" clause, 9
  safe workplace requirement of, 17,
    191
O'Connor v. Ortega, 225
Omnibus Crime Control and Safe
    Streets Act of 1968, 213
Omnibus Drug Initiative Act of 1988,
    9
Omnibus Transportation Employee
    Testing Act (OTETA), 205, 208
operative meetings, 101
operatives. *See* investigators
organizational culture, 53–54, 67
organized labor, 159–162, 163–172.
    See also union organizing
  agreements, reviewing before
    investigations, 48–50
  difficulty of penetrating union
    workshops, 29–30
  employee rights under, 160–162,
    184–186
  gathering information about, 73
  grievance/arbitrations and, 165–171
  legality of investigations and,
    159–161
  precedent/past practice and, 50–52
  surveillance cameras and, 212–213
  unfair labor practice claims and,
    160, 200–201
  union notification and, 163–165
  winning arbitrations through
    criminal prosecution and,
    170–171
overtime pay, 38

patience, 31–33
  case managers and, 83–84
PCP, 259–260
*Phillips v. Smalley Maintenance
    Servs., Inc.*, 218
photographs, 205
placement, investigator, 31–32, 67–69
  and cover stories, 69–70
  defined, 67
  in theft investigations, 147–148

planning
  for drug investigations, 125–129
  importance of, 79
player identification, 131
policies
  common omissions from, 48–49
  distribution of, 74
  ensuring compliance to, 124
  reviewing, preinvestigation, 48–50
  search, 227
  substance abuse, 123–124
political hires, 69
polygraph testing, 223–225
precedent, 50–52
preinvestigations, 39–40
  final preparation in, 72–74
  preparation for, 56–61
"preponderance of evidence"
    standard, 47
prescription drugs, 260
press statements, 172–173
prevention, theft, 157
prevention plans, 129
prevention programs, 123–124
privacy rights, 202–217
  definition of privacy in, 203
  drug/alcohol testing and, 202,
    205–210
  email monitoring and, 216–217
  fingerprints/photographs and, 205
  phone call monitoring and, 213–216
  public policy violations and,
    203–204
  visual/video surveillance and,
    210–213
private sector security. *See* contract
    security
productivity, 114, 237–239
Professional Law Enforcement (PLE),
    7
progression, 17–18
progressive discipline, 122
proposals, 56–57
  sample, 247–254
prosecution, 42–43
  deterrent value of, 43–44
  in drug investigations, 137–138
  winning arbitrations through,
    170–171

psychologists/psychiatrists, 19
psychopaths, 20
public policy, 49–50
  violations, 203–204
public records, 172
public relations, 165, 172–173
  case shutdown and, 179–180
  media response kit, 269–271

quid pro quo harassment, 198

Racketeer Influenced Criminal
    Organization Act (RICO), 45
ramping up, 19
rationalization, 107
  doper logic and, 8–9
  in theft, 142
reasonable accommodation, 196
"reasonable conclusion" standard, 47
recoveries, 180–181, 239–240
  civil litigation for, 181
  in theft investigations, 156–157
  third-party, 143–144
relationship-building phase, 28–30
reports, 59, 88–101
  altering/editing, 93–94
  electronic, 99–100
  as evidence, 166
  incident/buy, 97
  information gathering for, 88–89
  Investigative Summary, 94–97
  organization of, 89–90
  security issues for, 101
  special, 97, 98–99
  structured narrative format for,
    89–93
  timeline/chronological format for,
    89, 90
reputation, 59
research, 127
Research Triangle Institute, 4
resources, 33–38
respondeat superior doctrine, 194–195
restitution, 45–47
  vs. criminal prosecution, 46
results
  analysis of, 237–239
  attorney involvement in
    determining, 75

leveraging, 239–240
measuring, 41–47, 233–241
prosecution, 42–43
restitution, 45–47
termination, 43–45
Ribas v. Clark, 215
risk
in theft investigations, 145–147
of undercover investigations, 25–26
Robinson v. Hewlett-Packard Co.,
211
rock cocaine, 4

searches, 225–228
conducting, 226–228
security officers
as cover position, 64–66
involved in criminality, 66
self-directed work groups, 30
service contracts, 57–58
settle-down meetings, 190, 273
sexual harassment
ensuring freedom from, 23–24
failure to investigate, 40–41
lawsuits, avoiding, 198–200
types of, 198
Simpson, O.J., 166
*Simpson v. Commonwealth
Unemployment Comp. Bd. of
Review*, 226
*Skinner v. Railway Labor Executives
Assn.*, 202
snitches, 62
*Solis v. Southern Cal. Rapid Transit
Dist.*, 195
special reports, 97, 98–99
splits/split purchases, 131–132
sponsors, 30, 130
traits of, 130–131
standards of proof, 47–48
for criminal prosecution *vs.*
employment action, 45
statements, 183–187
State v. Bonnell, 211
statutes of limitations, 50
Steinberg, Donald, 4
stimulants, 257–258
sting operations, 153
street gangs, 13–16

strikes, labor, 200
substance abuse
defined, 107
destructive behaviors in, 115–119
failure to investigate, 39–40
human cost of, 106
measuring effects of, 234–235
policies, 48–49
prevention of, 123–124
progression of, 110–115
theft and, 149–150
understanding, 107–110
workplace opportunities for,
112–113
surveillance
electronic, 126–127
physical, 126
restrictions on, 50
rights to privacy and, 210–213
for supporting investigation,
135–137
in theft investigations, 155
video, 135–137
"Survey of Criminal History
Information Systems," 12

tape-recordings, 155, 183–187
target hardening, 73–74
Taylor v. O'Grady, 209
team meetings, 101
telephone communication, 100–101
monitoring employee, 213–216
temporary positions, 67, 243
terminations, 43–45
allowing resignations instead of,
186
assessing impact of, 178–179
company policies and, 49–50
cost savings through, 237–239
for threats of violence, 230
vs. prosecution, 44
wrongful discharge claims and,
231
testifying
in arbitration/grievance procedures,
167–170
testimony preparation for, 167–
170
willingness to, 59

theft
  conversion in, 143–144
  opportunity in, 142
  perceived need in, 142
  prevention of, 157
  process of, 141–144
  rationalization in, 142
  reasons for employee, 139–141
  substance abuse and, 113–114,
    149–150
theft investigations, 139–157
  buy-busts/sting operations in, 153
  evidence corroboration for, 154–
    156
  evidence markers in, 154
  lures in, 152–153
  multiple buys in, 155–156
  operative placement for, 147–148
  operative selection for, 144–147
  recoveries in, 156–157
  risks in, 145–147
  tactics for, 148–154
  time required for, 31
  use of associates/third parties in,
    150–152
  the wedge in, 149–150
theft powder, 154
theme development, 183
third-party recovery, 143–144
"thirty-day rule," 50
threat management, 19–21
threats of violence, 228–230
"three-day rule," 50
training
  agency, 58
  employee, 124
  to work in union environments,
    160–161
transportation, investigator, 71–72

undercharging, 35–37
undercover investigations. *See*
    investigations
undercover investigators. *See*
    investigators
unemployment benefits
  drug testing and, 207
  hearings, 172

  opposing, 178
unfair labor practices, 160
  avoiding claims of, 200–201
union organizing, 53, 160–161. *See
    also* organized labor
United States
  drugs in culture of, 1–2
  impact of drugs on business in, 5–8
  war on drugs, 2–5
United States v. Maxwell, 216–217
United States v. O'Reilly, 211
Unruh v. Truck Ins. Exch, 196
U.S. Chamber of Commerce, 12,
    139
U.S. Code Title VII, 23–24
U.S. Drug Enforcement Agency
    (DEA), 105
U.S. General Accounting Office,
    139
U.S. Justice Department Bureau of
    Justice Statistics, 12

values, 139–140
Vandiveer v. Charters, 220
video-recordings, 155
  of interviews, 186–187
  privacy rights and, 210–213
  surveillance, 135–137
  vmail, 99–100
violence
  categories of workplace, 228–229
  of drug culture, 108–109
  gangs and, 13–16
  identifying likely perpetrators of,
    20–21
  investigating threats of, 228–230
  motivation for, 18–19
  prevalence of workplace, 192
  prevention of, 21–22
  profile of aggressors, 17–18
  women and, 16
  workplace, 16–25
vmail, 99–100

war on drugs, 2–5
wedges, 149–150
Weingarten rights, 161–162, 184, 185,
    200–201

Wilkinson v. Times Mirror Corp., 206
wiretapping, 213–216
work ethic, 30, 140
work groups, 30–31
workplace evaluations, 190, 245

workplace privacy, 202–217
workplace searches, 225–228
work teams. *See* work groups
wrongful discharge claims, 231

Yunker v. Honeywell, 194